specially by Leaving a Key Under It) • Find
g Clamshell Packaging wi[   ]Yo
Fake Antique • Clean You[   ]tho
asher Don'ts • Don't Just [   ]Dirt Aro
use • The Freaking Remote Is Dead—Agai
ants • Wash Your Dog without Taking a B
papering Fails • Misadventures in Paintin
• Don't Be Driven Mad by a Dripping Fauc
n't Screw Up with Your Screwdriver • Don'
cipes • Don't Waste Money at the Grocery
Don't Get Burned by Your Freezer • So Yo
kes • Don't Let Your Guacamole Look Unh
ud Watermelon • Don't Take Your Lumps
Yes, It is Possible to Open aCoconut • Do
w Mein in Your Lap Trying to Use Chopstic
e Birds—Not the Squirrels • Pitch a Tent w
rnt • Don't Be a Mosquito Magnet • How
m a Hike without Blisters • OMG, Is That S
ur Head • Don't Suffer from Epic Sunbur
k Your Sweaters • Don't Waste Money on
nks • How Much Should You Pay for That
Be Embarrassed by Yellow Pit Stains Aga
ur Ankle Wearing High Heels • Keep a Sna
ace While Shaving • Don't Regret Your Ta
rance? That Doesn't Mean You Can't Get

DON'T SCREW IT UP!

AVOID 434 GOOFS
TO SAVE TIME, MONEY, AND FACE

LAURA LEE

Reader's Digest

The Reader's Digest Association, Inc.
New York, NY/Montreal

All illustrations (except those listed below): ©Shutterstock Images LLC
Tina Cash-Walsh: 13, 17, 27, 35, 41, 65, 69, 75, 79, 81, 85, 101, 104, 123
Joshua Kemble: 135, 141, 153, 157, 163, 167, 176, 189, 199, 202, 215, 229, 238

Library of Congress Cataloging-in-Publication data is available upon request.

ISBN 978-1-62145-005-4

We are committed to both the quality of our products and the service we provide
to our customers. We value your comments, so please feel free to contact us.
    The Reader's Digest Association, Inc.
    Adult Trade Publishing
    44 South Broadway
    White Plains, NY 10601

For more Reader's Digest products and information, visit our website:

    www.rd.com (in the United States)
    www.readersdigest.ca (in Canada)

Printed in China

10 9 8 7 6 5 4 3 2 1

NOTES TO OUR READERS

The information in this book should not be substituted for, or used to alter, medical therapy without your doctor's advice. For a specific health problem, consult your physician for guidance.
    Reader's Digest publishes the advice of expert authorities in many fields. But the use of a book is not a substitute for legal, accounting, or other professional services. Consult a competent professional for answers to your specific questions. This publication is sold with the understanding that the contributors and the publisher are not engaged in rendering legal advice. Laws vary from state to state, and readers with specific issues should seek the services of an attorney.
    This publication contains the opinions and ideas of its author and is designed to provide useful information to the reader. It is not intended as a substitute for the advice of an expert on the subject matter covered. Products or active ingredients, treatments, and the names of organizations that appear in this publication are included for informational purposes only; the inclusion of commercial products in the book does not imply endorsement by Reader's Digest, nor does the omission of any product or active ingredient or treatment advice indicate disapproval by Reader's Digest. When using any commercial product, readers should read and follow all label directions carefully. The publisher and the contributors specifically disclaim any responsibility for any liability, loss, or risk (personal, financial, or otherwise) that may be claimed or incurred as a consequence, directly or indirectly, of the use and/or application of any of the contents of this publication.
    The author and publisher specifically disclaim any responsibility for any liability, loss, or risk (personal, financial, or otherwise) that may be claimed or incurred as a consequence—directly or indirectly—of the use and/or application of any of the contents of this publication.

WARNING

All do-it-yourself activities involve a degree of risk. Skills, materials, tools, and site conditions vary widely. Although the editors have made every effort to ensure accuracy, the reader remains responsible for the selection and use of tools, materials, and methods. Always obey local codes and laws, follow manufacturer's operating instructions, and observe safety precautions.

CONTENTS

INTRODUCTION

*"For every evil under the sun
There is a remedy or there is none
If there be one, seek till you find it.
If there be none, never mind it."*
—Mother Goose

The working title of this book was *How Not to Screw Up Just About Anything*. When I was asked to write it, my first thought was, *That is a book no one is qualified to write.* Certainly I am not qualified to tell you how to have a perfect life. In fact, like most people, I keep a tally of all of my past screwups in a special place in the back of my mind that I can't help running through when I feel apprehensive about something. A bit of free advice from the "do as I say" file: don't do this. You can't fix past screwups, but you can learn from them and try not to make more.

So let me tell you off the bat that I am not a certified expert in home repair, sports, etiquette, parenting, relationships, managing money, or avoiding run-ins with deadly snakes and bears. What I am is a person who knows how to screw up, but who also knows how to research and ask real experts how to avoid doing it again. To paraphrase Will Rogers, we are all screwups, only in different areas.

My second concern with writing this book was that if God enjoys irony, I am setting myself up for some sort of disaster down the line. In addition to this book, I have written a book on how to avoid dangerous things and a book on schadenfreude, which is a German word for the pleasure one gets from the misfortune of others. I can picture the "Odd News of the Day" headline now: Author of Books on Avoiding Dangers and Screwups Dies in Freak Dishwasher Accident.

Thankfully, A. A. Milne, the author of *Winnie the Pooh,* put my mind at rest on this account. He pointed out in his book *Not That It Matters* that "Fate does not go out of its way to be dramatic." This leads me to another point about screwups. It is the dramatic and stunning screwup that makes headlines. As a result, we make a number of false associations that lead to a whole new set of screwups. As we are stressing and worrying about avoiding highly unlikely mishaps, such as abductions and mad cow disease, we trip over a crack in the sidewalk and fall in front of a bus. In this book, I tried to avoid repeating alarmist advice and to dispel some common misconceptions that can lead you in the wrong direction. If you are too scared of making a mistake you will never do anything at all, which in itself is a serious error.

We changed the title from *How Not to Screw Up Just About Anything* in recognition of the fact that such a book would be impossible to write. There is too much "anything" out there to screw up. If we were aiming for completeness, I would have to write something like the *Encyclopædia Britannica*, a 32-volume set. Even then, some haphazard reader would find a new way to err, and I would have to get to work on volume 33. A book of that size and scope would be a bit costly for you, dear reader. So this exploration into the world of human error will have to be limited and the selection somewhat subjective.

I started my research by focusing on the mistakes that seemed the most common and important, for example, not screwing up your first date or a job interview. Next I addressed things that are tricky to get right, like driving a stick shift or eating with chopsticks. There are everyday activities that could be done much better, like doing laundry or washing the dishes. I tried to combine these with a few screwups or hints and tips that were chosen for their interest and entertainment value—I do want you to enjoy reading the book. I tried to steer away from obvious advice as much as possible, which also shaped which screwups I included. Your particular favorite mistake may not be in here, but hopefully you will discover a few new processes and ideas that will allow you to move through the world with a bit more finesse.

Sincerely,
Laura Lee

YOUR HOME

don't put out the
welcome mat for **ROBBERS**
(Especially by Leaving a Key Under It)

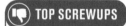
TOP SCREWUPS

- Letting the house look empty
- Leaving your door unlocked (seriously, people!?)

You don't need to live in a fortress to keep your home safe from burglars. You just need to think like a thief, which isn't hard because they generally aren't very bright. A few underhanded thoughts and some common sense will keep your possessions from walking out the door.

No to Newspapers

Imagine you're a burglar. What type of house are you going to target? Burglars generally do not want to run into homeowners, so they pick houses that look empty. If you go away over a long weekend and let the newspapers pile up at your door, you have given intruders a big, flashy sign that no one is home. 👎 **Giving a neighborhood kid a couple of bucks to pick up your papers could save you big in the long run.**

The Higher Utility Bill Is Totally Worth It

Simple light timers can create the impression that people are at home. Think about it: it's highly unlikely that human beings would turn off all the lights in a home at the same moment. Thus you will better fool would-be burglars if you have two or more lights on timers set to go on and off at different times. 👍 **A turned-on TV is a good way to announce you're home,** but you probably don't want to leave yours on while you're gone. Fear not! You can buy a device that simulates the glow of a TV and works on a timer. (Premium-channel simulators are extra.) There are also motion-sensitive alarms that play the sound of a barking dog when anyone approaches the house. A few inexpensive dog toys scattered across the lawn can be a similar, but quieter, ploy.

Why Not Just Leave the Door Open?

You shouldn't need to be told this, but 🔒 **lock up when you are not at home.** A surprising number of burglaries occur with no forced entry. Thieves just walk through unlocked doors and help themselves. And remember, thieves know about ladders. If you lock the front door and leave the second floor windows open, your home is not secure. All someone needs to do is put on a jumpsuit and carry a paintbrush; then they can climb right in your window in broad daylight as your neighbor barbecues next door.

Despite your—and a vigilant neighbor's—best efforts, a burglar can still target you. Your stuff may just be too cool to resist! Find out exactly what to do if you come upon a thief in your house on page 324 of the "Worst-Case-Scenerio" chapter. Best to do that now instead of waiting until an occasion to need the info arises.

THE PERKS OF A NOSY NEIGHBOR

Speaking of neighbors, home security is a great reason to get to know your neighbors. A neighbor you've never met might think that guy wandering around your yard is part of the family. A neighbor who has spent time with you at backyard picnics may just know better and call you or the police. And remember, if you put up a big hedge or fence to wall yourself off from a nosy neighbor, the price of your privacy is that you're providing the same protection for no-goodniks.

finding LOST ITEMS
without losing your mind

You are about to curl up and read the copy of *War and Peace* that you checked out of the library. (OK, it's actually *Harry Potter.*) You brew a cup of tea, find a comfortable place on the couch, wrap up in a blanket, open the first page, and . . . "Oh, man. Where are my reading glasses?"

Don't Panic!

We have a way of hiding things from ourselves and then working ourselves into a house-wrecking frenzy when we're about to start a project that requires the use of said things, or when we're about to head out the door and can't possibly afford to be late to where we're going. (Car keys are a major culprit.) **Don't panic. As long as you are systematic in your search, you and your things are likely to be reunited.**

Before you even start looking, take a moment to calm your nerves and clear your mind. Running around the house and pulling things out of drawers that haven't been opened in two years does not help. When you're in an agitated state, you can look straight at an object without seeing it.

Don't Overlook the Obvious

Start by checking where the object is supposed to be. Are your keys on the key hook? Even if you do not think you left it there, someone else may have put it away. If your item has not been put away, try to remember where you used it last. There is a good chance it is still there. These may sound like *duh, I already did thats*, but focusing on these two places works. How many times have you found something exactly where it should be, but just under something else that *shouldn't* be there? Did someone put a newspaper down on top of your reading glasses? Could your pen have rolled under your computer printer?

Work Backward

Still at a loss? Retrace your steps. Try to remember what you were doing and thinking when you last had the object. Were you distracted? Did you get a phone call? These could be important clues. Think about what you were wearing. Check the pockets.

Could the item be where something else is supposed to be? Could you have put the can opener where the stapler belongs and the stapler where the can opener should be?

WHEN ALL ELSE FAILS

If none of this works, call off your search (and possibly call to cancel your appointment), focus on something else, and let your subconscious work on it. You may remember where you put the item later in a flash of inspiration.

opening clamshell **PACKAGING**
without losing a finger

It's your son's fifth birthday, and he tears the paper off his present and starts jumping up and down when he sees the Transformers Robo Fighters Optimus Prime doll he has been begging for. He is ready for some serious robot play, but you are the one about to do battle. You have now entered the clamshell wars. Can you get the toy out of the plastic before your son has a complete meltdown *and* without slicing a couple of fingers in the process?

Your Adversary

Scissors are often no match for this tough material, and thousands of Americans are admitted to emergency rooms each year with packaging-related injuries. Some of these injuries are from knife slips. Many, however, are from the sharp edges of the plastic itself.

In response to consumer complaints, some manufacturers have

WHY, FOR THE LOVE OF GOD, DO COMPANIES USE THEM?

Clamshell packages, those polyvinyl-chloride plastic coverings sealed around the edges, are popular with manufacturers because they keep the products from moving about as they're being shipped from their country of origin. They also serve as a theft deterrent, not to mention as a being-able-to-use-the-thing deterrent.

started to package their products in shells that are easier to open. Before you pull out the tools, check the back of the package to see if there are any perforations or tabs that you can use to pull the plastic apart easily.

An Unlikely Ally

If there are not, go find your  **can opener.** Open one side of the packaging as if it were a can. The opener will not go around corners, so you can either repeat the process on each side or **carefully use a utility knife— inserted into the open side, facing toward the center of the packaging—to carefully cut the rest open.** This carries some risk, but not as much as the traditional method of stabbing the plastic in frustration and prying the knife in through the small hole it created.

don't get suckered in by a
FAKE ANTIQUE

It's oh-so-easy to get duped into buying an "antique" that was actually made last year. So whether you're on a mission to find a particular antique to put in that perfect spot in your living room or you just happen upon an impossibly good deal, there are a few tricks you can use to avoid going home with a knockoff.

Are There Age Spots?

Old things look, well, old.  **Wood shrinks with the grain, which will cause joints to separate over time. If the joints are too crisp, it should raise a red flag.** The color of the wood will vary in each of the drawers of an old piece because each drawer is exposed to a different amount of light. The middle drawers, which get less exposure to light, will be darker than the bottom drawer, which gets the most. The backboards of old pine chests likewise become darkened with age and exposure to air and dirt. If it has a very thin veneer, it was made after 1850. Before that, pieces were cut by hand and it would be rare to find anything that was less than $1/16''$ thick. Old mirrors will have wavy glass that causes breaks in the reflectivity.

WAIT FOR IT

If you're looking for antique bargains, the experts say the best times to shop at auctions are in June, July, August, and December. These are the slow months at most auction houses.

An Antique Is Not a Fixer-Upper

If you are hoping to sell grandma's chest of drawers, do not do anything to "fix it up." **It might seem like it would be nicer with a fresh coat of paint or a leg that is less wobbly, but in the eyes of an antique collector, that touch-up might reduce the value substantially.** One of the most common alterations to old furniture is removing old hardware, such as drawer pulls and feet. You can see if this has been done by looking for extra sets of holes. If the original hardware has been replaced, by you or anyone else, the piece is less valuable.

TOP TIP

One of the most common alterations to old furniture is removing old hardware, such as drawer pulls and feet.

KNOW YOUR STUFF, OR AT LEAST SOME STUFF

If you do not want to be taken in by fakes, take some time to learn the signs of legitimacy and fakery.

Legit

- Drawers that have dovetail joints and numbers written in pencil
- Color inside drawers and on the back is consistent
- All the surfaces of pieces in a set match
- A nutty smell

Big Fat Fake

- Shellac or finish on the inside of the drawers
- Glue that might indicate a repair
- Legs don't match
- A paint smell

CLEAN YOUR WINDOWS
without leaving streaks or breaking your leg

The whole point of cleaning a window is to be able to see through it. Yet after you spray and wipe with your blue window cleaner and a paper towel, you are left with streaks, spots, and little bits of paper lint. What the heck is going wrong?

The Wrong Tools for the Job

You are making one fatal error: using the wrong tools. Grabbing a few paper towels and a bottle of window cleaner just doesn't get the job done right. Counterintuitive? Yes. Easy to fix? Also yes.

The window cleaner is fine for interior windows, but it cannot do the job alone. **Professional window washers have a secret weapon: newspaper.** Newsprint is full of a naturally absorbent substance called lignin, which is also the stuff that makes old newspapers turn yellow, which is why it is removed from most consumer paper products.

MORE IS NOT ALWAYS BETTER

Spraying way too much cleaner for a job just gives you more junk to wipe up. You're wasting your energy and money and inhaling extra cleanser. Over time, breathing in all of those cleaners has been known to cause respiratory problems in some people.

Finish the Job

You may now have squeaky-clean glass on the inside, but if you stop there, you're really only doing a half-glass job. To  **clean the outer side of your windows,** you need a few more tools: a squeegee that has a sponge edge, windshield wiper fluid, a razor blade, a bucket, a ladder if you have a two-story home, and a chamois cloth (the type of towel used to wash cars). The last one is essential for not leaving streaks behind.

❶ Fill your bucket with a mixture of six to eight parts water to one part windshield wiper fluid.

❷ Climb the ladder. **DO NOT** try to climb the ladder with your hands full. That is just a massive screwup waiting to happen.

❸ Have someone hand you your supplies ·····▶ through an upstairs window.

❹ Use the sponge end of the squeegee to cover the window with the liquid.

❺ Razor off any sticky chunks while the window is still wet.

❻ Turn the squeegee and use the rubber side to wipe the liquid from the window, drying the squeegee between each swipe.

❼ Use the chamois to wipe the excess water off the rubber after each pass.

❽ Enjoy your brilliant, clean windows (without having to use a pencil to itch your leg under your cast).

DISHWASHER don'ts

Dishwasher design has changed a great deal since your parents' day. Yet most people learn what to do once in life and never revisit their dishwasher technique. If you read the directions in your machine's manual, or even on the box of soap, you will probably discover that you are doing things at least a little bit wrong.

Rinsing Does More Harm Than Good—Seriously!

You remember how your mom was always telling you to rinse your dishes before putting them in the dishwasher? The experts (a "senior dishwasher design engineer" quoted in the *New York Times*) say she was wrong. You weren't being lazy. You had an instinctive sense that detergent was created to dissolve food, and if it's in there without food, it will start attacking the glasses. **Duplicate rinsing just wastes water,** so say the dishwasher authorities.

Soap Overdose

The number-one mistake (which goes for the laundry, too, as you will see on pages 116–117) is putting in too much soap. Dishwashers use less water than they did in days gone by, and **detergents are more concentrated. This means you need less soap.** Not only are you spending more than you have to on something that's literally going down the drain, but also, too much soap leads to cloudy glasses.

Dishes Come Out Worse Than When They Went In

Do your dishes come out of the washer with a frosty white film more often than they used to? This is a residue of minerals that new phosphate-free detergents leave behind. You can wash the dishes a second time by hand to get it off, but if you're going to do that, why not just hand wash everything to begin with?

Instead, try this mineral-removing trick: Put two cups of white vinegar into a bowl and place it in your dishwasher's bottom rack. Run the washer without detergent. Once it has completed its cycle, run it a second time to remove the leftover vinegar.

Dishwasher Overload

When it comes to your loading technique, if yours is screwed up, then chances are that only a small percentage of your dishes are getting clean. **Place large items at the side and back to prevent them from blocking water and detergent from other dishes. The dirtier side should go toward the center, where it will have more exposure to spray.**

To avoid damage, hand wash wooden bowls and spoons and anything that is delicate or valuable, like your china. "It seems that you really shouldn't put anything in a dishwasher that was made before dishwashers were invented, which was in 1886," wrote author Andrew Martin in his home-management book *How to Get Things Really Flat.*

DON'T IGNORE YOUR SPONGE

Chances are your sponge is the dirtiest, germiest thing in your kitchen. More than a billion germs can grow in an uncleaned sponge in twenty-four hours. When you work with a dirty sponge, you're not cleaning. You're spreading germs around. To avoid that, throw your sponge in the dishwasher when you run a load, or moisten and microwave it for one minute. (Don't leave it in longer, or it might burn up. A charcoal brick isn't great for cleaning either.) Replace it every week or two, or whenever it gets discolored.

don't just PUSH THE DIRT
around your house

 TOP SCREWUPS

- Letting dirt in too easily
- Using the wrong broom
- Practicing bad form
- Leaving that little line of dirt behind

The Dirt on Dirt

Before you start working on getting dirt out of your house, take a moment to see how easy you're making it for dirt to come in. A nice welcome mat gives guests a place to wipe their feet, but **a second mat inside the door will catch a lot of the dirt they knocked loose outside.** Be sure to shake the dirt off of them from time to time, otherwise you're just giving your guests a place to pick up debris to track around your house.

You might also consider adopting a shoes-off policy for your family. Keep a pair of slippers for each family member near the door so you can change from your outdoor to your indoor footwear.

But unless your home is fitted with bio-containment doors, you're sure to track in a bit of the outdoors with you. And let's not forget about the general shed of skin, pet hair, and clothing fibers that are an everyday part of life.

Choose Your Weapon

The cleanest sweep begins with broom selection. Brooms for the house come in two basic designs: made with either soft plastic bristles or straw. Straw brooms are best for rough, worn flooring, but they are too harsh for delicate finishes. If your floor is new and (as yet) undamaged, you will want to use a plastic model. ◐ **Select a broom with an angled head if you need to get under cabinets.** Before sweeping, don't forget to turn off any fans or other devices that might blow the dust around the room.

Assume Formation

Now that you're ready to sweep, stand with your feet shoulder-distance apart. ◐ **Grasp the handle near the top with your dominant hand. Use the other hand to hold the handle farther down near your waist.** Allow the bristles to make full contact with the floor, but don't push so hard that they bend. Too much pressure will scratch the floor and weaken the broom. Too little pressure and the dust will simply laugh at you and stay put.

Use a Strategized Sweep Attack

If your room is square, use the perimeter method. Pick one corner and sweep inward along the walls. Then work around the room spiraling inward until you have a neat little pile of dirt in the middle of the room. If your room is more rectangular, start at one end and work toward the other. You'll end up with a series of small dirt piles at the end of each row, which you can combine into one at the very end.

TOP TIP

Too much pressure will scratch the floor and weaken the broom.

CLEAR THE LINE

So what do you do with that little line of dirt that just won't get into the dustpan? ◐ **Pull out your handy hand vacuum and suck it up, or use a moistened towel to mop up the last line of the dirt's defense.**

how to de-stinkafie a
STINKY HOUSE

TOP SCREWUPS

- Trying to cover up odors
- Allowing odors to get worse

Sniff, sniff. You smell that? Ugh, that stink just won't quit! Whether you moved somewhere new and are dealing with someone else's leftover odors or you live with a smell factory (like a litter box or a smoker), there are a number of ways to deal with a malodorous event aside from a clothespin on your nose.

What Can't Coffee Do?

Have you ever been to a perfume store? You may have noticed that they keep jars of coffee on hand **to keep the air from being overwhelmed with competing smells by absorbing them. This is a much better way to deal with smells than trying to mask them with other smells.** Coffee can absorb your household odors, too. Keep an open can of coffee near the cat's litter box or in the corner of the laundry room, and your nose will thank you.

Smoke Is a Killer

Tobacco smoke is a particularly stubborn smell. If you are the smoker and you continue to smoke in the house, you will not be able to remove the scent completely, but an electric air purifier can help. If a smoky essence has been left by a previous tenant, you can freshen things up with a thorough cleaning. It's not easy, though, and you will have to bring in a professional to steam the carpets, curtains, drapes, and upholstered furniture.

Walls also absorb smoke, unfortunately. You can implement the technique experts use in buildings that have absorbed smoke from fires: Seal the walls and ceilings with shellac or a shellac-based primer—this helps lock in the odor—and then repaint. If your landlord is top notch, you may be able to get him or her to pay for it.

Don't Even Let the Stink Happen

Better than dealing with an odor, of course, is preventing it from happening in the first place. One of the most common—and most disgusting—stinks is caused by mildew, which thrives in areas with prolonged moisture. **If you want to prevent it from growing in your bathroom, get the air circulating when all that post-shower steam is in the air.** A dehumidifier or an exhaust fan will do it. Also make sure you hang your damp towels separately so they can dry more quickly and thoroughly.

Speaking of, ugh, wet-towel smell, here's how to get that particular stank out: mix equal parts of Borax and laundry soap and pour the mixture into the washing machine with the offensive towels. Start the water, and then pause the cycle to let the towels (or clothing or shoes) soak for about twenty minutes before you run the machine on the regular cycle.

DON'T CLEAN YOUR HOUSE TO DEATH

There are many commercial cleaners available for mildew and all sorts of grime. You may be tempted to mix these chemicals together when you're dealing with stubborn filth that no single product is curing, but this is the biggest mistake you can make. Certain cleaning agents, such as bleach and ammonia, are great on their own, but they can have deadly chemical reactions when mixed. Most people have heard not to mix straight ammonia and bleach—the gas can inflame your airways and damage the lining of your lungs—but they might not read the label of that great new toilet cleanser and the fantastic toilet scrub or know that the chemicals in them, when mixed together, can create potentially deadly chlorine gas.

the freaking
REMOTE IS DEAD—again!

TOP SCREWUPS

- Buying old batteries
- Storing them improperly
- Leaving them in energy-sapping devices

You are watching your favorite program when a horribly loud commercial for a miracle cleaner blares through the speakers. The baby just got to sleep. You reach for the remote control and push the volume button and nothing happens. Don't let this happen to you! Follow these tips to keep your batteries from running out of juice and, not incidentally, prevent them from exploding.

Don't End up with a Battery Bomb

We should probably begin with the exploding thing first. Yes, alkaline batteries sometimes do explode. In fact, if you look at the packaging for your AAs, you will probably see a small-print warning advising you of this potential danger. This is, it should be noted, very rare, but it does occasionally happen.

These occasional blasts are why you may have heard you should not mix new and used batteries or different types of batteries (non-chargeable with rechargeable, for example) in the same device. When batteries have different levels of charge, the stronger cell will discharge rapidly to compensate for the weaker cell, which can cause it to overheat and, on rare occasions, go boom.

But They Seemed So Young

Now that we've gotten the explosions out of the way, why might your batteries be losing power so quickly? You may have bought old batteries to start with. **If you shop in a store with a low turnover, it is possible that the batteries have been gathering dust for a while before you came along.** The batteries at closeout and odd-lot stores may have already been sitting on the shelf at another store before they even got to yours.

Buying in Bulk Won't Save You This Time

Even though you want to be prepared, it doesn't help to buy batteries in bulk and stock up. Even if they are not in use, batteries degrade and lose their charge over time. **Buy what you need and a backup set, then replace your spares when you use them.**

Don't Let the Good Die Young

It is a myth that batteries last longer if you store them in the refrigerator or freezer. In fact, prolonged exposure to extreme cold or heat reduces battery life. When you store batteries, you want to be sure that they are not making a connection. Store them so that they are not touching other batteries or anything metal. Don't carry batteries loose in your bag or purse because they might roll around and come into contact with a metal object.

TOP TIP

When batteries have different levels of charge, the stronger cell will discharge rapidly to compensate for the weaker cell, which can cause it to overheat and, on rare occasions, go boom.

LEAVING THEM IN WEARS THEM OUT

Batteries drain more quickly when they are in an electronic device, even if the device is off. **If you have a camera or battery-operated gizmo that you only use from time to time, take the batteries out until you think you'll need them.** If you have a device that runs on both batteries and electricity, take the batteries out and store them while you're using the wall plug.

stop murdering your poor, innocent
HOUSEPLANTS

Every year thousands of houseplants are killed by well-meaning individuals with brown thumbs. They're so lush and green when you pick them up, but soon they droop, grow spots, get moldy, or just wither away to a husk. But you can mend your murdering ways if you just take the time to get to know your new roomie.

Who's Thirsty? Not the Plant!

You think you're doing a good thing. Your poor philodendron is looking sad and yellow. "You must be thirsty," you say to the plant, and you run to get your well-used watering can. The next day Phil is looking even more peeked, and with love you douse it again. A few days later, Phil is dead. You murdered him!

Warning Signs That Your Plant Is Drinking Too Much

Everyone knows you can kill a plant by under-watering, but many people get overzealous in the other direction. **You can recognize an overwatered plant by its yellow leaves, brown tips, and limp appearance.** A chronically overwatered plant also begins to shed its leaves.

Plant roots make no value judgments. They will suck up all of the water you provide them and pass them up through the stem to veins in the leaves. When the leaves are already saturated, the cells stretch to accommodate the extra water. Keep adding more and the cells will burst. At this point, some of the roots will rot and die. Plants need a direct proportion of root to leaves, so if the roots die, an equal number of leaves will go.

How Much Is Too Much?

At some point someone might have told you that houseplants should be watered once a week. This is not true. A plant needs water when it is thirsty, and this varies by plant species, season of growth, and the relative humidity where the plant lives. 🌀 **The simple way to determine if your plant needs water is to touch the soil. If it feels dry, the plant needs water.**

Nursing Your Victim Back to Health

If you have overwatered your plant, the one way to bring it back is to bring the root to leaf ration back by pruning. If you catch it in time, the remaining root system will recover enough to take care of the remaining leaves on the plant, eventually creating new roots and foliage.

WHEN ALL ELSE FAILS

If you do not trust this tactile method, you can buy a moisture meter. Don't leave the meter stuck in the soil all the time. Just poke it in when you think the plant might be ready for a drink. Plant experts say to ignore the booklet that comes with the device about various houseplants and their watering schedules. Let the soil itself give you the information.

WASH YOUR DOG
without taking a bath

 **TOP SCREWUPS**

- Throwing an unsuspecting pup in the tub
- Not brushing out the knots first
- Getting caught unprepared
- Cleaning only the easy parts

All you want is to be able to pet Lulu without holding your nose. You end up soaking wet, with a flooded bathroom, wet paw prints throughout the house, and a squirmy, soapy dog shaking suds all over your living room. It could have gone better.

Easing into the Bath

The trick to avoiding bathing battles is not to spring the idea on your dog all at once. Often a pet never sees the inside of a tub until someone throws her into it—all of a sudden she's in chest-high warm water and being doused in soap. You would protest, too, if someone did that to you.

You should start preparing for Lulu's first bath long before she gets dirty. **Teach your dog that the bath is a positive place. Start with a dry tub.** You can lift a small dog into the tub. If you have a fairly large dog, it will make your life much easier if she gets into the tub herself. You can lure her there with a treat. Play with the dog with a special toy, or pet her and speak in a soothing voice. Then take her back out.

Almost There

A few days later, try it again with a small amount of water in the tub. Then try it with a little more. Keep the water lukewarm so that it is comfortable for her. When you get to the point that the dog will let you wet her down without a fuss, you're ready for bath time! Almost.

Don't Get Caught Unprepared

Here are a few things you need to do to make sure a doggy bath goes swimmingly:

- Before you give your dog her first full bath, 🖓 **brush out her coat to be sure all mats have been removed.** Any knots that are left will become tighter once they are wet.

- Be sure you 🖓 **have the towel you will use to dry the dog handy.** You do *not* want to have to go looking for it with the dog still in the tub, especially if the dog is trying to get out of the tub.

- You need to use a special shampoo formulated for dogs, not the stuff you use on your own hair. Human shampoos have the wrong pH balance for dogs.

Water, Water Everywhere

Don't ignore the hard-to-reach parts of the dog. If you just scrub her back and sides, she isn't really clean. You'll need to 🖓 **wash her underside (this is where the most dirt collects) and her head and face, too.** The bath is a good time to check the dog's skin for lumps. If you find anything suspicious, have it checked by the vet.

TOP TIP

You need to use a special shampoo formulated for dogs, not the stuff you use on your own hair.

Don't Get Run Over

If your dog becomes nervous and tries to make a run for it, you need to be gentle but firm. Do not stop to soothe her because this will only reinforce her anxiety. Instead, keep bathing her while speaking in a calm voice. When she has calmed down you can praise her and maybe even offer her a treat.

It's Finally Over

Rather than rubbing her dry with the towel, which will tangle the coat, pat her dry and squeeze out any excess water. When it is all done, brush your dog again and enjoy the pleasures of the company of your squeaky-clean dog.

MAKE THINGS EASIER FOR YOURSELF

Your job will be easier if you have a handheld showerhead or spray nozzle that attaches to your bath faucet. You can use a plastic cup to scoop water from the bath to rinse the dog, but a spray nozzle does a better job of penetrating the fur. Also, if the dog is quite dirty, you will simply be dumping the dirt that came off back on.

don't let the cat
SHRED your furniture

The instinct to scratch is deeply embedded in your cat's DNA. Somewhere in the feline subconscious is the memory of an African plain, where lion ancestors sharpened their claws and marked their territory by scratching trees.

Evolutionary Psychology for Kitties

Your ten-pound kitty's territory may be nothing more than the inside of your house or apartment, and there may be no competing cats to impress or scare away. In theory then, Patches should not need to compulsively mark her territory with obsessive furniture shredding, but she still does. (Just as you do not need to eat as though you lived in the wild where food is scarce, but you do anyway.)

🖐 **Scratching not only leaves a visible mark, but it also releases scent markers through glands in the cat's paws.** This is why even declawed cats will make scratching motions. They are still able **to mark their territory** with their scent this way.

Furniture Defense

With this much evolution working against you, it is unlikely you can persuade your cat to stop. If you do not want to declaw your cat and you don't want tattered,

🗨 **TOP SCREWUPS**

- Not knowing the why of the scratch
- Trying to only change the cat
- Reinforcing negatively

scraped furniture, you will have to doctor the furniture, at least for a while.

Cats like to scratch anything that has a satisfying texture. The wooden legs of your dining room set or your upholstered armchair feel nice to Mitsy. **One way to spare your table or chair legs is to make your furniture less appealing to your cat by putting double-faced masking tape or a plastic cover over a favorite scratching spot.** You can also use citrus sprays on the furniture—cats hate that stuff!

Replacing Bad Habits

Since cats have an innate need to scratch their territory in particular spots, **place a scratching post near the area that your cat loves to claw.** Once she has become accustomed to using the post, you should be safe to uncover the furniture.

Discipline Fail

Cats are infamously hard to train, though not impossible. They do not respond to negative reinforcement though, so yelling at her may stop her from what she's doing at the moment, but it probably won't teach her not to do it in the future. Physically reprimanding a cat will never ever work and will only breed hostility and further bad behavior. The best way to train your cat to scratch a post and not your couch is by enticing her to do so. **Rub some catnip on the post, put some treats on it, and include it in playtime.**

DON'T SCREW UP

YOUR DIY

WALLPAPERING fails

TOP SCREWUPS

- Running out of paper
- Skipping crucial prep work
- Getting bubbles, peels, and curls

Presumably you want to hang wallpaper to make your room look better, not worse, but nothing can ruin the look of a room like a shoddy papering job.

Don't Underestimate the Job by Overestimating Your Skills

You don't want to run out of paper before you get the job done and run back to the store only to find your pattern is no longer in stock. When you are shopping, keep in mind that it is possible you might screw up with a roll or two before you get the hang of things. **Buy 30 to 40 percent more than you think you'll need, especially if your paper is from a discontinued line or has a pattern.** You're more likely to waste the patterned stuff because you might put it up only to realize the pattern doesn't align and have to start over. Make sure the batch numbers on all of the rolls match. You don't want to find yourself surrounded by two shades of almost the same color.

Start with a Clean Slate

One key to keeping out puckers and blisters is to make sure that the wall underneath is smooth and clean. Sure it's tempting to plaster over those little bits of the old paper you couldn't quite get off, but you'll be sorry if you succumb to the siren song of shoddy work. **First you should make a point to cover and fill any holes and cracks. Then wash the walls to get rid of any grease and grime. Next, prep the walls by painting them with a primer.** You may be saying, "But I'm papering so I don't have to paint." If you don't, however, there is a greater chance you'll end up with a bumpy, uneven surface.

Another option is to line the walls with lining paper to cover imperfections. Hang the lining paper horizontally so the seams do not fall in the same place as the wallpaper.

Glue It Good

Use a pasting table and brush, and apply a generous amount of wallpaper paste to the paper, making sure you paste right up to the edges and corners. This will prevent the seams from curling up on you later.

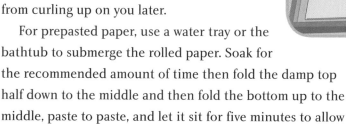

For prepasted paper, use a water tray or the bathtub to submerge the rolled paper. Soak for the recommended amount of time then fold the damp top half down to the middle and then fold the bottom up to the middle, paste to paste, and let it sit for five minutes to allow the adhesive to activate and the paper to relax.

Smoothing It Out

Hang your first strip along the guideline you created using a level and plumb line, and not your crooked wall. Use a paper-hanging brush to smooth out any bubbles, working from the center out. Stand back and take a look.  **If it seems to be puckered and uneven, take a deep breath, gently pull it down, and start again.** This will happen. More than once. Deep breaths. After you hang another strip to your liking, seal the matching edges with a seam roller.

To get a nice straight edge along the ceiling, bottom of the walls, and the corners, use a spatula to make a crease along the edge. Peel back the paper, and use scissors or a utility knife to cut along the crease.

misadventures in **PAINTING**

When painting a room, your goal is to get the paint in a nice, even coat on the walls, not to give yourself a rage attack as you make a mess.

Paint without Creating a Jackson Pollock Imitation on the Floor

The key to not dripping paint around the room is surprisingly simple. **Don't dip the brush very deeply into the paint.** See? Simple. The more paint on the brush, the more there is to drip off, flick around, and generally get out of control. To maintain the upper hand, hold the handle close to the brush head, not at the end. You may not think of it this way, but you are operating a lever. The longer the lever, the wider the arc of the swing and the harder it is to control. Physics! Not as simple . . .

As you work, paint will automatically be pushed toward the base of the brush and accumulate there. If you stroke outward from time to time, you can keep that buildup from dripping. Don't make grand gestures with your brush hand or finish off your strokes with a flourish. This will just spray little drops around the room.

Don't Take Your Lumps

A low-tech way to avoid lumpy paint is to cut a circle of window-screening material to the right circumference for it to fit inside the can. **After mixing the paint, lay the screen on top of the paint. As the screen sinks, it will carry the lumpy paint particles to the bottom of the can.**

Roll with It

Unless you're going for a spin-art effect on the walls and your face, bring some paint up into the slanted part of the tray and use this thin coating to cover your roller. Roll it back and forth several times, pressing firmly, to make the roller grip the paint. You want it to soak in evenly. If you have excess paint on the surface of the roller, it will not only drip and splatter, but it will also go on the wall unevenly and produce dreaded paint streaks.

Now roll slowly. Put some muscle into it. **For even coverage you really have to press as you go.** This is especially important for ceilings. If you're painting these, you'd better get some goggles.

There's Always a Next Time

Now that you have a lovely streak-free paint job, plan ahead to make your life easier next time. Rather than leaving the leftover paint to dry up in the paint can, pour it into a clean airtight container such as a plastic milk jug. Remember to label the outside of the container by manufacturer, color, number, and storage date, and keep it somewhere it will not be mistaken for food!

Before you pack everything away, take a piece of cardboard the size of a piece of office paper—the cardboard from the back of a lined notepad works well for this—and give it a few coats of paint. Now you have a sample of the wall color to take with you when you're shopping for furniture and other decorative items for the room.

TOP TIP

. . . bring some paint up into the slanted part of the tray and use this thin coating to cover your roller. Roll it back and forth several times, pressing firmly, to make the roller grip the paint.

NOW YOU SMELL IT, NOW YOU DON'T!

If you actually want to enjoy your beautiful new room—instead of just nodding in satisfaction and then fleeing for fresher air for a few weeks after you paint—you need to get rid of that paint-fume smell. To do this, place several charcoal briquettes in a pan, leave them in the center of the room, and close the door. The smell will be gone as soon as the next day!

your beautiful piece of **ART**
is hideously hung

There is one painting hanging on your living room wall. Itis above the sofa, sort of, but a little bit off to the side. If you cock your head at just the right angle, you can almost pretend it is hanging straight. Next time perhaps you should try a different technique.

Don't Just Start Banging Away

Before you start pounding holes into the wall, make sure your final product is not going to come crashing down. **A nail and hook is fine for smaller frames, but if you have a larger frame, you will either need to buy some hollow-wall anchors,** which distribute the frame's weight and grip the drywall more securely, or you will need to nail directly into a stud. Use a stud finder to see if there's one in the wall where you'd like to hang your frame. Expect to make or hear jokes along the lines of "The stud's right here!" This is inevitable.

Finding the Sweet Spot

Your art will look best if you hang it so that the center is approximately at eye level and so that it follows the lines of furniture or windows. Don't hang a tiny picture on a huge wall—it'll just seem lonely. One way to get an idea of how it will look is to trace around the picture on a piece of paper, cut it out, and then stick the paper version on the wall.

Now you can back up, gaze at it, and see if you like its position without driving a bunch of nails in, deciding you hate it, patching the holes, and doing it again. Once you've got it where you want it, mark the top edge with a pencil.

Next, you need to measure the space from the top of the frame to the hanger. Be sure to pull the wire taut before you measure, or it will not hang where you intended. Measure out the same distance down on the wall from the top of the mark you made and make another pencil mark there.

Hammer Time!

A rookie mistake to make at this point would be to pound the nail into this spot. This is actually the spot where the wire is supposed to rest. So put the bottom of your hook on the pencil mark, mark above it where the nail needs to be, and pound your hook into the wall there. Hang the picture. Marvel at the beauty.

THE DANG THING JUST WON'T STAY STRAIGHT!

Some frames will have a tendency to droop, forcing you to constantly adjust them, thus driving you crazy in proportion to your need for neatness and order. There are two ways to keep a picture prone to tipping in its place:

1. The first involves the wire on the back. The painting will slide around if the wire is too smooth. You can fix this by wrapping a little masking tape around the part of the wire that goes over the hook. The texture will keep the wire from slipping.

2. The other technique is to secure the bottom corners with poster tack, museum wax, or rubber feet. These should provide just enough stickiness or friction to keep the picture in its place.

don't be driven mad by a
DRIPPING FAUCET

TOP SCREWUPS

- Waiting for someone else to fix it
- Having dirty aerators
- Letting the faucet seat get worn out

The sound of water is usually relaxing. People spend good money on "nature sounds" CDs and white noise apps to hear ocean waves and babbling brooks. But you will never find "faucet drip" title among these soothing sounds.

Who Cares?

If a dripping faucet has you ready to climb the walls, chances are you are a woman. This isn't because the fairer sex is less handy, though. Psychologists have found that there are certain noises that bother women more than men, and a faucet drip is one of them. They can only speculate as to why this would be.

What we do know is that throughout the nation people are having conversations like this:

"I thought you said you were going to fix that faucet."

"Yes, dear, I'll get to it."

"Isn't it driving you crazy?"

"I said I'd get to it."

So, ladies, instead of waiting for him, break out the toolbox yourself. Here is how to fix a leaking faucet *and* avoid an expensive plumber's fee.

Start with the Simple Stuff

Before you disassemble your sink, check to see if you have a blocked aerator. What's an airgator you say?

⚪ The *aerator* is the little device on the end of your **faucet** that softens the flow of water by introducing air into the stream. That little screen can get clogged, and when it does, the faucet will run slowly when hot and cold are both turned on. It will also trap water that will drip, drip, drip, drip. If this is your problem, it's an easy fix.

👍 **Unscrew the aerator, clean it out, and put it back on.**

Still Suffering a Drip?

If your problem wasn't that simple, you've probably got a washer that's all washed out. To replace it, you're going to have to remove the faucet, but first you'll need to turn off the water supply. You do not want a geyser of tap water to the face when you take apart the faucet. Look under the sink for the water valve, and turn it counterclockwise. Turn the faucet on to let out any water that remains in the pipe. Now for the real fun.

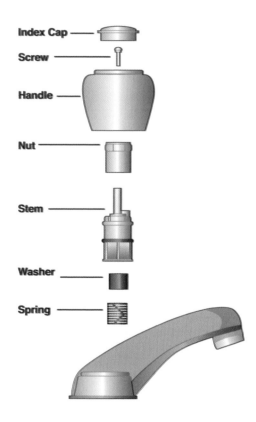

Index Cap

Screw

Handle

Nut

Stem

Washer

Spring

⚪ Sink Surgery in 7 Simple Steps!

❶ To begin the operation, you need to take the top off the faucet. Nearly all handles are fixed with a screw (or screws if you have individual hot and cold handles). If you do not see it, it may be hidden under a decorative cap, which you can pry off with a small screwdriver.

WHEN ALL ELSE
FAILS

If the operation was a failure, fear not—you have not lost the patient yet. It is possible the seating is worn. In this case, you will need to buy a valve-seat dresser from a hardware store. Take the faucet apart again and then push the end of the tool into the faucet. Adjust the cutter so it touches the seat and rotate it to grind down the metalwork. Put the faucet back together, and it should be drip free!

If that made you cock one eyebrow and/or tilt your head, you will probably need to ask a few questions at the hardware store. If you're still feeling less than confident, it's time to call in a professional.

2 Loosen the locknut inside the faucet with a crescent wrench.

3 Once the nut is loose, pull out the stem. Be sure to remember the order in which the parts came off—you will need to put them back on!

4 Use a screwdriver to pry off the old rubber washer at the bottom of the stem. The washer may be held in place with a small screw. If it is, remove the screw.

5 Push a new washer of exactly the same size into place and screw the nut back onto the faucet, being careful not to overtighten it.

6 If you did not know in advance what size washer you would need, you will now need to take a trip to the hardware store to find one that fits properly.

7 Replace the parts you took off in the previous steps, turn the water back on, and enjoy your drip-free faucet.

SOME ASSEMBLY required

You bought what you hope will be a bookshelf at your favorite Swedish furniture store. Now you're home with a box of ambiguous parts and instructions that read like they were written in Japanese and translated into Korean before ending up in English. You are sensing the beginning of a headache. So how can you get part A into slot B without pulling hair C out of head D?

Don't Let the Bell Toll for Thee

The biggest mistake when it comes to putting together kit furniture is not giving yourself enough time to tackle the task in a relaxed manner. Launching into assembly after spending five hours in an IKEA can turn the closet organizer that's supposed to make your life simpler into a chore that makes your life shorter.

Besides being absolutely infuriating, working in these conditions will make for a shoddier bookshelf. If you're in a hurry and/or exhausted, you're not going to be as careful and thorough as you should be. You may end up with something that either looks like garbage or actually ends up *in* the garbage.

Whoa There, Overeager Peter

It is not uncommon for an overly enthusiastic amateur furniture assembler to stab the packaging with a box cutter only to find that (s)he has sliced the tabletop and the instruction manual, too. **Before you open**

the box—which you will do while carefully avoiding its contents—check it for damage. If the box is banged up, your furniture might be, too.

Make a Positive ID

Once you've managed to open the box without incident, find the instructions before you throw it out. The manual may be on one piece of paper, and it might be stuck to the side of the box. (You should really keep the box until you've managed to put the whole thing together in case some parts are missing and you need to take the whole dang thing back.)

Spread out the contents and see what you've got. You're probably not going to be too confused as to which piece is the table leg, but you may get tripped up by the small pieces. There are probably a few different kinds of screws and bolts that look reeeeeallly similar. To avoid confusion down the line, separate the small parts and put them into the wells of a muffin tin (use bowls for larger small parts). Label them with the part's identifying number from the instruction manual.

Easy Now!

Because kit furniture is often made of particleboard, your biggest challenge is to make sure you use the right screw in the right hole. Otherwise you might strip the threads or chip the material. Then your cheap piece of furniture becomes an expensive piece of trash. This is why making a positive ID of all the parts is so important.

You should 👍 **try to assemble your furniture on a carpet or towel.** The finished surfaces of particleboard furniture are infamously easy to snap off, and if you're banging pieces around on a hard floor, you're just asking for damage.

SO YOU BROKE IT

Don't feel bad. Breaking some flimsy piece or stripping a hole is pretty much a guarantee. Here's what you do:

Screwup ······▶ Big Fix

- You stripped a screw hole.
- Gently hammer as many toothpicks as you can into the hole. Use some strong scissors or a small handsaw to cut off the ends so they are flush with the edge of the piece. Screw away!

- You broke one of those cheap dowels, and they only gave you the precise number you need.
- Tape together a bunch of toothpicks to the gauge of an unbroken dowel. Use scissors to trim your Frankenstein piece to the length of the dowel. Use as a dowel.

- A surface chipped, and now you can see the ugly particleboard.
- You can fill deep gauges with wood putty and you can repair the surface with replacement veneer, which comes in a huge selection at most hardware stores.

TOILET terrors

TOP SCREWUPS

- Letting panic cause a flood
- Using drain cleaners
- Using the wrong plunger
- Being afraid of snakes

Nothing will spoil your day like an overflowing commode that floods your bathroom ankle-deep in, well, stuff you don't want to wade in.

Act Fast, as in Right This Second!

Jump into action as soon as you become aware the toilet is going to overfill. Sometimes, if you have a plunger at the ready, you can unclog the drain before the liquid has a chance to get to the bowl's rim. If your initial attempts are not successful, you will want to stop the water from rushing out of the bowl, which unfortunately means getting all up around it.

Reach under the left side of the tank and you should find a shut-off valve. Turn it off at the source, and the bowl will stop filling. You can also lift the lid off the tank and raise the floater. You have to keep holding the floater, though, this is only a stopgap measure in case you are having trouble getting the valve to turn quickly.

It's Tempting to Go for the Hands-off Approach

Of course you want to avoid coming in contact with the yucky water. This leads many people to reach for liquid drain cleaner, such as Drano, in the hopes that it will magically sort out everything. Unfortunately, this is not what these liquids were designed to do. They do a poor job on large pipes, such as those under the toilet. They can even eat holes through the pipes if they're used often, and then you'll get toilet water leaking in your walls. Fun!

Plunge On In There

Put a bit of Vaseline on the lip of the plunger go get a good seal. Insert it into the water on a diagonal so the air escapes out of the rubber bell.

Use plunging strokes that create force inside the trap (the hole in the bowl leads to a narrow passageway called the trap) without splashing the water in your face. If beginning with a push isn't working, try the opposite approach: Slowly push the plunger down over the opening, then pull back fast to create negative pressure in the trap. With any luck, the obstruction will be cleared.

Snakes—the Good Kind

If your toilet is clogged by something too large for a plunger to handle—for example if your son tried to flush his toy car—you will need an auger, also known as a "snake," to get it out.

To avoid making ugly black scratch marks on the porcelain, insert the auger into the bowl with the cable fully retracted in its protective shaft. While applying downward pressure onto the handle, crank the cable clockwise. The spring on the end of the auger will break up paper clogs or snag wayward items. You'll know when the obstruction has been reached because the crank will become hard to turn. Don't crank the snake backward or you'll lose what you've caught. Instead, slowly try to pull the item back through the trap.

WHY WON'T THIS PLUNGER WORK!?

If you can't get the plunger to create any suction action, you might be using a sink plunger and not a toilet plunger. There is a difference. Who knew, right? A sink plunger has a rubber cup that is usually eraser-colored. A toilet plunger has a protruding smaller bell coming out of the cup (like the little head that comes out of the big head in *Alien*). The commode variety is usually black. Explanation of color choice is pretty self-explanatory.

don't screw up with your
SCREWDRIVER

Your screwdriver may not look as scary as a chain saw, but this handheld tool beats that producer of horror-movie sound effects when it comes to the sheer number of injuries it causes each year. The Royal Society for the Prevention of Accidents estimates that 3,800 Britons injure themselves each year with screwdrivers—more than with welding equipment, axes, circular saws, power drills, chain saws, blow torches, or heat guns. In fact, the only household tool that causes more injuries is the hammer.

It's a Bad Fit

One common screwdriver mishap involves a screwdriver that is not quite the right size for the respective screw. If you use a small driver in a screw with a large slot, it is likely to slip. This is bad in many ways. Even if it doesn't slip and stab you in the hand, which it absolutely can, you may damage the driver's blade. If the blade is too large for the screw but you force it in anyway, you might snap off the screw and will probably damage the wood as you try to turn it. A bad fit in either direction can strip the screw's slot, and then you *really* have a problem.

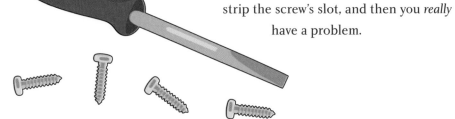

The Wrong Tool for the Job

If you're faced with the common problem of having a Phillips screw and a flat-head screwdriver, 🛠 **just wait until you can locate the right kind of driver.** If you try to turn the screw with what you've got, you may manage to get it to turn a bit, but in the process you will damage your screwdriver's head and maybe strip the screw hole. Either of these outcomes will be frustrating down the road.

Don't Screw Up the Wood

Another common screwing screwup is splitting the wood. Avoiding this is easy. All you have to do is 🛠 **drill a pilot hole.** Using a drill, an awl, or an ice pick, make a hole slightly smaller than the diameter of the screw. Always use a drill if you're going to be placing the screw near the end of a board.

Wood always splits along the grain. So another method to prevent splitting is to clamp the edges of the wood before screwing. This reduces the outward pressure on the grain and keeps everything together.

WHAT A SCREWDRIVER ISN'T

A Screwdriver Is Not a Hammer

Another way people injure themselves with screwdrivers is by using them for things they were never intended to do. One of the most common is when a person lacking a hammer tries to use the plastic handle of the screwdriver to whack a nail into place. The plastic is not hard enough for the task and can shatter into pieces that can fly into a person's eye.

A Screwdriver Is Not a Mini Crowbar

Don't use your screwdriver to pry things up. Screwdrivers have been known to snap in half under the pressure, sending their owners reeling. A screwdriver should only be used for its namesake, driving screws.

don't get stuck with **SUPERGLUE**

Krazy Glue, Super Glue, and similar glues with different brand names are great for sticking two pieces of broken china together and just as effective at bonding your index finger to your thumb and your hand to the plate.

The Glue for You

Using the right glue for the right job is important. There are different types of glue available, each of which is best suited for a particular material. There are superglues designed to work with wood, plastic, and ceramic. Choose the appropriate type and the appropriate applicator for the task at hand. Read the instructions carefully.

How to Use Superglue without Getting Too Attached

THIS LIP BALM TASTES FUNNY

When you are finished using the glue, put it back where it belongs. You do not want to leave the tube someplace where it could be confused for any other product. This might seem unlikely, but it happens so often that physicians needed to create an official term for it: "inadvertent self-administration of superglue."

- Cover your work surface with cloth or metal foil. This will prevent any spilled glue from remaining on the work surface for the rest of your life.

- You need only one drop for a square inch of surface area if you're using one of the major brands. Using too much will increase the likelihood of finger-sticking mishaps, do a worse job holding your object together, and increase drying time.

so you GLUED YOUR FINGERS together

Hey, it happens to the best of us. If you started building a model rocket and are now struggling to turn these pages with a little plastic booster cemented to your palm, here is what you need to get unstuck: acetone.

TOP SCREWUPS

• Trying to yank your glued parts apart

Here's Hoping Someone in Your House Does Her Nails

Acetone is most commonly found in nail polish remover, but not all nail polish removers are acetone based. Check the bottle before you pour. **A small amount of an acetone-based nail polish remover on a cotton swab applied to the glue is all it takes to dissolve the bond.**

Acetone Alternative

If you do not have any nail polish remover handy, **immerse any bonded skin in warm soapy water, then peel or roll the skin apart. Take your time.** You may have to dunk the glued skin in the water several times.

Don't Use Your Muscle

If your fingers are stuck together, do not try to pull them apart. The commercials you've seen are no joke. Superglue is so strong that several drops can hold a two-ton truck in the air. (An Australian television science program demonstrated this.) Your skin will separate from your finger before it will break its bond with the glue.

CASES OF MISTAKEN IDENTITY

If you have mistaken your superglue for your lip balm (see previous entry on page 50) apply warm water to your lips and also wet your lips from the inside with saliva. Peel or roll the lips apart. Do not try to pry them from each other. If the glue becomes stuck on the inside of your mouth, saliva should lift the adhesive in one to two very long days.

If you have mistaken your superglue for your artificial lash glue, you have a bigger problem. The good news is, it appears that there are no documented cases of superglue in the eye causing permanent damage, but you do not want to be the first! Do not try to pry the eye open. Wash with warm water and apply a gauze patch. Have someone drive you to the doctor.

DON'T SCREW UP

YOUR FOOD

don't FALL SHORT on RECIPES

You are expecting company in two hours and are preparing a beautiful meal from a recipe you found in a magazine. You have chopped the vegetables, preheated the oven, the sauce is already cooking on the stove, and suddenly you realize that when you went shopping you forgot to buy coriander. What can you substitute? Cloves start with "c"—maybe that will work. You glance ahead to see if you have forgotten anything else, and your heart sinks when you see, "chill overnight."

Learn from the French

I have three words for you: *mise en place.* Mise en place is the French way of saying "putting in place." It is a term invented by restaurant chefs and refers to the 👍 **first step of any meal prep: arranging all of the ingredients that will be needed for that evening's cooking.**

Start well in advance of your meal and 👍 **read through the recipe, noting any ingredients you will need, their amounts, and what must be done with them.** Most printed recipes begin with a list of ingredients and quantities, and perhaps a cooking time. It is easy to make the mistake of reading those two pieces of information and thinking you're ready to go. But sometimes a cookbook author sneaks in a crucial bit of information in the process part of the recipe. For example, the cherries must be frozen ahead of time or the meat must be marinated for several hours.

Prep Like They Do on Food Network

Once you've gone through the recipe and noted that the carrots are chopped, the garlic mashed, and the cheese grated, you can begin by preparing these items. Measure out the quantities you will need and set each aside in individual bowls or measuring cups. Set them on your counter like you're Paula Deen.

Now as you go through the steps of your recipe, when it calls for "three eggs beaten," you just need to pick up the right bowl. When it comes time to sift in the flour, you do not have to stop to measure. 👍 **Doing all the prep work upfront allows the cooking portion of your evening to be, well, a piece of cake!**

IF YOU FIND YOURSELF WITHOUT . . .

No matter how conscientious you try to be, you're bound to forget or run out of something from time to time. So,

If You Don't Have:	Then Use:
1 egg	2 tablespoons milk mixed with ½ teaspoon baking powder
1 cup sour cream	1 cup plain whole yogurt plus 3 tablespoons melted butter
1 cup milk (baking only)	1 cup water plus 1½ teaspoons melted butter
Vegetable oil	Olive oil
Honey	Corn syrup

don't waste money at the
GROCERY STORE

TOP SCREWUPS

- Failing to plan
- Skipping over bargains
- Not knowing if a deal is really a deal

Most articles on budgeting will tell you to plan your shopping list in advance and stick to it no matter what. The idea here is to avoid the temptation of putting a lot of impulse buys in your cart. But this strategy can backfire when you pass up bargains and buy more expensive options from your list instead. As former president and famed strategist Dwight D. Eisenhower once said, 👍 **"planning is everything, the plan is nothing."**

Don't Get Hung Up

Having some low-cost recipes to shop for will save you money if you do that instead of grabbing convenience foods, but 👍 **if you planned pork and discover your local shop is having an incredible sale on beef, you're better off getting the bargain** and preparing meals with what you bought.

Go by the Book—Your Book

Of course, to take advantage of bargains, you have to know if you're really getting a bargain. Shops do all kinds of marketing tricks to make you think you're saving when you're really spending. The only way to be sure is to 👍 **have a good idea of what various products cost at different stores in your area.** Keep a price book with sections that correspond to the aisles in a typical grocery store, or you can try to arrange the pages alphabetically—apples followed by apricots, and so on. Knowing how to space it this way can be a challenge, but use whatever system makes sense to you. You'll become familiar enough with the prices to know if a product was marked up first in order to be marked down later.

Make More Than One Stop

Chances are no one store in your area has the best prices on everything. After a while, you'll start to see some patterns. You will know that store A has better prices on dairy and store B on paper goods. These days you can also find smartphone applications that allow you to find out where the best deals are on individual products.

Here's the Plan

Now that you are well educated and you know which shops have the best prices, you can set a realistic upper limit for the items you buy regularly. This is your strategy. 🕐 **Plan your meals and make a grocery list. Decide which stores to go to based on which are likeliest to have the best prices for the major items on your list.** If you discover that those items are priced higher than you're willing to pay, pass them up and go for something else.

SMARTER THAN COUPONS

Coupons are useful if they are helping you to save on items you would normally buy, but not if they are enticing you to buy things you usually don't. (See pages 236–237.) One of the most overlooked ways to save money is personal relationships. Instead of just clipping coupons, stop and chat with the staff at the stores where you frequently shop. If you're friendly with the employees and you let them know you're a bargain shopper, they will point out all of the best deals and special offers. They can give you insider information about what days new stock comes in or when prices are changed. And they sure won't let you miss the coupons in the circular that you can really use.

reheating LEFTOVERS
without ruining them

TOP SCREWUPS

- Overusing the microwave

Life is full of small disappointments. For example, you have a delicious but huge meal at a restaurant, so you ask to take the leftovers home in a box. The next day you get the Styrofoam out of the fridge, looking forward to a delicious treat at lunchtime, but after a quick zap in the microwave, your gourmet meal has turned into mush that is fiery hot on the outside, icy cold on the inside.

Don't Always Go for the Microwave

Microwaves are great for fast heating, but they do not always do the best job of keeping yesterday's foods appetizing. If you have the option, **you will usually get better results reheating your leftovers in a traditional oven.** Fried foods are notorious for becoming soggy in the microwave. Instead, wrap your fried chicken and french fries in aluminum foil and stick them under the broiler. Broilers provide top-down heat, which can make them crunchy again.

Pizza becomes soft and doughy in the microwave. To keep the crust crisp, bake the slices on an aluminum foil–covered baking sheet in an oven set to 450°F (232°C). Or try heating it on the stovetop. Heat a pan or skillet on medium-high for one minute; place the pizza in the pan; cover and heat for another two to three minutes. A toaster oven also works well, if you have one.

Microwave the Right Way

While fried foods come out of the microwave a bit gummy, some foods, like rice or turkey, come out tasteless and dry. To combat this problem, just add moisture. You can do this by **placing a small mug filled with water, or even a damp paper towel, in the machine with your food. This will release steam and rehydrate the leftovers.** For an even better flavor, wrap your poultry in aluminum foil and heat it in a conventional oven.

The same property that makes the microwave so bad at reheating makes it an excellent tool for bringing back stale chips. Leftover chips generally become inedible because they soak up too much moisture. Pop them in the microwave for thirty seconds to dry them out and give them a little more life.

 TOP TIP

. . . wrap your fried chicken and french fries in aluminum foil and stick them under the broiler. Broilers provide top-down heat, which can make them crunchy again.

DO NOT RESUSCITATE

Of course, no cooking method can improve upon food that is spoiled. Most cooked foods last only four days when stored in an airtight container in the refrigerator. To maximize your leftover's refrigerator shelf life, keep the fridge temperature below 40°F (4.5°C). Spread the food evenly in the container so the cold air hits it consistently, and leave space between items in your refrigerator so that the cold air can circulate around them. Be aware that a food may not be safe to eat even if it has not yet started to smell bad. If you are planning to keep food longer than a few days, store it in the freezer. (But see the entry on freezer burn on pages 60–61.)

DON'T GET BURNED
by your FREEZER

TOP SCREWUPS

- Not wrapping food well enough
- Keeping food for waaaay too long

Freezer burn should probably be more accurately described as freezer dehydration. A freezer-burned pork chop is one that has lost its water molecules through a process called sublimation. When the chop freezes, its water content becomes ice crystals that then become vapor without first changing into liquid water. Water molecules then spontaneously migrate to the coldest possible place. If there is any way for the water to escape from the food's wrapping it will make a beeline for a place like the freezer's walls. The pork chop is left with a dry, white frost.

Staving Off the Bite

No packaging is completely airtight. Eventually, if it is kept long enough, any food will become frostbitten. To hold it off longer, be sure to use a wrapping material that is designed for freezing. **The ideal packages are vacuum-sealed thick plastic packages, like Cryovac. If you do not have something like this, opt for freezer paper or well-fastened plastic wrap.** Check what material your cling wrap is made of. Polyvinylidine chloride (the stuff they use in Saran Wrap) is preferable to films made of polyvinyl chloride. Polyethylene wraps and sandwich bags do not do a very good job, but **polyethylene "freezer bags" are thicker and should do a fair job, as long as you do not keep them too long.** Uncooked red meats should be used within three months of freezing, while poultry can last as long as nine months.

It's All in How You Wrap

Once you've selected the right material, be sure you do an effective job with the wrapping. If you leave air pockets, the space inside the package will allow the water molecules to float out of the food and onto the inner surface of the packaging where it is colder. **Wrap foods as tightly as you can, and push all the air out of bags.** Do what you do when you dress for freezing temperatures: use a few layers.

TOP TIP

Polyvinylidine chloride (the stuff they use in Saran Wrap) is preferable to films made of polyvinyl chloride.

DON'T BUY THE BURN

When you're in the frozen foods aisle, pick up a package and feel for "snow" inside. Any ice crystals in the packaging were sucked out of the food, which means the food itself is probably dehydrated. It is safe to eat, but it will not taste as good as a package without the snow.

so your **BROWN SUGAR**
turned into a brick

Why Does This Keep Happening!?

The first time you open your bag of brown sugar, it is a lovely soft package of sweetness. The next time you go to use it, it has more in common with a doorstop. How did you screw that up!? The short answer is that you let the moisture out. Brown sugar consists of white sugar crystals coated with a thin film of molasses. Molasses absorbs water vapor, which gives fresh brown sugar its soft, dewy quality. When it is exposed to the air, the molasses starts to lose its moisture and the sugar crystals bond together to form the sucrose cement you have before you.

Now What?

At this point you can get out a hammer and pound away, but there is a way to un-screw up your mistake: restore some of the moisture. To do this, **seal the sugar in an airtight container with something that gives off moisture,** for example a damp towel, a piece of fruit, or a cup of water.

It will take a day or more for the sugar to be restored to

its pre-brick state. If you need to unscrew up your brown sugar more quickly, you can use the microwave to heat and soften the molasses. Put it in for a minute or two on high, checking every half-minute or so to see if it's soft yet. You can do the same in a conventional oven set at 250°F (121°C) for ten to twenty minutes. Once you've heated it up, you have to act fast, though, because this is just a quick fix. The sugar will turn into a brick again as soon as it cools.

DIY Sweet Stuff

If you are frequently confronted with a brown sugar brick in spite of your best efforts, why not avoid the problem all together? Brown sugar is plain sugar with molasses, and making your own is easy. Measure one cup of sugar for every tablespoon of molasses and blend well in a food processor until it looks like, well, brown sugar. For dark brown sugar, you guessed it, add more molasses.

 TOP TIP

If you need to unscrew up your brown sugar more quickly, you can use the microwave to heat and soften the molasses.

SIDESTEPPING THE WHOLE ISSUE

If you want your brown sugar to stay sugar instead of cementing into a rock in the first place, you need to store your brown sugar in a vapor-tight container, like a plastic food storage box with a tight lid or a jar with a screw-top lid.

CAKE mistakes

TOP SCREWUPS

- Using the wrong size pan
- Not preparing your pan correctly
- Skipping crucial prep steps
- Letting too much air in there

Your friend has just gotten a promotion, and you want to help her celebrate by baking a special cake. You imagine her delight as you present a perfect confection to her. In the end, however, you apologize as you set down an uneven concoction with ugly icing and a center that is not quite firm. Why do people refer to easy things as "a piece of cake" when making a cake correctly is so hard?

A Pain in the Pan

You can ruin your cake before you ever take out the flour by choosing a pan that is the wrong size. If your pan is too small, the cake will expand over the top and cause a mess or bulge up in the center like a chocolate camel.

It does not matter how beautiful a cake is if you cannot even get it out of the pan. You do not want to bail your lava cake out of the pan with a spoon, but this is what will inevitably happen if you fail to properly prepare the pan. Most cake recipes say to **grease and flour the pan before pouring in the batter. Don't skip this step!** If you are making an especially gooey cake, you should consider lining the pan with parchment paper.

The Perfect Mix

Unless you want a cake that is full of dry lumps, do not skip the flour sifting. It may seem as though it is a waste of time, but sifting gets the lumps out of the flour and distributes the leavener evenly throughout the mixture.

Undermixing is one of the major cake-baking errors. If you do not take the time to thoroughly combine the ingredients with the flour, you will end up with swirls of ingredients in the finished cake. On the other hand, you do not want to overmix the batter. If you get too much air in there, you run the risk of making the cake fall. A good rule of thumb is to fold the dry ingredients into the sugar and butter as gently as possible and then to stop mixing when all of the flour has been absorbed.

Don't Forget to Air Out the Batter

Once the batter is mixed, pour it into the pan and be sure to smooth it out. This works out the large air cavities and makes sure the top of the cake bakes evenly. Here is the step that is most often missed: **tap the pan. The reason for this is to get rid of any remaining air bubbles trapped in the batter.** If they're left in, they could cause the cake to fall or form little craters in the surface.

Patience Is a Virtue

Especially when it comes to baking a cake. Fight the urge to keep opening the oven to see how the cake is doing. When you do this you cause the heat to fluctuate, which can cause the cake to collapse. This is especially important with cheesecake and flourless cake.

You also need patience when the cake comes out of the oven. It needs to finish baking from within and acclimate itself to room temperature. Let it cool in the pan until the top feels firm. Next, turn it out onto a cooling rack. Don't frost it until it's completely cool, or your frosting will become a drippy mess. Throwing the cake in the fridge to cool it quickly will only make it fall, so you'll just have to wait if you want to enjoy the fluffy goodness.

don't let your
GUACAMOLE look unholy

 **TOP SCREWUPS**

- Preparing it too early
- Not sealing it up

You are planning a small party, and you plan to wow your guests with your homemade guacamole. You spend the afternoon chopping, mashing, and seasoning until everything tastes just right, but by the time your guests arrive, you are looking at a bowl of unappealing brown mush. What happened?

Timing Is Everything

You obviously started making your guacamole way too early. It takes about six hours for an avocado exposed to the air to start changing color. Avocados and other fast-browning fruits, such as apples and bananas, are full of a class of enzymes called polyphenol oxidase. When you cut into the avocado, you open some of the cells allowing the enzyme to react with the oxygen in the air. The chemical reaction produces a brown pigment and makes your guests search for something else to dip their corn chips in. **If you do make an avocado dish early, be sure to keep it in an airtight container.**

It's Not the Pits

There is a popular misconception that you can prevent browning by leaving the pit in the fruit. Some people even go so far as to drop the pit into the center of a bowl of guacamole. The pit has no magical greening properties. The only thing it does is to keep the oxygen away from the avocado it touches, so you'll get a few green spots surrounded by brown.

One Thing You Can Do

The acid from a lemon or lime will slow, but not stop the browning. This is why lemon juice is often an ingredient in guacamole. Dripping a bit of lemon juice on that uneaten avocado half before you wrap it up and store it could give it another day or two of green life.

TOP TIP

Dripping a bit of lemon juice on that uneaten avocado half before you wrap it up and store it could give it another day or two of green life.

PRO TIP

There is a very easy method to stop fruit rust. Chefs who need to prepare avocados in advance of restaurant service cut them and then immediately immerse them in ice-cold water, which keeps them away from oxygen. They stay fresh this way for up to four hours. So you can get your guac all set up and just mash in the pre-peeled and diced avocado at the last minute.

don't cry over
CHOPPED ONION

TOP SCREWUPS

- Working in close quarters
- Using a knife that is too short
- Chopping fingers with onions
- Cutting the onion in half horizontally

You're making a beautiful meal for loved ones. You're drinking a class of cabernet, things are simmering, and everyone's commenting on how good it all smells. You start cutting up some beautiful onions, and— BAM—sulfenic acid in your eyes! All of a sudden you're seasoning the food with your salty tears.

At Least Open the Window

Sulfenic acid—a cousin of sulfuric acid, which is used in antifreeze and fertilizers and to wash away impurities during the refining of petroleum—is the compound in those tasty onions that brings tears to your eyes. But there are ways to fight back against this chemical warfare. **Onion experts recommend working in a well-ventilated room.** If that's not an option, work near the stove with the ventilation fan on. You can also chill the onion in the refrigerator before cutting, heat the onion in the microwave for one minute before cutting, wear goggles, cut the onion under running water, or chop near a flame (these last two are not klutz-approved).

Up Your Game

If you want to take your chopping skills to the next level, you could do what the pros do: cut so fast that you're done with the onion before the vapor has time to get you. Getting that good will take some practice, but here's what to do to get there:

1. 👍 **Begin with a sharp knife that is at least twice as long as the onion.**

2. Position the onion on your cutting board so you can see both the root and the stem. 👍 **Aim to cut it in half vertically, through both the root and stem ends.** Cutting the onion in half horizontally, so the stem ends up on one half and the root the other, is a big mistake. It will be nearly impossible to keep the onion together if you cut it this way.

3. Start the cut and then stop to make sure the blade is lined up properly. Take your hand off the onion and place it on top of the knife so if it slips it won't cut you.

4. When you've cut the onion in half, place each half on the board, cut-side down, and cut off about ½ inch from the tops and discard them. Do not cut off the roots. Remove the peel.

5. 👍 **Hold half of the onion against the cutting board with one hand, curling your fingertips under to keep them away from the blade.** Hold the knife in the other hand with the flat of the blade (flat, top edge of the metal) parallel to the board.

6. Cut the onion almost through in horizontal slices. Be sure they are still connected at the root end.

7. Point the tip of the knife away from yourself and cut vertically toward the root to make something that looks like a stack of sticks. Then cut across the onion to make a dice. Repeat the process with the other onion half.

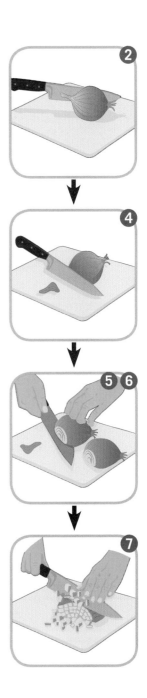

To get a finer dice, hold the knife with one hand and place the fingers of your other hand on top of the knife by the tip. Press the tip lightly into the cutting board, then use a rocking motion with the tip acting as a hinge.

KEEP YOUR ONIONS FRESHER LONGER

By the way, you can make your onions last longer by storing them in the leg from an old pair of panty hose. Put one onion in the leg and tie a knot above it. Slide another onion into the leg and tie a knot above it. Repeat with each onion. The knots keep the onions separated, which lets air circulate between them. This keeps them from rotting. When you need an onion, just cut the lowest-hanging one free. The rest will stay in their little bundles ready for your next—hopefully tear-free—onion recipe.

don't buy a dud WATERMELON

You may have heard something in your distant past about thumping on a watermelon to tell if it is ripe. You may even have stood in a grocery store and rapped on a melon yourself. The question is, did you have any idea what you were listening for?

Size Matters

If a watermelon is plucked from its vine before its time, you will have to eat it before its time, too. So how do you tell if a melon spent enough time on the vine? To start, the larger it is, the more time it probably spent on the vine. Next, 👍 **look at the discolored side of the outer skin. This is the side that was sitting on the soil. If it's light green, it is not ripe and you will not get that great, juicy summer flavor. Look for creamy yellow.**

Knock, Knock

Once you've selected the best shell, it's time to listen to the interior. Rock it a little and listen for any sloshing. Watermelons are ninety percent water (hence the name), and when they are overripe the fiber starts to break down, and you'll hear it sloshing around in the melon. If you don't hear that, rap on the rind. 👍 **The melon should have a hollow sound.** If it emits a high-pitched tone, makes a solid thud, or if anyone knocks back, try a different one.

DON'T FORGET TO WASH UP

Before you cut into your perfect new melon, be sure to wash the rind with running water. Unlike most fruits, melon is not acidic, so any bacteria you transfer from the outer surface to the inside will thrive. Be sure to refrigerate your melon within two to four hours of cutting it.

don't take your lumps
with your GRAVY

TOP SCREWUPS

- Failing to separate
- Using the wrong ratio

Sticky flour islands in a pool of grease. Yum. If your attempts at making gravy produce such unsavory results, here is what's going wrong: basic science. Oil and water don't mix. Gravy is usually made out of drippings, which are a combination of yummy melted meat fat—that's the oil—and a water-based liquid that comes from other cooking juices, such as broth, vegetables, and non-fat meat juices. A delicious gravy incorporates the flavors from both kinds of liquid. But it is hard to get them to play nice together.

You Need to Separate Those Two

In order to make smooth gravy you will need a fat separator. This is a kitchen tool that looks like a pitcher. Pour the liquid in the container and wait for it to settle so that the oil and watery liquids separate. Then you can pour off the water-based liquid. Wait! Don't just dump it out. Pour it into a bowl, and stop just before the layer of fat floating on the surface reaches the opening for the spout.

Get the Ratio Right

Now get your flour. It is important to have the right mix of fat and flour. If you don't use enough flour, it will not be able to absorb all of the fat, and your gravy will have pools of grease. If you use too much flour, you get lumps.

You want to keep the amount of oil and flour as equal as possible. Next, mix the flour into some of the fat, creating a blend called a roux. Mixing the flour with the fat coats each grain of flour with oil. Brown the roux in a pan for two to three minutes.

Mixing Them Up

Stir the water-based liquids into the browned roux and voilà! Oil and water blended into a smooth sauce. This is because the water can't get through to the flour's protein. Thus, when you stir the water-based juices into the roux, the flour grains are dispersed rather than clumping together. For a perfect consistency, use eight or more parts of liquid juice or stock to one part flour and one part fat. You may use a bit more or less depending on how thick you like your gravy.

Finally, simmer the sauce for a few minutes while stirring to break down the flour grains and release their thickening starches. Pour your delicious homemade gravy over mashed potatoes and enjoy.

TOP TIP

It is important to have the right mix of fat and flour. If you don't use enough flour, it will not be able to absorb all of the fat, and your gravy will have pools of grease.

WHERE DO LUMPS COME FROM?

This is where the thickening agent comes in. Most commonly, this is flour. If you just dump the flour into the juices, it will turn into a gooey sludge. This will not impress your guests. Here's why that happened: Flour is made up of the proteins glutenin and glaidin. When they absorb water, they form a sticky substance called gluten. Because the sludge is water-based, the oil cannot get in, and that equals lumps.

slice the **BAGEL,**
not your hand

TOP SCREWUPS

- Being too tired to use a knife
- Using a dull knife

You wake up bleary-eyed and craving a quick carbohydrate-laden breakfast. So you grab a bagel. With your other hand you pick up a slightly dull knife. You start sawing into the bagel toward your own palm, and in your morning fog, you fail to stop slicing when the knife has made it through the breakfast snack and into your skin. You spend the rest of your morning in the emergency room. This is not a good way to start the day.

How Sharp Are You?

Knife slips are more common with dull equipment because it takes more force to get the job done. The extra pressure tires out your cutting arm more quickly, which can also lead to accidents. So keep it sharp. **With a sharp knife, you should not have to saw back and forth. You can use a long, swift motion and be done with it.**

Where's This Screwup Going?

Whenever you use a knife, think about the "failure mode." Where is this knife going to end up if it slips? Hint: the answer should not be "into my forearm." If you're holding the bagel, though, this is just about the only answer. So don't cut the lazy way. Instead, rest the bagel on a cutting board or at least a plate. Make sure your bagel is going to stay still by placing a towel or slip mat under it.

The Right Way to Do It

The proper bagel-cutting technique is to place it flat on the counter with one hand on top. Don't curl your fingers around the bagel as you cut parallel to the counter. For those who prefer technical solutions to problems, there are special kitchen devices available for slicing bagels without resting them in the palm of your hand.

TOP TIP

Knife slips are more common with dull equipment because it takes more force to get the job done.

GOOD KNIFE TECHNIQUE

If you want to know the right way to use a cooking knife, watch one of the many cooking shows out there. Notice how the pros curve their fingers so they don't get cut? Use their technique as an example and keep the fingers of the hand holding the item curled back. You can even rub the upper side of the knife against your knuckles to get better control over the knife. Note this is the upper side, not the blade. For even greater control of the knife, you can use the "pinch grip." Hold the handle of the knife in your hand and tuck your middle finger against the finger-guard. With your thumb on one side and the index finger curled up on the other, pinch the heel of the blade.

yes, it is possible to
OPEN A COCONUT

 **TOP SCREWUPS**

- Not having the tools for the job
- Failing to drain

The coconut is a staple of tropical diets. Some cultures use almost every part of the tree. Coconut milk is an indispensable ingredient in many Thai recipes, and some people use it as a dairy substitute to keep kosher or vegan. The liquid inside of a coconut is sterile and was even used in emergencies as an intravenous solution during World War II. And, of course, you can't make a perfect piña colada without fresh coconut. There is only one problem with the coconut: getting into it.

You Need a Few Things to Start With

Getting into a coconut will take a bit more muscle than, say, peeling an apple, but it is not as hard as you might think. **You will need a hammer, a screwdriver (that you need to clean before using), a knife, and a container for the milk.** Safety goggles and gloves are not a bad idea either, as your tools could slip.

The Best Way to Make a Mess with a Coconut

If you want a coconut mishap, try to chisel it open without first draining the liquid. Go ahead, have fun. But if you want things to actually go well, start by looking for the three dark "eyes" on the coconut's smaller end. (A coconut is not entirely round—it is shaped more like an egg.) **Take your screwdriver and place it on one of the eyes. Use your hammer to tap the screwdriver into the** nut. **When you can move the screwdriver in and out of the coconut easily, it means you've broken through the shell. Do this into a second eye to allow air pressure to get in and push the milk out**—sort of like opening a can of juice. Now you can tip the nut to drain the milk into your waiting container.

Find Its Weak Spot

Now you need to find the natural stress point where the coconut's outer shell will easily split open. To do this, pick a spot about two to three inches from the place where you drained the liquid. Take the screwdriver by the shaft, and tap the spot with the handle, using some force, a few times. Next turn the coconut and tap the same distance down from the other end. Keep tapping and turning, and a small crack should eventually appear in the outer shell.

Once it does, insert the point of the screwdriver into the break and tap it with the hammer to pry it open. Congratulations, you're in! Now you can use your knife to cut out the yummy white coconut meat.

TOP TIP

. . . you need to find the natural stress point where the coconut's outer shell will easily split open.

WHEN ALL ELSE
FAILS

If this seems like too much work—and you don't mind making a big mess and losing all the coconut milk—a less elegant way to get into a coconut is to bash it with a hammer or mallet until it breaks. This method is preferable after a bad day.

don't screw up your
HAMBURGERS

TOP SCREWUPS

- Buying bad beef
- Fiddling with them as they cook
- Cooking in a dry pan

The ubiquitous hamburger seems like it should be the easiest food in the world to prepare, yet somehow you always seem to end up with a thick, dry, tasteless hunk of meat with a half-melted piece of processed cheese on top.

The Dry Burger

If your burgers come out dry, it may be that they started out that way. The perfect burger begins with the perfect beef. Yes, lean ground beef is good for your health, but for flavor,  **choose a ground chuck that has about twenty percent fat content.**

You can also dry out your meat if you knead and pack it too much. Don't try for a perfectly flat little fast-food–style patty. Instead, take seven ounces of beef per patty and slap it down onto a flat, cold surface, such as a plate. Form it gently and season each side with a little salt and pepper.

For the Indoor Burger

Preheat your pan over a medium flame for three to four minutes and add a little fat or olive oil to keep the meat from sticking. **Slide the patties onto the pan and then do nothing for three to four minutes.** If you keep moving them around and fiddling with them you will not get a nice even outer crust.

Before you flip the burger, check to see if the pan looks dry. If it does,  **add a small amount of oil to the spot where the flipped burger will be.** If it looks like it still has oil, skip this step. Approximate cooking times on the second side are two minutes for rare, three for medium-rare, four to five for medium, and six to seven for well done. If you like your hamburgers burned into charcoal briquettes, keep them on longer.

THE PERFECT CHEESEBURGER

If you are making a cheeseburger, you can avoid that half-melted look by putting a metal cover over the burger until the cheese is melted. Just be sure that whatever you use does not seal the pan completely, or you will end up with a steamed burger, which will taste a bit like something at a sports arena concession stand, but hey, maybe you're into that.

don't drop chow mein in your lap
trying to use **CHOPSTICKS**

Whether you want to impress your foodie friends at a sushi restaurant or you want to be like the people in the movies who eat Chinese takeout from paper boxes when they work late, you will need to operate a pair of chopsticks without scattering shrimp across the room. Eating with chopsticks does not come naturally to most Westerners. There is a learning curve. Then again, you weren't born knowing how to use a fork, either. With a little practice you can get it right.

The Ancient Art of Chopsticks

The main mistake chopstick amateurs make is trying to move both of the sticks like a pair of tongs. **The trick is to only move the top chopstick and use the bottom one as a base.**

1. Begin by holding out your hand with the index and middle fingers extended and the last two fingers curled so they are perpendicular to the extended ones. The little fingers should now form a 90° angle.

2. Now lay a chopstick between your thumb and index finger across the web of your hand so the

tip of your ring finger is in the center of the chopstick. Hold the stick in place with your thumb. This is the chopstick that will remain stationary.

3 Take the second chopstick. Put it on top of the first stick and hold it between the thumb and index finger the way you would hold a pencil. Operate it as though you were writing.

It takes some practice to master, so in order to avoid any undue embarrassment on your first attempt, you might try it at home with Chinese restaurant takeout.

CHOPSTICKS HAVE A PRETTY SERIOUS BACKGROUND

There are a few chopstick etiquette tips to bear in mind so you do not set off an international incident. Chopsticks were originally used only in religious ceremonies, and they still hold a sacred place in certain rituals today. If you want to enjoy your food without insulting tradition, you should:

- Never store your chopsticks vertically in your rice bowl when you're not using them. This is a serious insult.

- Not pass food to another person using only chopsticks. Put the food on the other person's plate.

- Use the wide end of the sticks to take food from a communal dish. You do this for the same reason you should not double dip a chip.

- Not ask for chopsticks in a Thai restaurant, as chopsticks are not used as utensils in Thailand.

don't trip up making TEA

TOP SCREWUPS

- Using the microwave
- Not taking your time

Hot water and a tea bag. What could go wrong? Tea is easy to make and also easy to make poorly. To make a perfect cup of tea you need a third ingredient that people often leave out: patience.

Don't Settle for a Microwave Boil—You May Get Burned

To begin with, the microwave is not the best device for making tea. Even when microwave-heated water looks as though it is boiling, it is not as hot as water heated in a kettle, and boiling hot water is needed to get all of the color and flavor out of tea. Microwaves heat only the outer inch around the cup. The water in the middle warms up slowly from the heat of the outer portions. So when you see the water on the outside boiling, you are tricked into thinking your cup is hot all the way through.

Microwave-heated water can even be dangerous. Sometimes, as the cup is jostled when you take it out of the oven, some of the superheated outer liquid mixes with cooler liquid and causes it to boil suddenly. The hot liquid splashes all over. Whenever you see liquid boiling in the microwave, wait a few moments after you turn it off to take the cup out. To be extra safe, you can put a spoon into the cup to set off any superheated areas before taking it out.

Kettles Rock!

But a **kettle will produce a full, even boil of around 212°F (100°C),** because the heated water at the bottom rises and is replaced by cooler water, and that bubbling mixes the water to create a nice uniform temperature throughout.

Give It a Minute, Actually Six

The team from the University of Northumbria's School of Life Sciences in the United Kingdom concluded that most people screw up tea by taking out the tea bag too soon. **The tea bag should be left in the hot water for at least two minutes but no more than seventeen.** If you drink your tea with milk, you should take out the bag after two minutes, pour the milk in, and let it sit for another six minutes before your first sip so the whole mixture can reach an ideal temperature of 140°F (60°C). But don't leave it too long or it will cool down to the point that it will, in the words of the study's authors, reduce the "all round sensory experience."

TOP TIP

Whenever you see liquid boiling in the microwave, wait a few moments after you turn it off to take the cup out.

THE BRITISH KNOW THEIR TEA

To figure out the perfect timing for tea, the team at the University of Northumbria's School of Life Sciences spent 180 hours testing, and their enlisted panel of volunteers consumed 285 cups of tea in the laboratory to come up with the recipe for the perfect cup. The British have a keen interest in the science of tea brewing. The British drink 165 million cups of tea per day, or 60.2 billion a year.

getting the meat out of a
LOBSTER OR CRAB

TOP SCREWUPS

- Attempting unorganized attacks
- Succumbing to frustration

After paying "market price" for lobster or crab on a seafood restaurant menu, the last thing you want is to fail breaking through the shell barricade between you and deliciousness and end up with a meal that consists of almost no meat. Eating lobsters and crabs can be frustrating.

Lobsters First

Lobster is a bit easier, so let's start there. **First, remove the legs.** Grab the lobster by the back and then twist off each leg and put them aside. Now use the same twisting motion to remove the claws at the first joint. You will need a nutcracker to get into the claw. Place it around the top of the large section of the claw and squeeze firmly. Once it is open, push the meat from the top of the claw out of the end that was attached to the arm.

DEALING WITH LIVE LOBSTERS

If you are doing the lobster cooking yourself and you have to pick up a live lobster, here's how to do it without getting pinched. First off, lobsters are cold blooded, so if you keep it in icy cold water, it is going to be a much more sluggish adversary. Come in behind the animal and seize it in one motion from above by the shell just where the lobster's last two legs join his tail.

Going for the Big Prize: the Tail

Take the tail in one hand and the back in the other, and twist until the two parts separate. Once it is free, turn the tail over. Put your finger into the end of the tail that was not attached to the body. You should be able to push all of the meat out in one piece. Peel off the top and look for a long black vein. This is the digestive tract. Remove it before you eat the tail meat.

You Can Crack the Crab

The claw is the meatiest part and also one of the toughest to crack. You will be tempted to try to get in with brute force, pounding on it with a hammer or a nutcracker. What usually happens if you do this is that the meat inside is mashed and you end up with a mixture of shell pieces and crab-meat strands. 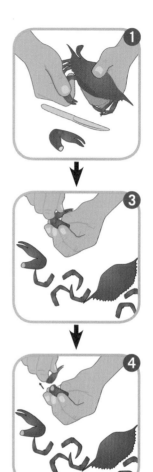 **Instead, use a knife *and* a mallet.**

Start by putting the claw on the table with the inside of the pincers facing up. Now place the knife slightly behind where the pincers meet. Use the mallet to tap lightly on the knife until you have **cut the claw about halfway through. Do not cut it completely in half. Once you've made your cut, pick up the claw in both hands and snap it in half.** This should let you pull out the claw meat with little mess. Repeat this technique on the claw arm. Dip the meat in melted butter and enjoy.

Nice Legs

Getting the meat out of a crab's legs may seem like a lot of work for not a lot of reward, but if you have good technique, this part can actually be a lot of fun.

1. Start by breaking off one of the legs where it attaches to the body.

2. The leg consists of four sections. Most of the meat is in the top piece, the upper thigh. The lowest part of the leg, the part that looks like a foot, contains no meat at all. Most people start with the meatiest part, but a better strategy is to **begin at the foot end.** There is a tendon that

runs about halfway up the length of the leg. If you pull out the tendon first, the meat will come out more easily. Snap off the bottom section, pull out the tendon. Don't eat it.

3 Now you can break the leg apart at the joints. Taking a section of leg between your thumbs and forefingers, try to crack the shell of only the side that is facing away from you. 👎 **Do not break it all the way through.**

4 Once it is cracked, turn it around and repeat the process, cracking the other side. Now you can remove the shell without damaging the meat, allowing you to take it out in one piece. If you crack it all the way through at once, you will damage the meat and have to scoop it out with a fork.

DON'T SCREW UP

The (Not Always So)
GREAT OUTDOORS

is **MY LAWN**
supposed to be brown?

TOP SCREWUPS

- Trying to grow the wrong grass
- Waging chemical warfare
- Misting often instead of soaking occasionally
- Depressing the lawn
- Letting dog piddle cause spots

The lawn began as a status symbol of wealthy Europeans, who used it to show they had so much land that they didn't have to use it all to grow crops. Of course, it is not a very effective symbol of status if it is brown and overgrown with weeds.

Is Your Grass Right for You?

If you have trouble maintaining a lush lawn, it may be because you have the wrong kind of grass. Traditional bluegrass has a shallow root structure. Almost all of its roots stay within five feet (one and a half meters) of the surface. A few inches farther down, the soil maintains a steadier level of moisture, which makes grasses with deeper roots—like tall fescue or red fescue—a better bet. They require less watering and are less susceptible to disease. If you already have bluegrass and do not want to dig it up to start over, try overseeding it in spring or fall with a heartier bluegrass variety.

You Don't Need a Chemical Treatment

You do not have to pay a fortune or spray truckloads of chemical fertilizer to keep your lawn green. A mower that mulches the grass and leaves it on the lawn provides natural fertilizer. A thick lawn should choke out weeds of its own accord. Then 🕐 **proper irrigation should be**

enough to keep things in order. To see if the soil is moist enough, poke it with a screwdriver. It should be moist to a depth of four inches (about ten centimeters). 🖐 **Instead of misting every day, give it a good soak less frequently.**

Seeing Spots

Not every yellow spot on your lawn was caused by a pest. Many of these spots just need a little bit of compost. (See pages 112–114.) A low spot in your lawn can turn yellow, especially after a heavy rain. Putting a little soil over the indentation to raise it up to the level of the surrounding ground will fix the problem.

So *That's* Why You Call Him Patches

If you have a dog, however, your yellow patches could be caused by the nitrogen in his urine. Even though nitrogen is a common ingredient in fertilizers, the concentration that is emitted from a dog is too much for the grass and can kill it.

The only way to solve this problem is to 🖐 **dilute the dog's urine—not while it is in the dog, of course, but after it is on the lawn. Pour water on the spot on the grass within eight hours** of the deposit, and that should stop circles from forming.

THE GREAT AERATE DEBATE

Do you need to hire a company to aerate your lawn? It depends on whom you ask. Many lawn experts swear by the procedure. You do not have to hire pros, however. You can rent the aerator and get out there yourself to drill little holes in the soil to keep it from becoming too compact. There are even special shoes with extra long cleats that you can use to walk-aerate your lawn. Then again, doing so might not be necessary at all. Trey Rogers, a professor of crop and soil sciences at Michigan State University, told Kiplinger's Personal Finance that aerating a healthy lawn is like taking Rogaine when you have a full head of hair.

are you tempted to turn the DEER in your garden into Jane Doe's?

 **TOP SCREWUPS**

- Having a fence that is too short
- Having plants that are too tempting
- Spraying deterrents that just wash away

What lovely, majestic animals. Truly one of God's most beautiful creatures—but if they break through your garden defenses one more time, you're afraid you might have to introduce them to their maker.

Building a Perimeter

If you built a fence but you still see Bambi chomping on your prize-winning tulips, you didn't make the fence high enough. Deer are excellent jumpers, so to keep them from bounding right in, **be sure your fence is at least eight feet high.**

A Repellant Idea

Perhaps you stunk up your yard with chemical deer deterrents that you sprayed onto your plants. The deer might have stayed away because the fragrance is offensive to them, but if an animal that revels in the sweaty pheromones of an unwashed buck is turned off, odds are you're not going to be enjoying your green space anymore either. Bar soap can serve the same purpose without the nasty odors or toxins. You can either sprinkle soap shavings on the dirt or dissolve the soap in water and spray it on the plants. The problem with this method is that the effect of any scent-based deterrents is temporary, because they are washed away by rain. If you work it into your maintenance routine, great, but screw it up once and there goes your bumper crop of heirloom tomatoes.

Second Line of Defense

If your barrier and scent lines of defense fail to do the trick, you might 🔘 **try a sound deterrent.** Deer don't like loud noises, and desperate gardeners have had some success with clock radios in the garden set for the music alarm to come on slightly after sunset. Hubcaps or pie tins hung from cords so they bang against each other in the wind can also work, though you might screw up your own sleep on a windy night if you go for this method.

If you're past caring about what your garden looks like, then covering your plants with plastic mesh might do the trick—deer hate sticking their tongues through mesh. Some upside down plastic laundry baskets can work for individual plants if they are held securely in place, and you can lightly wrap plastic netting around the taller greens.

If none of this works with your stubborn deer population—deer tenacity is not to be underestimated—plan ahead and plant things that deer don't like. 🔘 **They are not fond of highly aromatic herbs like mint, lavender, thyme, rosemary, and sage** (you can play "Scarborough Fair" on loop if you want to combine tactics). 🔘 **Flowers that make unpopular deer snacks include begonias, ageratum, cornflower, marigolds, cleome, and salvia.** They also tend to steer away from plants with thorns, though roses might be harder to not screw up than keeping the deer away. Your local nursery is a good place to ask about plants that deer will hate.

that seed is 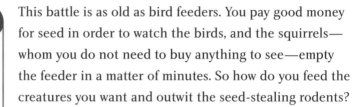 **FOR THE BIRDS—**
not the squirrels

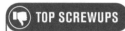 **TOP SCREWUPS**

- Underestimating your opponent
- Getting the wrong feeder
- Putting the feeder in a squirrel-friendly spot

This battle is as old as bird feeders. You pay good money for seed in order to watch the birds, and the squirrels—whom you do not need to buy anything to see—empty the feeder in a matter of minutes. So how do you feed the creatures you want and outwit the seed-stealing rodents?

Who Wants It More—You or the Squirrels?

Remember that you are battling for the sanctity of your seed, but 👍 **your opponent is battling for the ability to eat and stay alive.** The squirrel is thus highly motivated and is ready to face almost any obstacle.

Don't Get the Wrong Feeder

There are many squirrel-proof feeders on the market. In fact, about four million dollars' worth are sold each year. They have various success levels based on their design. You can get an idea of which ones work and amuse yourself by watching the many squirrel and bird feeder videos on YouTube.

Baffle Them

Remember that 👍 **no feeder is squirrel-proof unless it is at least six feet off the ground and at least ten feet away from trees.** Once you have chosen your spot, the most effective squirrel deterrent is a baffle. A baffle is a wide plastic disc that fits around the pole, looking something like a hovering UFO. A squirrel can climb up to the baffle but can't get around it. A dome-shaped baffle above the feeder keeps squirrels from climbing down onto the feeder from above. If you don't want to buy a baffle, you can make your own out of anything of a similar shape, for example a flowerpot or a 2-liter soda bottle.

Guerilla Squirrel Warfare

Squirrel fighters have come up with a number of more do-it-yourself solutions, including attaching one end of a Slinky toy to the top of the pole and letting the rest hang so the pole runs through the center of the toy. Squirrels who try to jump onto the poll will grab the Slinky and get dumped to the ground. After a while, however, some of the more clever squirrels figure out the trick. They can climb the pole while pushing the slinky ahead of them with their noses.

Another idea is to 🕐 **mount the bird feeder not on a pole but on a length of PVC pipe, the surface of which is too slippery for squirrels to get any traction**. Hanging bird feeders from a wire generally does not work because squirrels are impressive aerialists. If you string the line with plastic soda bottles, however, the squirrels will find it hard to cross.

A Nocturnal Opponent

If you seem to be keeping your squirrels out of the feeders but the seeds disappear overnight, your problem is most likely a raccoon. Raccoons are omnivorous, clever bird-feeder raiders, and they weigh ten times as much as your typical squirrel. Keep them out of the feeder using the same techniques you use for squirrels—just be sure that the baffles are wide enough to foil this larger animal.

WHEN ALL ELSE FAILS

If none of these technological solutions work, you might try changing your seed mix. Squirrels may gobble your sunflower seeds, but they're not fond of safflower. They will also leave the tiny black niger thistle seeds that fill tube feeders for finches. Finally, plain white suet, a favorite of woodpeckers, is not tempting to your rodent nemesis.

PITCH A TENT
without pitching a fit

 **TOP SCREWUPS**

- Failing to prep
- Picking a bad site
- Getting too rough with the poles

There are few things more frustrating than arriving, exhausted, at your campsite after a long hike and then spending an hour trying to pitch your tent in the rain, only to discover that two of the tent poles are missing.

Before You Start Your Wilderness Adventure

Perfect camping begins before you step foot into the woods. **When you are buying your tent, put a set of paints or colored tapes in your cart. You will use these to mark the various joints.** Your color-coding will be much easier to follow than a set of soggy instructions. Keep track of all of your tent pieces by tying them directly to the tent body. If you know you're prone to losing things, order some extra fly poles and connecters now. While you're at it, spare yourself any unpleasant surprises by packing duct tape, a nylon patch kit, and a coil of parachute cord.

Conduct a Dry Run

Set up your tent in your backyard when you are not wet, hungry, or tired. Most tents come with a two-tier roof system consisting of a vented peak and a rain fly that hangs over the vent. As the name suggests, the rain fly is designed to keep the rain out. It also lets the condensation out. Be sure you understand all the pieces so you don't end up stuffing something back in the bag, only to realize when you wake up soaking wet how important it was.

Picking Your Site

If you do not want to be soaked from the ground up, 🖐 **be sure to pitch your tent on level ground.** Even small depressions will fill with water if it rains. If the ground is wet to begin with, it helps to put a tarp down first and pitch your tent on top of that.

Unless you like sleeping with hard things poking into your back, 🖐 **clear the area beneath the tent of as many rocks and branches as you can.** Of course you will also want to steer clear of anthills, poison ivy, and suspicious holes that could be burrows of small animals. Pile dead grass or pine boughs underneath the tent. This provides a softer bed and keeps you warmer as you will have less direct contact with the ground.

Proper Orientation

If possible, pitch your tent facing east or southeast. This way you will get the sun's morning rays and have shade in the afternoon. Lay out your tent and check that the front flaps are overlapped and joined, as you will want them to be when the tent is up.

Raising the Roof

Now place stakes for the guy lines and raise the tent poles. 🖐 **If you have shock-corded poles, do not shake them out before you snap them together. Slide the ends together gently,** lest you crack them. String guy lines to stakes or tree bases from each corner.

DON'T GET SCREWED BY SMOKE AND WIND

To avoid turning your tent into a giant windsail, pin down the corners with tent pins. If you're trying to put up your tent on soil that is too sandy, you can bury a log and use it as a base for the pin.

To avoid turning it into a smokehouse, your campfire should be upwind and at least ten to fifteen feet away from your tent. Even "fireproof" tents will ignite if a big enough spark lands on them. (See Build a Fire Without Getting Burnt on pages 96–97.)

BUILD A FIRE without
getting burned

TOP SCREWUPS

- Rubbing sticks together
- Picking a dangerous spot

You plan a weekend camping trip with visions of roasting marshmallows and telling ghost stories around a roaring fire. Nothing can ruin your night like a pile of soggy, smoldering logs that refuse to light.

Playing the Match Game

When you're loading your backpack, unless you want to try to start the fire by rubbing two sticks together (possible, but your time is better spent enjoying your barbeque), you will need to take something along to start the blaze. A lighter is smaller and much more consistent than matches.

Don't Make Smokey the Bear Tell You Again!

Assuming you do not want to start a forest fire, it is important to choose a good spot for your blaze. 👍 **You will need a clearing far away from houses, trees, dangling branches, your neighbor's tent, and so on. An area at least ten feet (about three meters) in diameter is a good rule of thumb.** Create a perimeter of rocks about three to four feet (one meter) around the center of the place you plan to build the fire. This is to keep the fire contained should it escape the pit. Remember that sparks can rise on the air and land a good distance from your fire. If conditions are especially dry, you may want to consider camping out another day. Dry grass can start burning in all directions much faster than you think and quickly get out of control.

Get It Going

The main things that will keep your fire from burning bright are using the wrong fuel and stacking the wood so that the air cannot circulate. The kindling has to burn long enough and hot enough to release more and more gas from progressively larger amounts of fuel to get the fire going. Good kindling is a lightweight material such as old papers. If you're out in nature without a stack of old bills, look for some of these standbys: birch or cedar bark, dry grass and leaves, dry moss, dead evergreen needles, down from milkweed, or pussy willows or cattails.

A Pyramid Scheme That Works

Small sticks and branches should be broken up and placed around the kindling in a pyramid. It is best to use resinous softwoods, such as pine, for kindling and switch to hardwoods for the long haul. Softwoods are smoky and throw sparks, but they light quickly. Hardwoods take longer to ignite, but they provide a steady heat and burn down into satisfying embers.

Don't try to light the fire from the top. It won't work. Start with the kindling at the bottom and watch it spread and grow. Add more hardwood logs as it really gets burning. One thing you do not want to add under any circumstances is a rock, especially a nice smooth rock from a stream. Rocks seem solid, but they can be filled with water that can expand and cause the rock to explode, turning your campfire into a non-directed cannon.

THE MOST IMPORTANT PART

Once you've lit the fire, your job is only half done. It is considered a rather egregious breach of camping etiquette to start a forest fire. Unless you want to do this, you need to be sure your fire is completely out when you leave the site. Drench the fire with as much water as you can, then throw dirt on the coals. Before you toss the dirt, though, be sure it does not contain any small twigs and leaves. They can be ignited by hot coals hours after you think the fire has gone out. Before you leave your campsite, hold your hand over the pit and see if you can feel any heat. If you can't, you're free to go.

don't be a
MOSQUITO MAGNET

Are you one of those people whom others invite to outdoor parties so the mosquitoes will fly away from them? You'll be glad to know it's not all in your head. Scientists have determined that some people are, in fact, more attractive to the insects. The bad news is, they don't know why. The even worse news is that the only surefire way to keep a mosquito from finding you is to stop breathing, which is, I am sorry to say, pretty impractical.

Don't Blame Them All

In fairness, it is only a part of the population that gives the rest of the mosquito community a bad name. Males never bite, and even the female sucks blood only when she needs the nutrients to develop fertile eggs. The rest of the time, both male and female mosquitoes are satisfied with sugar from plant nectar. Humans are not even her favorite choice of host. She prefers birds, rodents, and large mammals like cows and horses. This is not a great comfort, though, when you are at a backyard party in Minnesota (land of 10,000 lakes and 100 billion mosquitoes).

She Can Smell You Forty Miles Away

A mosquito can detect carbon dioxide from up to forty miles away, according to some sources. 🌓 **She localizes** a breathing animal by flying in a zigzag fashion across the stream of CO_2. As she approaches, she sniffs for water vapor and lactic acid. Thus, the way to keep a mosquito away is to interfere with her sense of smell.

For those who prefer to avoid commercial repellants with DEET, there are a number of natural deterrents you can try. Pennyroyal essential oil, peppermint, vanilla, bay, clove, sassafras, lavender oil, and cedar all have their adherents. You could try burning rosemary and sage at your next barbeque; some swear this keeps mosquitoes at bay. Rub some fresh parsley or apple cider vinegar on the skin. Another homemade bug repellant can be concocted with one tablespoon citronella oil, two cups white vinegar, one cup water, and one cup Avon Skin-So-Soft bath oil.

TOP TIP

Males never bite, and even the female sucks blood only when she needs the nutrients to develop fertile eggs. The rest of the time, both male and female mosquitoes are satisfied with sugar from plant nectar.

Cut Them Off at the Source

Even better, if you have control over the environment, is to prevent being bitten by preventing mosquito breeding in the first place. You can get rid of their breeding ground by eliminating standing water. The mosquito's hunting ground is about 100 to 200 feet from where she begins her life cycle. If she breeds far away, she'll bite far away, too.

MOSQUITO MYTH

There is a popular myth that if you let a mosquito drink her fill, she will remove the anticoagulant that she injected before she leaves and the bite will not itch. There is no truth to this, but there is at least one reason to let a mosquito finish. If she has not had her fill she may come back. The result is two welts, not one. For your edification: It takes about three minutes from the time she bites you for the spot to swell and start itching.

how to not get
LOST IN THE WOODS

It is a lovely afternoon, and you decide to take a leisurely hike in the woods. After an hour or two you decide it is time to head back, so you turn around. Where did that fork in the path come from? It didn't fork on your way in. No worries. You pull out your trusty compass. Will it help? There is a good chance it will not. Here's why.

Which Way Is East? That's Easy.

Orienting yourself to the north, south, east, or west is a fairly easy task, with or without a compass. **You know (or you should) that the sun rises in the east. If the sky is clear and you have an idea of the time of day, you can figure out which way is east.** If you want to go north, then you just have to turn 90° to the left.

OK, Now What?

All of this is well and good except for one thing: Knowing which way is north will not help you if you do not know which way you came into the woods to begin with. In other words, if you don't know if the parking lot is to the east, west, north, or south, a compass will be about as useful as a wind-up monkey that plays the cymbals. The monkey might even be more useful, because at least it would make some noise and alert nearby hikers to your presence.

What You Need to Do

👍 **As you hike, you need to check your compass and look for landmarks periodically as you go.** Then when you're tracking back, you will know that the big rock where you saw the frog was due east of the purple wild flowers, which was near the path that leads to the place where you parked your car.

It is a good idea not to rely entirely on the compass to get you home. Keep a map in your backpack so if you do stumble onto a roadway in your confusion, you can pull out the map and figure out exactly where you are.

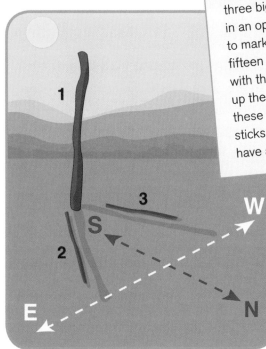

BUILD YOUR OWN COMPASS

If you're a bit unsure of the time of day but there is enough light to cast a shadow, you can make your own sun compass. Find three big sticks. Drive one into the ground in an open area. Then use another stick to mark the line of its shadow. Wait about fifteen minutes, then mark the new line with the last stick, about half of the way up the shadow. Now draw a line between these two sticks (if you have run out of sticks, you can use your finger). You now have an east-to-west guideline.

getting home from a hike
WITHOUT BLISTERS

 **TOP SCREWUPS**

- Not breaking in your boots
- Wearing the wrong socks

Blisters are caused by the following conditions: moisture, heat, pressure, and friction. To avoid blisters you need to eliminate or reduce some of these ingredients.

These Boots Were Made for Walking—Eventually

The obvious place to start is with your hiking boots. One mistake that new hikers often make is to buy a pair of stiff new boots and wait until the first hike to break them in. It is much better to find out if your boots rub you the wrong way when you're in your house than at the bottom of a canyon with a three-hour climb ahead of you.

It may look strange, but 👎 **break in your boots by wearing them to the grocery store and around the house as you do your cleaning. Try going up and down stairs in them, and don't forget to see how they feel when you're carrying your backpack,** because the extra load can change how your foot moves inside your shoe. You should have enough space to wiggle your toes, but not enough for your foot to slide around.

Finding the Right Socks

Stay away from cotton socks. They absorb moisture, one of the blister ingredients. Instead, 👎 **get some synthetic "wicking socks."** These are specially designed to keep the moisture off your feet. If your feet sweat a lot, bring an extra pair and change them when they get too damp.

Don't Get Dehydrated

Although it may seem contradictory since blisters are caused by moisture, be sure to drink lots of water. If you don't drink enough, when your sweat dries, the tiny salt crystals stay on your skin and create friction.

Duct Tape to the Rescue!

Many hikers swear by duct tape. 👍 **Wrap the parts of your foot that are blister-prone in the all-purpose tape,** and it creates a slippery barrier between boot and skin. (Duct tape also removes warts. The only thing it is not good for, apparently, is sealing ducts.)

WHAT ABOUT ANTIPERSPIRANTS?

You may be wondering if covering your feet in a good antiperspirant will keep you blister free, after all it stops the sweating that leads to both moisture and salt-friction. Maybe, but it may not be a great solution anyway. A study conducted at the West Point found that reducing moisture with antiperspirants did minimize the frictional forces that cause blisters. There is one catch, though.

They divided the cadets into two groups. One used antiperspirants, the other a placebo. Of those who had the antiperspirant treatment, twenty-one percent got blisters. Among the placebo group, forty-eight percent had them. Here's the catch. Of those in the antiperspirant group, fifty-seven percent reported skin irritation.

OMG, is that snake
POISONOUS!?

You're working in your garden. You reach down to pull some weeds and you jump when you spot a black snake close to your hand. Is it a harmless garter snake, or could it be a poisonous viper? This is one identification you do *not* want to screw up.

It's in Their Heads

The key to identifying a poisonous snake is the head. Nonpoisonous reptiles—such as your garden-variety garter—have long, narrow heads. 👍 **Almost all poisonous snakes in North America are pit vipers, which have wide triangle-shaped heads.** Pit vipers also have long hollow fangs and use "pits" on the sides of their

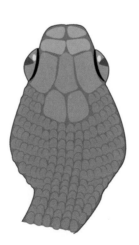
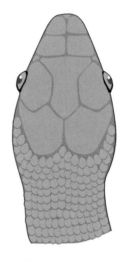

Venomous **Nonvenomous**

heads (hence the name) to sense the presence of warm-blooded creatures that they hope will make good snacks. Rattlesnakes, copperheads, and water moccasins are all pit vipers.

Nonpoisonous Snakes Aren't Necessarily Safe

Whether a snake is poisonous or not, it is wise to give it a wide berth. Even nonpoisonous snakes will strike if they feel threatened. **You do not have to run far to get away from a snake. Snakes can strike only about half of their own length.** Leave the snake alone and it will slither away on its own. If you feel that you must remove the snake from your yard, spray it gently with the hose while keeping your distance. Never pick up a dead snake. It may not be quite dead yet.

If you are bitten by a snake, even if you are absolutely certain it is not poisonous, you should see a doctor right away. The bite may not kill you right away, but many snakes carry germs that can lead to serious illness or infection if the wounds are left untreated.

THE SOUTHERN EXCEPTION

In North America there is only one exception to the wide-head rule: the coral snake. It lives in parts of the southern United States and Mexico, including the entire state of Florida. You are not likely to encounter it though, because it hunts underground. Just to be safe, remember what the coral looks like: it has red, yellow, and black rings with red outlining yellow. There is a nonpoisonous snake, the king snake, which also has red, yellow, and black rings, but its red rings are outlined by black. There is a mnemonic to help you remember this distinction: "Red on black, friend of Jack. Red on yellow, kill a fellow." Coral snakes are highly venomous and deadly to humans, so you will want to move a safe distance from any striped snake while you are trying to remember the rhyme.

don't CHOP DOWN A TREE
onto your head

TOP SCREWUPS

- Not wearing safety gear
- Cutting in a straight line
- Doing an amateur job

Here is how *not* to chop down a tree. First you take a chain saw. You will, of course not be wearing any protective goggles or gloves. Turn on the chain saw and listen to its powerful *whrrr*. Exciting! Then with a bit of pride and your lumberjack prowess, you start to saw into the bark cutting across the tree in a straight line.

What Happens Next?

The tree leans back in the direction of the cut and pinches the chain saw between the still-standing tree and the stump. No matter how much you try to pull, the tree is too heavy. The blade is completely stuck. In order to get it out, you need to go find another saw or axe and start hacking away. You manage to get enough of the wood cleared away to make a good tug on the chain saw and get it loose just as the entire tree starts to tumble in your direction.

What You Should Have Done

First, make sure the area around the base of your soon-to-be ex-tree is clear of debris and underbrush that might get in your way and cause you to trip while operating a deadly, deadly chain saw.

Ideally, you want to use the unique condition of the tree itself. If it is leaning to the south, you want it to drop that way. Don't underestimate the effect the wind might have. Even if it is fairly calm down on the ground, up in the branches there may be significant wind power.

Know When to Call in the Pros

Even for the best-trained professionals felling a tree is not an exact science, so be prepared for it to come down somewhere slightly to the side of where you plan for it to land. In short, 🕐 **if there are any houses or things you do not want crushed nearby, you might want to leave it to the experts.**

The Wedge Method

🕐 **Begin by cutting a wedge on the same side where you want the tree to fall. This should not be deep, no more than halfway through the tree. Remove the wedge, and then cut down at an angle from the opposite side.** The tree should fall in the direction of the wedge you cut. You can help it along by stopping frequently to nudge the tree gently with your shoulder. When it starts to make falling noises, turn off the chain saw and get out of the way. Be aware that limbs and branches might rain down.

Sometimes a tree lands on top of brush and other trees that keep it from tumbling all the way to the ground. If your tree rests this way, do not start cutting it into sections until it is all the way down. A sudden fall could crush a foot or knock your chain saw in an unpredictable direction.

ROPE TRICK

There is a method for nudging a tree away from a house, but it is tricky. To do it you need to attach two ropes up as high as possible on the tree and then have two people each holding the other end of a ropes while standing as far away as the tree is tall at quartering angles. The tree should fall between them, but it is absolutely crucial you make sure the ropes are long enough that no matter which way the tree falls, there is no danger of it falling on your amateur lumberjacks—unless you don't like them, then give them whatever length of rope you have lying around.

don't suffer from epic SUNBURN

The surprising mistake that people make when it comes to sunburn? They use sunscreen. More accurately, they trust sunscreen as an absolutely infallible method of prevention.

Sunscreen Is Not Made of Magic

A number of recent studies have found that people who use sunscreen have higher rates of skin cancer and develop more moles than people who don't. People who use high-protection sunscreen—that is, sunscreen with a sun protection factor (SPF) of 30—stay out in the sun longer, and get the same number of sunburns as those who used an SPF 10 formula. Using sunscreen appears to give people a false sense of security.

Other studies have shown that most people use too little sunscreen to do them any good. They put on a little dab of SPF 30, and think they are protected all day long when they may not be protected at all.

How to Use Sunscreen Realistically

So 👍 **slather on the sunscreen, and be sure you get a nice, even coat. Apply it again after you swim or sweat.** But don't rely on sunscreen alone. Keep your shoulders covered and wear a hat with a big brim. You may not look like the models in swimsuit catalogs, but you will avoid a painful sunburn and have healthier skin for life.

Sunburn? They Should Call It UV-Burn

People often forget, or don't realize, that you can get sunburned on an overcast day or in the winter when the sun reflects off the snow and ice. The only thing that is required to get sunburn is prolonged exposure to ultraviolet rays. You may be exposed to more intense rays through your car window on the way to the beach than you are playing in the surf.

A Single Burn Can Do Real Damage

Another mistake that tourists make is that they forget about their exposure to the sun as soon as they get home. A fair-skinned man working in a dark office in London who goes on an occasional holiday in the south of France is at a fairly high risk. Experts say that even one blistering burn can double the risk of developing melanoma, an often lethal form of skin cancer. Yet our traveler forgets about his brief sun exposure a few days after he uploads his holiday pictures to his computer.

That is why even though more people in Australia—which is known for its beach culture—get melanoma more often than people in England—which is known for its umbrellas—more of the English die from it. Australians are aware of the dangers of sunburn. When an Australian spots a suspicious mole, she is more likely to go straight to the doctor to check things out. This 🙂 **early detection leads to a greater survival rate.**

TOP TIP

. . . **you can get sunburned on an overcast day or in the winter when the sun reflects off the snow and ice. The only thing that is required to get sunburn is prolonged exposure to ultraviolet rays.**

HOT FASHION TIP

If you're going to be walking around in the sun, consider wearing a dark blue or red T-shirt. When researchers dyed lightweight cotton different shades of blue, red, and yellow and measured the amount of UV rays that penetrated them, they discovered that darker colors blocked out more than did lighter shades.

don't bust your butt on the **ICE**

TOP SCREWUPS

- Doing the opposite of what you should do
- Being way too tense
- Taking long steps

When most people venture out onto the ice, they make the mistake of tensing their muscles because they are worried about falling. The fear becomes a self-fulfilling prophecy. They over-straighten their bodies and lean back. Then they lose stability and down they go.

Keep Calm, Carry On

If you prefer to remain upright, you should **just relax. Bend your knees a bit, and lean slightly forward.** This way, even if you do miscalculate and fall, you'll go down forward, which is way less dangerous than falling backward.

Learn from the Children

Your kids might be able to teach you a thing or two about falling without getting hurt. Have you noticed how they seem to be able to come crashing down, and then they stand right back up and giggle? This is because they tense their muscles less than adults do.

Do the Inuit Shuffle

As for ice-walking technique, a shuffle beats a normal step. **Inch your way forward, taking tiny steps. If you're still having trouble, turn sideways and shuffle along that way.** If all else fails, sit down, and slide along on your seat. This is a particularly good method for icy stairs. It's not the most glamorous way to go, but it is slightly more dignified, and less dangerous, than an arm-waving *whooooah* followed by a flop.

TOP TIP

Have you noticed how kids seem to be able to come crashing down, and then they stand right back up and giggle? This is because they tense their muscles less than adults do.

A QUICK GUIDE TO STAYING UPRIGHT

It's not hard, as long as you aren't in a rush!

Screwup ········▶ Big Fix

Screwup	Big Fix
• Tensing up	• Relaxing and staying loose
• Leaning back to keep your balance	• Leaning forward—because that's the better direction to fall in
• Using your normal stride	• Taking tiny, shuffling steps

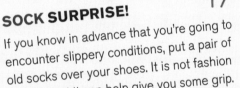

SOCK SURPRISE!

If you know in advance that you're going to encounter slippery conditions, put a pair of old socks over your shoes. It is not fashion forward but it can help give you some grip.

COMPOSTING
without the stink

 **TOP SCREWUPS**

- Having too much of one thing
- Not having enough of another
- Building a fly haven

You love the idea of composting. Compost can help control plant diseases like fungus. It gives plants a nourishing soil and uses food waste that would otherwise go into a landfill. Yet every time you try to compost, you end up with a stinky pile of rotting foodstuffs that attracts flies and scares away barbeque guests.

What Is That Smell!?

Your problem is most likely either too much moisture or too much nitrogen-rich green material in the pile. Either will cause a bad odor. To keep it under control, 👎 **be sure you keep your compost covered to keep moisture out.**

Turning Over an Old Leaf

You need to 👎 **turn the pile regularly. If it starts to smell bad anyway, add in more brown carbon-based material, such as dead leaves, hay, or straw.** Keeping the balance of brown and green right will give you a stink-free product. You can even compost paper, cardboard, and sawdust. Shred the paper first, and break the cardboard down into a slurry by ripping it to pieces and adding water. Just avoid glossy paper and sawdust from pressure-treated wood. Pressure-treated wood can leak arsenic into the soil—not ideal for your vegetable garden.

Involuntary Bug Invitations

Maintaining the right mix of brown and green material should also help keep your pile from becoming a fly magnet. Fruit flies and fungus gnats are the most common flying insects found around compost bins. They are not harmful, just annoying. Fruit flies seem to appear in huge numbers overnight as if by magic. This is because we buy their larva along with our fruit in the grocery store. The fruit fly lays eggs that are too small for humans to see. They are found on the peels of bananas and other fruits, and they hatch in our fruit bowls. Throw an egg-coated banana peel into your compost, and you will have hundreds of fruit fly hatchlings.

Say Goodbye, Fly

You can 🕐 **capture fruit flies and get them out of the house by exploiting their attraction to bananas.** Place a banana peel inside a clear plastic container (like a leftover takeout soup container) and use a toothpick to make three or four holes in the cover large enough for a fruit fly to crawl through. Place the plastic near the fruit bowl or the indoor compost bin (wherever the fruit flies are congregating). The flies will find their way into the banana but will not be able to get out. Within twenty-four hours, about ninety-nine percent of the fruit flies will be inside the plastic

DON'T SLIP UP WITH BANANA PEELS

Banana peels are a good source of potassium and are beneficial to flowering plants such as roses, but they are also one of the most common bearers of fruit-fly larvae. If you are a banana eater, and you have a big problem with fruit flies, keep the peels out of the compost and bury them directly in the soil around the plants you want to fertilize. Do not bury more than three skins per rose bush per week.

container, so you can take the trap outside and let the flies out.

TOP TIP

If you are making compost in a warm season, the center of your compost pile should be warm or even hot to the touch. If it isn't, this is either a sign that the pile is too dry or that it is too small.

Gnat Your Problem

Fungus gnats are harder to eliminate. Rather than get rid of them entirely, you can get them to hide. The bugs are attracted to moisture and fungus, both of which are needed in the composting process. If you are bothered by gnats, keep your compost bin uncovered long enough to let the top layer of bedding dry out, but make sure that the layers underneath still have the moisture they need. The fungus gnats will stay below the surface and should not bother you.

If Your Compost Is Just a Pile of Trash

If your compost problem is not a bad smell or flies, but has to do with inaction—the pile just sits there and doesn't break down—it may be too dry. In this case, uncover it and let the rain fix the problem. If you are making compost in a warm season, the center of your compost pile should be warm or even hot to the touch. If it isn't, this is either a sign that the pile is too dry or that it is too small to get hot enough.

HOW YOU LOOK

LAUNDRY lapses

 **TOP SCREWUPS**

- Using too much detergent
- Failing to get stains out
- Wearing out fabrics prematurely

Are you pouring cash down the drain by using too much laundry detergent? Allowing your favorite clothes to go in the trash because of stains and wear? These common screwups are easier to avoid than you might think.

Are You Laundering Money?

Most people guess how much detergent they need or just fill the cap up to the top, a practice that wastes more than half of the loads a detergent bottle could wash. Extra suds in the machine can lead to the development of odor-causing residue and can cause high-efficiency machines to use extra water and extend the cycle length, which costs you even more money.

Fighting Stains from the Outside In

When it comes to removing stains, the biggest mistake launderers make is working from the center where the stain is deepest to the outside. This can cause the stain to spread. Instead,  **start from the outer edges and work your way in.** If you do not have a spot remover handy, try a solution of two parts water to one part rubbing alcohol. Simply soaking your stained clothes overnight in warm water should help get the stains out, too.

Don't Get Set in Your Settings

Before you push the start button, look at your temperature and load settings. When was the last time you changed them? Some people are satisfied with a single tried-and-true setting, and they wash everything with it.

👍 **Assuming you want clean clothing that lasts, sort your clothes according to the washing instructions on the labels and change the settings on the machine accordingly.** As a general rule, clothes that are soiled with body oils are best washed with hot water; colors should be washed in cold to keep them from running and losing pigment.

Brighten Your Whites Instead of Turning Them Pink

If you want to really brighten your whites, launder them in cold and add a spoonful of cream of tartar to the wash water.

Of course, you already know not to wash that bright red skirt in the same load as your white shorts, right? If you do have an item that is likely to bleed, soak it in salt water before washing it, or add a dash of vinegar to the wash cycle.

Are Your Towels Soft but Water Repellant?

Fabric softener smells great, but don't add it to the water in which you wash your towels. It can make them less absorbent. If you already doused them before reading this, you can bring them back by adding a cup of distilled vinegar to the rinse cycle. In fact, if you like homemade solutions, you can save money by replacing fabric softener with vinegar altogether—just make sure you have a good rinse cycle so you don't go around smelling like salad dressing.

TOP TIP

If you wash an item that is likely to bleed, soak it in salt water before washing it, or add a dash of vinegar to the wash cycle.

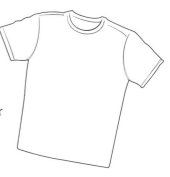

WHO NEEDS SOAP?

There are those who argue that detergent is not necessary at all, and that it is the agitation in the washing machine that cleans clothes just by pushing them around in the water. If you're feeling adventurous, or you just don't feel like spending money on detergent, give it a try and see if you notice a difference.

don't SHRINK your sweaters

TOP SCREWUPS

- Machine washing your wool
- Getting too rough while hand washing
- Putting your wet sweater in the dryer

You bought a new wool sweater that you absolutely love, and you got a great deal on it. Well done! You throw it in the washing machine for its first cleaning, and plan to air-dry it so it doesn't shrink. Good plan, right? Wrong! You'll discover your mistake when you remove a much-smaller garment from the machine, because it is the agitation of the washer—not the heat from the dryer—that causes wool to shrink. Even the gentle cycle can do it.

What Is Going on Here?

When wool grows on the back of a sheep, it all goes in roughly the same direction. This is why sheep coats do not shrink when it rains. Once the wool is woven into a sweater, however, the individual strands point in different directions. When they get wet and then dry, they latch onto one another and become locked. The technical name for this is "fulling." Whatever name you give it, you end up with an uneven, heavy piece of child-sized clothing.

Don't Suffer from Shrinkage

The only way to be sure you will not shrink your wool sweater is to wash it by hand. Always keep this fact in mind: It is not heat but agitation that causes shrinkage. This means that even when you wash by hand you need to avoid too much rubbing, kneading, and swishing. Washing a sweater, therefore, does not require a lot of work. A more apt description might be soaking.

1. Pour about a quarter cup of detergent into your sink and fill it with hot or warm water. Shampoo and liquid dish soap also work.

2. **Submerge your garment in the soapy water until it is soaked all the way through.**

3. **Do nothing. Leave the sweater in the water for about half an hour.**

4. When you come back, remove the sweater from the water and gently press out the excess water.

5. Then refill the sink with cold water. Put the sweater back in the water and let it soak for another half hour.

6. Repeat this step one more time to rinse out all of the remaining soap.

Don't Head for the Dryer Yet

Do not put a wet sweater in the dryer. The heat won't harm it, but the tumbling can cause fulling. Do not be tempted to twist or wring the sweater. (If you are tempted, resist.) **When you're done with all of the soak cycles, take the sweater out of the liquid and lay it out flat on a large towel.** Cover it with another towel, and roll all three up. Press the roll to push out more of the water.

Finally, unroll the sweater and put it on a sweater drying rack. If you do not have one, set it on another towel to dry. After a few hours come back and flip the sweater to let the back side dry. If you like, when the sweater has fully dried you can tumble it in the dryer to soften it up.

WHEN ALL ELSE FAILS

Sheep have another form of protection against matted wool fibers: lanolin. Sheep naturally produce this oil, which acts a bit like the conditioner you put in your hair to keep it from tangling. This leads to one thing you can try to unshrink a tiny sweater. Immerse it in a solution of water and hair conditioner for half an hour. With any luck the fibers will untangle and your sweater will magically expand to its original size.

don't waste money on unnecessary
DRY CLEANING

TOP SCREWUPS

- Believing only what you read
- Dry cleaning the wrong stuff
- Wet cleaning dry-clean–only clothing

The label on your blouse says, "dry clean," so you take it to the dry cleaner after every time you wear it. This makes perfect sense, but it is probably not necessary. There is even some clothing that should not be dry cleaned at all. For example, dry cleaning does not do a good job of getting out perspiration and oils from an everyday office shirt.

Misleading Labels

Labeling laws for clothing say that the manufacturer has to list at least one method for cleaning the fabric. This doesn't mean that they have to list every possible method to safely clean it.  **Even if it says "dry clean," there is a good chance you can hand wash the item and save time and money in the process. Many garments made of silk, satins, nylon, even woolens and rayon can be gently hand washed.**

Why Is Something "Dry Clean Only"?

Manufacturers are not supposed to use this warning unless they have "a reasonable basis indicating that the item will be harmed if washed." (Even then, you may have success hand washing, but there is a risk, so don't try it if you're not willing to face the consequences if it doesn't work out.)

The main thing that can go wrong when you wet clean a dry-clean–only fabric is shrinkage. This is most likely to happen with natural fibers such as delicate cotton and leather. If you use a detergent with the wrong pH balance, it can strip off oils and change the texture of the fabric.

Don't Overdo It

Your clothes will not last any longer if you dry clean them rather than hand wash them. Dry cleaning can damage buttons and eventually deteriorate the fabric. So 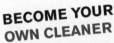 **you should not take a dry-clean–only garment in after every wearing, only when it is soiled. Keep your clothes wrinkle free and aired out by hanging them as soon as you take them off.**

BECOME YOUR OWN CLEANER

Use a gentle cleanser or baby shampoo and cold water. Do not wring the wet clothes. Rayon is especially prone to coming out a bit stiff and fuzzy if it is agitated too much. Once you've rinsed, don't throw the clothes in the dryer. Lay them flat on a drying screen instead. If you really miss that freshly pressed look, you can still hand wash your delicate clothes and then take them to the cleaners for a professional press from time to time.

IRONING out the kinks

TOP SCREWUPS

- Not knowing the secret language of iron labels
- Melting synthetic fabrics onto the iron's surface
- Ironing stains permanently into fabric

The iconic ironing disaster is the one you see in cartoons where a mislaid iron leaves a black iron-shaped imprint in the center of a white cotton shirt. You need an expert level of incompetence to achieve this stunning result. Although something similar, albeit less dramatic, can occur when using a hotel iron or an iron that was gummed up by a family member who is now pretending not to even know what an iron is.

Ironing Hieroglyphs

The first faux pas of the inexpert ironer is likely to be not reading or understanding the ironing instructions before putting hot metal to fabric. The iron instruction hieroglyphics are, in fact, quite easy to interpret once you know them. They are variations on a little iron symbol. If you're not supposed to iron it at all, the little iron has an X over it. If the iron has dots in it, they correspond to the number of clicks on your iron's thermostat. Two dots in the iron icon mean to set the real iron to the two-dot setting.

Gumming up the Works

Ironing things too cool is not disastrous, just ineffective. **Ironing too hot can cause woolen fibers to become shiny and may cause manmade fibers to melt.** If you touch a hot iron to a nylon jacket, for example, it will melt. In the process, the iron becomes coated in the liquid jacket material. Every time you fire it up, it will melt a bit of the gunk and transfer it to anything else that you iron. That is why you should always examine the surface of the iron before you start.

Degunking an Iron

If you find that you have a gunky iron, try this trick. Lay out a piece of aluminum foil and iron it. The buildup should stick to the foil after a few passes.

Ironing symbol

Don't Iron a Dirty Shirt

🕐 **If you press a dirty one, you'll set in the stain forever. For best results iron the clothes while they are still a bit damp from washing.** Remove them from the dryer or take them off the line before they are completely dry. If the item is entirely dry, spray it with a light mist of water from a spray bottle before ironing. If you're skipping the iron and going straight to folding, fold it as soon as it comes out of the dryer. If you miss that window, you may want to run the dryer on warm for a few minutes to loosen up the clothing before folding.

Iron at low temperature

Iron at medium temperature

Iron at high temperature

Do not iron

MINOR IRONING PERILS

Avoid the little ironing snafus that all launderers must face:

Screwup ················▶ Big Fix

Screwup	Big Fix
• Throwing freshly ironed slacks over the back of the chair, creating a new seam.	• Hang pants from the waist using pants or clip hangers.
• Scorching lighter fabrics after ironing heavy ones.	• Start with fabrics that need the coolest setting and progressing to those that need more heat.
• Breaking and/or melting buttons by ironing over them.	• Poke the point of the iron between each button, angling up and down with every pass.

how much should you
PAY FOR THAT SHIRT?

Everyone wants to look his or her best—or at least not his or her worst—so you probably do not want to be caught wearing 1980s shoulder pads and 1970s lapels to work. But don't let your quest for fashionable attire turn you into the best-dressed person in the poor house.

Go Classic

Invest in one high-quality piece of clothing that is not trendy and will last for years. Use this as a base and pair it with inexpensive, washable clothing that you get from the clearance rack or secondhand store.

Don't Undervalue Customer Relations

Chat with the clerks at your favorite clothing store. They are always happy to do a good job for a repeat customer. Once they get to know your taste, they will keep an eye out for the kind of clothing you like and let you know about upcoming sales.

Patience Pays Off

Never pay the first price. Early in the season, a department store will put a dress out on display with a preprinted price tag. Only ten to twenty percent of buyers actually pay this price. Thank them. They subsidize the rest of us. As the season wears on, the dress will be marked down and down until it ends up on the clearance rack

at a price that is close to what the retailer paid for it, because by this time, it is just taking up valuable floor space. You may end up with a wool dress in June, but cold weather will come back again and you will have paid half as much for it. Shopping experts also suggest hitting the stores on Thursdays to take advantage of weekend sales before the items are depleted, then you can go back once the sale begins and get the discount applied retroactively.

 TOP TIP

Shopping experts also suggest hitting the stores on Thursdays to take advantage of weekend sales before the items are depleted, then you can go back once the sale begins and get the discount applied retroactively.

Twins Separated at the Factory

One of the great secrets of the fashion industry is that clothing manufacturers often create two versions of their trendy new duds. The blouse may be exactly the same but it is shipped with two different labels, one for the department store and the second for the discount shop. You can find these duplicates by looking for a code that identifies the garment's manufacturer. On the tag of every piece of clothing you will find the letters "RN" followed by several numbers. Write down the RN number of the garment you like at the department store and look for that same number at the discount store. If the numbers are the same, so is the manufacturer.

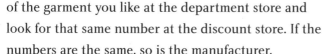

IT NEVER HURTS TO ASK

You may be able to get a discount you were not aware of just by asking. It doesn't always work, but when you are checking out ask, "Are there any discounts available on this item?" Worst-case scenario, there aren't, and the clerk looks at you a little funny. Best-case scenario, you save some money.

don't show up in your
FATHER'S SUIT

TOP SCREWUPS

- Wearing the wrong fit
- Wasting money on trends

The whole reason you buy a suit is so that people will say, "What a serious, grown-up looking man he is." So the last thing you want is to look like a kid playing dress up in his dad's clothes. Knowing what to look for in a suit can be a bit daunting if you've gotten by with your college sweatshirt and jeans up to now. First off, unlike those duds, suits are meant to fit your form perfectly.

There's a Lot to Consider

Here is how to avoid that "in my dad's suit" look:

- You will not get a proper fit if you are putting your jacket on over a sweater. When you go shopping, wear a dress shirt and dress shoes.

- Suits are measured by your chest and come in short, regular, and long. If you do not know your measurements, a salesperson should be able to take them and help you find a suit that fits.

- A proper fit begins with the shoulders. You don't want a suit that keeps you from moving your arms or swallows you up and wrinkles because it is too large. The suit shoulders should end at the end of your natural shoulder.

- With the suit buttoned, you should be able to just slip your closed fist between your chest and jacket. If you can't, the chest is too tight. If you have extra space it is too big.

- Stand with your arms at your sides. The bottom of the jacket should end at your knuckles. If you have to bend your arms in order to wrap your fingers underneath it, your sleeves are too short.

- You want your jacket cuffs to fall where your wrists meet your hands, and one-half inch of your shirt cuff should be showing through the bottom.

Sloppy Slacks

When the legs of your pants are too long, they bunch up, wrinkle, and generally give you that just-woke-up-in-my-clothes look. If they are too short, you will look like a teenager who just had a growth spurt. **Wear your slacks at your waist. The material should fall on top of your shoelaces and create a horizontal crease about one inch from the bottom of the pant leg with no bunching.**

Don't Dress for the Wrong Decade

Jackets come with one to four buttons, the number and placement of which tailors play with for the sake of fashion. The three-button look was popular in the 1990s, and single-button suits were most stylish when Duran Duran was popular. **Nowadays, a two-button jacket is your best option.**

Ask "Do I look Fat in This Suit?"

The wrong suit can make you look stubby or skinny or fat. Suits are tailored, and certain styles flatter certain figures more than others. Your suit should have at least one vent. If you're tall or wide, go for a jacket with a center vent.

If you're on the shorter side, choose one with double side vents. A four-button jacket will only work if you are especially tall and slim.

The Finishing Touches

⭕ **When you have selected your suit, hire a tailor to fine-tune it.** After it is altered, try on the suit one more time before you leave the shop to be sure it fits just right. Pair your new dark suit with a shirt that contrasts with the jacket. Try pale pink, lilac, or blue. Your tie is your accent color. Choose one that contrasts with the ensemble in a complementary way. Hint: ask a sales clerk for help.

Stand tall and hold your head high.

DON'T LOSE OUT ON A JOB BECAUSE OF YOUR TIE

You might assume that you're safe going with the most expensive and stylish tie you can find. Not so. Style experts caution against selecting an expensive woven tie for your big interview because it can come across as overpowering. You want to look like a professional team player.

Don't be a show off with the color, either. A purple tie screams "Look at me!" The interviewer is likely to see you as arrogant. Yellow is a bit better. It says you're not afraid to be different, but in a good way. Your best getting-employed colors, however, are navy and maroon, which exude calm confidence, and red, which calls to mind strength, passion, and masculinity. A brown tie says you are a reliable sort.

never be embarrassed by
YELLOW PIT STAINS again!

You probably assumed that the yellow stains under the arms of your T-shirts were caused by your potent sweat. It turns out that they are caused by the aluminum from antiperspirants combined with the salt in your sweat.

Prevent the Problem

If you are able to find an effective non-aluminum antiperspirant, your yellow pit stain problem should clear up. One suggestion is to **use a powder like Gold Bond that can reduce wetness without using aluminum.**

Or Treat the Effect

The biggest mistake pit-stain victims make is to reach for the chlorine bleach, which makes pit stains even more yellow. Instead **try an oxygen-based bleach such as OxiClean or a stain remover specially formulated to remove sweat stains.** A great home remedy is to mix one part baking soda to one part hydrogen peroxide to one part water. Rub the solution on the stains and let it set for at least thirty minutes before washing.

Don't Get Set in Your Stains

If you've had a sweaty day, wash your shirt right away; don't let it sit in the hamper. If it has some yellowing when it comes out of the wash, don't put it in the dryer. Instead, line dry the shirt in the sun if you can.

TOP SCREWUPS

- Using deodorants with aluminum
- Treating stains with chlorine bleach
- Letting the stains set

WHEN ALL ELSE
FAILS

If you're still bedeviled by yellow pit stains, invest in disposable underarm shields. These stick directly to the inside of the shirt to soak up the sweat and can be thrown away after use.

Or you could just switch to dark-colored shirts. They still get stained by the salt and aluminum mixture, but no one can see it.

does your **BRA FIT** correctly?

TOP SCREWUPS

- Measuring with an outdated method
- Having a band that is too tight
- Having a cup size that is too small

If you are a woman, you have no doubt heard the shocking figure that eighty-five percent of women are wearing the wrong bra size. Sometimes it is stated as eight out of ten or four out of five women. The origin of this statistic is a bit of a mystery, but it gained currency on a bra-fitting episode of *The Oprah Winfrey Show*.

It's the System That's Broken

The traditional method of sizing bras uses a tape measure, but the first scholarly ergonomic study of bra fitting in the United Kingdom, which was published in June of 2012, concluded that this method may actually be the problem. The majority of the forty-five participants in the University of Portsmouth study ended up with an ill-fitting bra, but not because they didn't know how to measure themselves. They found the wrong fit using traditional tape-measure sizing. Band size was overestimated for seventy-six percent of the participants, and cup size was underestimated for eighty-four percent of the participants. The larger a woman's breast size, the greater the discrepancy was.

Asking the Wrong Question

The real question is not "What is my correct bra size?" but "How should my bra fit?" It sounds as though these are the same, but they're not. Think about how you shop for other articles of clothing. You know that one manufacturer's size-twelve jeans will fit you perfectly, but another's may be a bit tight around the hips. So why would you accept a number over your senses when it comes to your underwear?

The Best-fit Method

Using a tape measure and having a ballpark size is the beginning of the fitting process, not the end. It gives you an idea of which sizes to try. It's important, too, to be honest about changes in your body and accept that the size you wore when you were twenty is probably not ideal for you today. So 👍 **take a wide range—like a 38C a 36D and a 40B—into the fitting room and check the following criteria:**

- Is the band too tight or too loose? You'll know it is too tight because it will be uncomfortable. You're not supposed to feel bound or to have flesh bulging over the band (aka back loaf). But if the band lifts when you raise your arms over your head, it is too loose.

- If the fabric wrinkles on the cup, then it is too big, but if you're busting out all over, it is too small.

- Check the straps. If they are digging in, they are too tight. If they're sliding off the shoulder and you can't adjust the length any more, you should look for another bra.

OUR CHANGING BODIES— NOT JUST A PUBERTY THING

"Alphabet sizing" is the traditional method of sizing bras. It was developed in the 1930s, and reached up to only a D cup. Since then, the shape of women's bodies has changed because of changes in the food we eat. Most striking is that there has been a substantial increase in the size of the average breast, from a 34B to a 36C.

don't break your ankle wearing
HIGH HEELS

You've met the man of your dreams, and he has invited you to a night at the opera. You spend a week dreaming of the night and what you will wear. You scour the shops for the perfect dress and a brand-new pair of gorgeous stiletto heels. You put on your ensemble, admire yourself in the mirror, and then trip down the stairs as you are leaving your house and end up in an ambulance instead of on the world's best date.

It's Not Exactly the Natural Look

Walking in high heels does not come naturally. It takes practice. So if you're unaccustomed to it, do not wait for your big night to strap on four-inch heels. **Shoe experts suggest you spend at least two hours walking in them to let the fabric stretch to accommodate the shape of your foot.** Then before you go out, spend twenty minutes walking in them in your house. You will, of course, need excellent posture and balance. (See pages 165–167).

You're Not on the Runway

Thanks to runway models, many women think the best way to look glamorous in heels is to strut. Do not try to imitate these fashion models. Unless you are actually a model on the catwalk, you will just look like you're stomping down the street. Plus a model's long steps are hard to achieve in heels. No one looks glamorous as she tumbles off her heels onto her posterior.

Twinkle Toes Is More Like It

Instead, envision a ballerina. If she can stand and move around on the very tips of her toes without tumbling over, you should be able to keep aligned over a pair of Pradas. Ballerinas on pointe 👆 **take tiny steps, not long strides,** ergo you will also have to take smaller steps than normal in your heels. And do not expect to move as quickly as you do in your gym shoes. Ballerinas also stand with their hips turned out all the way down to the toes. As you will not actually be walking on pointe, you do not need a full ballet turnout, but 👆 **pointing your feet outward slightly will help.**

 TOP TIP

Do not try to imitate fashion models. Unless you are actually a model on the catwalk, you will just look like you're stomping down the street.

Don't Be a High-Heel Hero

The higher the heel, the more danger to your foot health and balance. 👆 **Choose lower heels for everyday wear. Only unbox your stunning stilettos, if you must, for a few hours at a time.** Extremely high heels push heels up at angles of 60° to 70° and shorten the calf muscles, or the Achilles tendon, which runs from the back of the heel through the calf. Walking at such angles puts a disproportionate amount of weight on the ball of the foot, creating extra stress. Women who wear high heels are more prone to back pain, osteoarthritis of the knees, and bunions.

WHAT ARE THE ODDS?

According to the National Floor Safety Institute, which devotes most of its time and energy to the study of slip-and-fall accidents, each year about two million Americans are admitted to the hospital for falls. Of those, twenty percent (or 400,000 injuries) are related to slips from the heights of tall heels. That's one in every five falls! Most often the women (and a few men) are treated for broken feet and ankles, or lacerations that they got on their hands and arms as they tried to brace themselves as they fell.

keep a snagged sweater from
UNRAVELING

You're fighting with a jammed photocopier at work, and you feel the elbow of your sweater catch on the open feed tray. When you examine the spot, you find a small snag. If you do not act fast, you will soon have a long train of unraveled yarn hanging from your arm.

Don't Wait, Act Now!

Repairing a sweater snag is easy, as long as you act fast. If you don't, the snag will unravel the knit at a surprising rate, and then you might not be able to fix it at all. First, you need to take your sweater off and turn it inside out. (You will probably want to go into the restroom to do this.) Look at the snag and see if you can identify where it started. Do not pick up the scissors! If you cut the snagged loop, you will most likely end up with a big hole.

Parts May Not Be Included

You will need a crochet hook to perform this repair by the book. Depending on the size of the loop you may also need some thread. Manufacturers sometimes include some extra thread for just such an emergency. If you happen to have liquid ravel preventer, which is an adhesive safe for knit fabrics, this will also come in handy.

Performing Sweater Surgery

Using your crochet hook, or reasonable facsimile, ease the snagged loop through to the inside (now outside) of the sweater. Be sure you pull it through the same hole that it came out of, or you'll create a new stitch and pucker the fabric. Turn the sweater right side out for a moment to check your work. If you've done everything right, the hole will be gone, and the snag will be invisible. Good job! Now turn the sweater back the other way. Tie a knot in the loop from the snag. If it is large, you can snip the part above the knot away with a scissors. If it is too small to knot, you'll have to thread a needle with the matching thread you found (or bought) and carefully sew the loop flat.

If you have some ravel preventer, this is the time to use it. When you're done, turn the sweater right side out again and gently stretch it to smooth out any bunching. Or, if you are someplace where you have access to an iron, press both sides of the garment over a cotton cloth with the iron set to wool, and you're done. Your sweater should be good as new or at least not at any immediate risk of unraveling.

DON'T TRAVEL WITH A FIRST-AID KIT FOR SWEATERS? NOT TO WORRY.

If, by chance, you do not carry a crochet hook with you, find a paper clip, unwind it, and fashion it into a makeshift one. If you don't travel with a supply of thread, you may find some near the seams at the bottom of your sweater. You only need a tiny bit. Odds are if you don't have a crochet hook and thread at the ready, you probably don't have ravel preventer on you either. You may be like most people and not even know it exists. Clear nail polish can be your backup for this.

don't **WRECK YOUR FACE**
while shaving

Making a good first impression is vitally important, but it is hard to be impressive when you show up with little bits of toilet paper stuck to red spots on your chin. What is more, each year about 40,000 men in the United States manage to cut themselves badly enough that they end up in the emergency room! Here's how to avoid that fate and get a smooth, injury-free shave.

Be Sharp *and* Soft

It seems reasonable that a sharper blade is a more dangerous blade. Reasonable, but wrong. Dull blades inflame your skin and are, paradoxically, more likely to result in cuts. This is because you need to push harder on them in order to have any effect. Pushing too hard is one of the biggest shaving mistakes you can make. So **change your blade or toss out your disposable razors regularly. Shaving experts say you should do this every third shave.** (Of course, the experts in question are also the ones who sell razors.)

Long Live the Razor!

You can prolong the life of your razor by soaking it in mineral oil. The oil slows the corrosion that dulls the cutting edge. When you're finished soaking the razor, dip the corner of a cloth in rubbing alcohol and wipe the oil off.

Don't Push!

Be sure to rinse your razor regularly throughout the shave. Those little bits of beard gum up the works, and your instinct is to push down even harder to compensate. To really get around the pushing-too-hard problem, opt for an old-fashioned double-edge adjustable razor. It is heavier than disposables and requires much less pressure.

You Don't Want a Dry Run

If you do not want a shredded chin, do not apply shaving foam directly onto a dry face. **Wet the skin with hot water or apply moisturizing skin cream before you lather up.** You could also shave directly after taking a bath or shower.

The Lesser of Two Evils

Now comes the part where you have to decide which screwup you want to make. Do you want to take the chance of razor burn or do you want to risk leaving stubble? You will get a closer shave by going up against the grain, but shaving downward in the direction of the hair is easier on the skin. One suggestion for the best balance of closeness to comfort is to first shave with the grain on each cheek, then the neck, upper lip, and chin and follow up by shaving each area across and at a slight angle to the grain. When you've finished shaving, rinse your face and neck with hot water and then splash with cold water or aftershave to close the pores.

You Don't Have to Feel the Burn

If you want to avoid aftershave sting, choose a non-alcohol-based liquid. As you shave, no matter how careful you are, you create little nicks and abrasions in the skin.

Throw ethyl alcohol into the tiny wounds, and you feel the burn. The alcohol does serve a purpose. It acts as an antiseptic and, along with other ingredients, helps heal the cuts and smooth the skin. It is possible to make aftershaves that do not sting, yet the cosmetics companies that produce them have not met with much commercial success. Apparently, men prefer an aftershave that comes with a built-in stinging sensation. Companies speculate that this is because it feels more like the stuff is working.

Don't TP Your Face

If you follow these tips and still manage to cut yourself, don't make the mistake of stopping the blood with a little piece of toilet paper. When you pull it off, you will usually take the tiny scab with it and open the skin again. Instead, **scoop up the little bit of shaving cream that is left on the nozzle and dab it on the cut.** It will stop the bleeding and then dissolve.

PREP FOR THE PERFECT SHAVE

Assuming you want a baby-smooth shave, and not a 10:00 a.m. shadow, massage your skin in a circular motion to make the hairs stand up before you start cutting. Shaving cream from a can is fine, but if you want a really good shave, opt for a glycerin-based cream from a tub, which you put on with a quality shaving brush. A shaving brush exfoliates your skin and makes the whiskers stand out while providing a richer, more hydrating lather. Apply an even layer to the entire beard area. If you do use a shaving brush, avoid damaging the bristles by storing it with the bristles upright.

don't regret your **TATTOO**

You stagger home from yet another failed job interview wondering what you could have said to make a better impression. You loosen your tie, take off your jacket, go into the bathroom to splash water on your face. When you look in the mirror you think to yourself, "Maybe that skull and crossbones tattoo on my neck wasn't such a good idea after all."

Not Something to Bargain-Shop For

One of the biggest mistake potential tattoo-ees make is to go looking for the cheapest artist they can find. Tattoo removal is expensive, and you don't want to have to pay for the tattoo twice by having a better artist touch it up or cover it up entirely. **You will spend less in the long run by saving up now and getting what you want, not what you almost want.**

Research the Artist

When selecting something so personal and permanent, you would think people would put in at least as much time and thought as they do in purchasing a car. Instead, many people walk into the first tattoo studio they see. Be careful in selecting your tattoo artist. No one excels at everything. **Some artists are great at tribal tattoos but not as gifted at three-dimensional skulls. Ask around and check online. Find the right person for your job.**

You Have to Wear it Everywhere

In order to avoid a serious case of tattoo-rue, you have to think long-term. Try to imagine the design in different outfits and contexts. You might love the dragon on your arm when you're at the beach, but will you be as happy with it when you are wearing a sleeveless dress at a wedding?

Trends Come and Go, Tattoos are Forever

Remember that many things will happen over the course of a lifetime. People change in mind, body, and spirit. Your current passions and relationships, as difficult as it is to believe now, may not be as important to you in thirty years. That's why you should avoid branding yourself with images that have a risk of being ephemeral, like the name of your favorite band. Will One Direction rock forever? Imagine this is 1983—you might feel the same way about Kajagoogoo. Who? Exactly.

Your Tattoo Will Age with You

Another mistake is to forget that your body is going to change. You may plan to beat the odds and stay at your fighting weight throughout life, but just in case you don't, try to 🖐 **imagine what that Celtic knot on your hip would look like if you put on a few extra pounds. Remember, too, that skin changes as you age and some finely detailed tattoos can spread and become fuzzy.** Ask your artist for tips on which designs are likely to last longest. Or if you're set on something intricate, plan on how you can touch it up later in a way that will hide any blown-out details.

A Cute Gecko Can Become Godzilla

Women are more likely than men to express regret over a tattoo. Consider the changes that your body will go through if you decide to have children. Tattoos on the abdomen can be stretched and changed with a pregnancy. 👍 **You can avoid the worst ravages by applying cocoa butter a couple times a day throughout the pregnancy, which is a good idea for your skin anyway.** Things will still stretch, but they won't get destroyed.

Get a Translator You Trust

👍 **Before you get Asian characters etched into your skin, be sure you know what they say.** Many people are victims of what has been called "gibberish font" where the characters that supposedly say "peace" in Japanese actually say "sushi"—or worse. If your tattoo artist offers to spell out your name letter by letter using corresponding Japanese or Chinese characters, he doesn't have a clue as to what he is writing because those languages do not work that way.

polish your **NAILS,** not your fingers

Nail polish—or nail varnish as they call it in the United Kingdom (this is technically more accurate as you are applying color, not shining them up)—adds a touch of elegance or whimsy to your look when it is done right, but applying nail polish is easy to get terribly wrong. This is not surprising given that you are doing detailed painting with a tiny brush, and half the time you're using your non-dominant hand.

Fend off Frustration

Unless you want a pitted mess, you should remove the remnants of any old polish from your nails with a cotton ball dipped in nail polish remover. It is a good idea to start working on your dominant hand with your non-dominant hand. For example, if you are right-handed, start with the brush in your left hand. This way you're going from difficult to easy. You also fend off the frustration of having just completed a perfect manicure only to make a mess of things on the other hand. The more you work at it, the better your non-dominant hand's coordination will become.

The Best Method

Rest your dominant hand on a firm surface with the fingers spread. Start with the pinky and work your way in. Put a little less polish on the brush than you think you will need. It is easier to go back and touch it up with a bit more than it is to fix a thick glob.

Now you're ready to apply the base coat. Place a dot just above the little inverted moon at the base of your nail. Brush back toward the cuticle and then forward to the tip of your nail. Next, make a parallel stroke to the right, brushing from cuticle to tip and another on the left. 🖐 **When the first coat has dried completely, apply a second coat covering any gaps in the first.**

No More Chips

Now that you have lovely, colored, smudge-free nails, you want to keep them from chipping. 🖐 **Avoid quick-dry topcoats. They do make the polish dry more quickly, but they also make it chip faster.**

If your nails are dry and brittle, the paint can chip as your nails crack and peel. You can try adding moisture to them by soaking your nails in warm water for a few minutes, then coating them with olive oil or petroleum jelly. They act as a temporary sealant and keep water from evaporating from the surface of the nail. Do this when the nails are clean before you polish them.

TOP TIP

Unless you want a pitted mess, you should remove the remnants of any old polish from your nails with a cotton ball dipped in nail polish remover.

IF YOU'RE NO PRO

Until you get your self-manicure technique down, it is a good idea to start with a clear or subtle solid color. Most people will not pay enough attention to your fingers to notice if you messed up a bit unless you have smeared bright red all over your cuticles.

🖐 **A good trick is to apply Vaseline on the skin around your nails. That way if you screw up, you can wipe away any paint that went off your nails.** You'll be be left with a nice, neat manicure, and as an added bonus, the Vaseline will have softened your cuticles.

ZIPPER slipups

 **TOP SCREWUPS**

- Getting fabric caught
- Trying to use a misshapen slider

Unlike the straightforward button, which can basically only fail by falling off, the zipper has many potential places to become jammed or broken.

Slider Error

Most often it is the slider that causes a zipper to fail. If you find your zipper just won't zip, or if it has the unfortunate habit of leaving you exposed to the public, the slider is probably worn or bent out of shape. The slider is also to blame if the zip seems welded in place. The main way that a slider gets bent is that fabric gets caught in the mechanism. Don't just start yanking away. **Try to gently pull the threads out of the slider or the zipper's teeth. If you still can't get it open, try greasing the zipper with candles, soap, or lip balm.**

Work It Back into Shape

Once you get the offending item off, **you can fix the slider by gently squeezing it back into shape with a pair of pliers.** "Gently" is the active word here. You want to squeeze it just enough to keep it from sliding down the teeth or open it just enough to move freely, not enough to seal it shut or break it in half. If the zipper is missing teeth or is coming off the fabric altogether, this is more complicated and requires some sewing skill.

DON'T SCREW UP

YOUR HEALTH

don't give yourself an **ULCER**

TOP SCREWUPS

- Misunderstanding the causes
- Taking the wrong medication
- Livin' la vida loca

Here's the thing you need to know about ulcers: Contrary to popular belief, they are not caused by stress, or at least not by stress alone. The idea that you can worry yourself into an ulcer probably comes from the observation that stress sometimes causes the stomach to churn. Excessive stress, it is reasonable to assume, can burn a hole right through it. This seems logical, but it is wrong.

Drugs You Should Be On

While drugs that inhibit production of stomach acid are an effective treatment for ulcers, researchers found that fifty to ninety percent of ulcers come back as soon as the treatment is stopped. This has led gastroenterologists to conclude that while stomach acid irritates ulcers, it may not cause them. **The real culprit is now believed to be an infection with the bacterium H. Pylori. With an antibiotic treatment that kills H. Pylori, doctors are able to decrease the occurrence of ulcers by ninety to ninety-five percent.** That said, the majority of people who have the bacteria don't develop ulcers, so scientists are still investigating the complex combination of factors that make one person and not another prone to developing stomach ulcers.

They Don't Cause It, but They Don't Help Either

A daily routine that includes strong coffee to wake up, aspirin to get rid of a headache, and vodka at night to unwind might not be the best thing for your stomach. All these substances—coffee, both decaf and regular; painkillers such as aspirin and ibuprofen; and alcohol of all kinds—irritate your stomach lining. Therefore, they play an indirect role in the formation of ulcers. It doesn't matter whether the coffee has caffeine or not. It is the acid in coffee that can irritate the lining of the stomach. **Learning to relax will certainly not hurt, especially combined with a prescription for antibiotics from your doctor.**

ULCER MYTHS

You cannot give yourself an ulcer by eating spicy foods, nor can you cure one by eating bland foods or drinking milk. Any food—spicy or bland—will stimulate the production of stomach acid.

NO INSURANCE?
that doesn't mean you can't get care

If you have no insurance, don't go without care because you're worried about money. There are ways to get the care you need.

Talk Them Down

If you tell your health care provider you don't have insurance, they will probably negotiate a lower price for you. Few people do this, but most who try it are able to get a lower price. If possible, speak directly to your doctor, not the receptionist, and explain your financial situation. If you're worried about taking money away from your physician, bear in mind that insurance companies typically pay doctors one-half to two-thirds of the amount billed. Your doctor usually has the wiggle room to cut you some slack if the alternative is to go without vital treatment. Your doctor may also be willing to waive or reduce the fee for your follow-up visit if it is just to share results and will only take a few moments.

Go Straight to the Source

Consider getting routine tests done directly at a lab rather than at the doctor's office. When your doctor does a test, she charges you for the visit and a fee for drawing your blood, plus whatever the lab charges to run the test. Ask your doctor to give you the necessary paperwork and then go online and look for clinical, medical, and diagnostics laboratories in your area.

If you have a prescription that you cannot afford, look up the drug manufacturer's web page. Most pharmaceutical companies have programs that provide free drugs to people who qualify. The different programs have different criteria.

One-Stop Shop

Look for medical care at the drugstore. **Many grocery stores and drugstores are equipped with mini-clinics that can handle basic procedures.** Going there for treatment of minor health problems like bronchitis and rashes can save you a substantial amount compared to a full-service doctor visit.

Uncle Sam Can Help

If medical costs are still out of reach, **the U.S. Department of Health and Human Services maintains a list of federally funded health centers that will care for you, even if you have no health insurance.** You pay what you can afford, based on your income. Search for one near you at http://findahealthcenter.hrsa.gov.

IS ALL THAT REALLY NECESSARY?

Double-check that all tests are necessary. When a patient is fully insured, the doctor has the luxury of doing tests just to be sure that all bases are covered. Some of these tests may be nice to have, but not strictly necessary.

don't get OVERCHARGED AT THE HOSPITAL

If you have to go to the hospital, you probably have a lot on your mind besides the bill. That is why most people don't go over the bill until much later. By then you don't remember whether the doctors' visits and lab tests that are listed actually happened. According to the People's Medical Society, a nonprofit medical consumer-rights organization, as many as three out of four hospital bills have overcharges.

Keep on Top of It

👍 **When you are admitted into the hospital, tell a staff member that you want an itemized bill brought to you each day.** Hospitals are required to do this if you ask. If you see that you were billed for two doctor visits and you only remember receiving one, ask to speak to the hospital's patient advocate and ask him to explain any charges you do not understand. 👍 **Keep a sharp lookout for double billings. Hospitals often bill patients twice for the same thing. For example, if you're billed for scrubs and gloves worn by the surgical staff, ask your advocate if this is also covered under the cost for the operating room time.**

The Last Day Should Be on the House

You should not have to pay for the last day of your stay. **Hospital patients are charged the full day's room rate for the day they check in, even if they arrived at 11:30 pm. The trade-off is that they are not supposed to be charged for the last day.** Hospitals often forget this and charge for the last day anyway. Find out in advance if you will be charged for the last day. If the hospital tells you that you will not be charged if you are out by noon, ask your doctor if she can give you your final checkup in the morning so you can be out before then. If she can't, tell your patient advocate that you should not be charged because the late checkout was your doctor's doing.

WHEN ALL ELSE

FAILS

If your patient advocate is unable to help you and you still feel you were overbilled, you can hire an independent medical-billing advocate. They charge a fee for their services either per hour or as a percentage of the amount saved. The former will probably save you money, and the latter definitely will.

DON'T FART
in anyone's general direction

 **TOP SCREWUPS**

- Eating gas-producing food
- Eating bad-smelling-gas–producing food
- Eating too fast and not chewing enough

Everyone does it—an average of ten times a day, in fact. Some people pass gas more often, and others pass larger volumes less often, but the total volume remains roughly the same of up to 2 liters of gas a day (yup, that's a bottle of soda). Men typically expel a bit more than women. This has nothing to do with testosterone; they just eat more.

Lead Trumpeters

As long as you remain human, you will not eradicate this problem entirely, but you can mitigate the effects. Certain foods are infamous for their gas-producing ability. Beans, broccoli, cabbage, and apples contain complex sugars that can't be broken down by the digestive juices. Bacteria in the intestines ferment them, and the result is gas. Milk can also result in excess gas, especially if you are lactose intolerant. Other studies have pointed the finger at high-fructose corn syrup.

Lessening the Blasts

If you can't or don't want to avoid these gas-producing foods, 🔘 **try an over-the-counter enzyme tablet or drop such as Beano.** Swallow or drip it onto your food before a meal. Studies show it helps a little. If you're a bean fan, you can reduce their gas-producing magic by soaking them before you cook them. This reduces some of the complex carbohydrates. Cover the beans with water and bring it to a boil for a few minutes. Then turn off the heat and let the beans soak for four hours. The boiling step is important; it will remove much more sugar than soaking in cold water alone.

A Multi-Sensory Experience

Most of the gas you pass is odorless. It is primarily made up of nitrogen, oxygen, carbon dioxide, hydrogen, and methane. The stinky part is produced in the digestive system from bile and the linings of the intestines, and is predominantly composed of sulfur. 👄 **If you want to be less of stink machine, stay away from sulfur-rich foods like eggs, meat, and cauliflower.**

What Goes in Must Come Out

To avoid gas coming out one end, don't put it in the other. When you eat or drink, a bit of air goes down with the food. Some of it makes its way into the digestive tract and has to come back out. 👄 **You can keep excess gas out by eating and drinking slowly, and chewing food thoroughly.** Carbonated beverages and air-filled treats like sponge cake and soufflé will also add gas to your system.

Get It All Out at Once

If you have a big date or an important meeting and you're feeling bloated, you should try to get as much gas out as you can before you go. This technique is something you'll want to try when no one else is around. Kneel on the floor, bend forward, and stretch your arms in front of you. Form a triangle with your upper body and the floor and elevate your posterior high in the air. This position can force out unwanted gas and relieve pressure.

WHEN ALL ELSE FAILS

If none of this solves your social stink problem, invest in odor-eating underwear. They are not cheap, but underwear made with activated carbon fiber will absorb nearly all of the sulfur-containing gasses. They will still pass, but they will not offend anyone's nose. Thank you, science!

how not *HIC* to suffer *HIC* from hiccups

TOP SCREWUPS

- Eating or drinking quickly
- Employing silly homemade cures

Hiccups have been part of the medical literature since Hippocrates' time (the fourth century BCE). In all those years, physicians haven't quite figured out exactly what makes them happen. Of course, there hasn't been much serious study of hiccups because they come out of the blue and are usually very brief, making them hard to observe.

Slow It Down—Hiccup Prevention

The only thing you might be able to do to prevent them is  **avoid eating or drinking too much too fast.** It seems benign, self-limited hiccups, as opposed to the persistent or "intractable" kind, can be set off by eating too much or drinking carbonated and alcoholic beverages. This causes distension in the digestive tract, which activates the gastric branches of the vagus nerve or directly stimulates the diaphragm, causing spasms. A sudden change in body temperature or a high level of stress may also start the spasms.

When the muscle's movements get out of rhythm, you take in big gulps of air. As your lungs quickly fill, your throat closes. The "hic" sound is caused by a rush of air as the vocal chords snap shut.

Which Wives' Tales Have Merit?

There are endless home remedies of varying effectiveness for getting rid of hiccups. Dr. Charles Mayo of the Mayo Clinic once said, "There is no disease which has had more forms of treatment and fewer results from treatment than has persistent hiccups." 🕐 **Here are the ones that have at least a bit of scientific plausibility and a chance of working:**

- Breathing into a paper bag forces a hiccupper to suck in more carbon dioxide, which helps regulate breathing. But do this with caution because you could become light-headed. Also, never try this with a plastic bag. If you don't have a paper bag, just hold your breath.

- Sipping water from the opposite side of the glass stretches the neck and stimulates the vagus nerve in the brain, which helps in swallowing the breathing.

- If you don't mind looking a little foolish, stick a finger into each ear. This stimulates the vagus nerve, which runs from the brain to the abdomen and controls hiccups.

- Use a cotton swab to draw a line gently down the roof of your mouth. The tickling stops the spasm that causes hiccups.

Medical experts say these treatments may work, or they may just distract you until your diaphragm gets back to a normal rhythm on its own.

A TRUE CURE?

A 13-year-old Connecticut student recently filed a patent so she can produce a line of hiccup-killing lollipops called Hiccupops. She based the concept on her science fair project. If you don't want to wait for her company to get off the ground, you can try whipping up a homemade batch by mixing apple cider vinegar and sugar. The mixture is said to overstimulate nerves that cause the hiccup reflex and just a teaspoon's worth can cure you.

don't screw up SITTING DOWN

The humble chair may not seem like a tricky contraption, but believe it or not, it is the cause of a substantial number of injuries. Each year 410,000 Americans have seating mishaps. Perhaps someone you love is sitting right now, at risk of this scourge that is sweeping the world!

A Real Pain in the Chair

By far the biggest thing you can screw up just by sitting down is your posture. Bad form can lead to all sorts of neck and back pain. And then when people ask how you hurt yourself, it can lead to the embarrassment of telling them your injury was brought on by an easy chair and a *Law & Order* marathon.

👍 **If you want to be sitting pretty, you must:**

1 Make sure your butt is touching the back of your seat and your back is aligned with the chair back. If it's a deep chair, get yourself a pillow.

2 Sit up straight with your shoulders back and accentuate the natural curve of your back. Then relax just a little bit. Phew!

3 Make sure your sit bones (the bottom of your pelvis) are firmly planted and your weight is evenly distributed on them, no leaning to one side.

4 Your knees should be a little higher than your hips and bent at a 90° angle.

Get on Up

When you're leaning back in your chair, you have to bring your center of gravity forward to get up. A person usually does this by leaning back farther, then whipping her head and chest forward to get momentum. This is an excellent way to throw out your back. Instead, 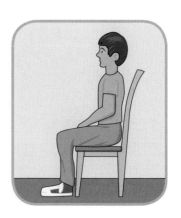 **do this:**

1 With your head and spine aligned, place your feet flat on the ground with your knees facing forward.

2 Imagine a string extending from the middle of your pelvis through your neck out the top of your head and onward to infinity.

3 Now imagine someone gently pulling up on this cord to lift you out of the chair. Lead with the top of your head, bend at the waist, and bring your upper body forward and up as you think of sending your knees forward and away.

4 Place your hands on the seat of the chair next to your thighs with your elbows slightly bent.

5 Keep your shoulders relaxed and your neck free as you rise in a single smooth movement.

Congratulations, you are safely out of your chair.

DON'T DRIVE YOURSELF TO BAD POSTURE

If you spend a lot of time behind the wheel, you might be tempted to fall into some bad sitting habits: slouching, slumping, sitting askew. It's hard to maintain a good position once you've been stuck in a traffic jam caused by one guy with a flat tire five miles up the highway, but your back will thank you in the long term if you keep your shoulders back, your head held high, and your chest out. It'll take a little work at first but you'll feel better and look better in and out of the car if you keep yourself held straight. Plus, it'll give you something to think about besides what the heck the vanity plate "MIBGNU" means.

what to do if you get
SOCKED IN THE FACE

If you have watched lots of 1960s sitcoms, you probably think you know how to treat a black eye already. Just get out a thick steak and lay it over the injured eye. Well, sort of.

What Happened to Your Eye

There is nothing magical about a piece of steak that draws bruising out of an eye wound. This old folk remedy sometimes helps a bit indirectly, though. Black eyes, known as periorbital hematomas to medical types, are caused by tiny broken blood vessels under the skin. If you apply something cold to an injury right away, it constricts the tiny broken blood vessels, which may potentially keep the blood from pouring out and creating a bruise.

Beef: It's Not Just for Dinner

This is where the steak comes in. **When you first take it out of the refrigerator, it is cold. That is the only black-eye-treating property it has.** Another thing the TV dads get wrong with this trick is that they often apply the thick steak to a full-blown blue bruise. Once the injury has turned blue, the only thing that can heal it is time, although continuing to apply cold will help reduce swelling. If you are going to put a raw slab of meat on your face, you should put it in a plastic bag first so as to not get meat juice in your eye and skin flakes on your steak.

The Vegetarian Version

Instead of using an expensive cut of meat, the best way to treat a shiner is to sit down, tilt your head back, and use a plain ice bag, five minutes on and five minutes off. You will want to do this gently, of course. The eye will be sensitive and sore. If the ice bag is too cold to hold over your eye, wrap it in cloth. If you want to take something for the pain, try a pain reliever such as acetaminophen instead of aspirin. Aspirin reduces blood clotting, which can make a bruise worse.

If both of your eyes are black (like a raccoon) or if there is bleeding, get to a doctor. These could be signs of a damaged skull or another serious medical condition.

 TOP TIP

Once the injury has turned blue, the only thing that can heal it is time, although continuing to apply cold will help reduce swelling.

COVERING UP THAT SHINER

If you don't want to explain to everyone you see how exactly you ended up with a black eye, you can try concealing it. This is tough to do, but you can try it with a yellow-green liquid or cream concealer if you're working on a fresh bruise. It may seem counterintuitive, but these shades will offset the red and blue of the shiner. Dab on the makeup and spread it evenly. After it dries, you may need a second coat. After that dries, apply foundation that matches your skin tone. If you're a lady, now may be the time to try that dramatic, smoky eye shadow style you've been thinking about.

what not to do when you get a
SPLINTER

It is a myth that splinters will work their way out themselves. According to Dr. Ted Broadway of the Ontario Medical Association, 👍 **splinters should always be removed because nature will not do it for you.** If you do not remove them, they will likely become infected in a day or two.

You May Have to Get All Up in There

Tweezers usually aren't enough to remove a splinter on their own. Most are poorly made, and the tips don't touch. Unless the splinter has barely pierced the skin, using tweezers alone usually leaves fragments behind, which can lead to infection. 👍 **To get the job done right, you will also need a needle.** Begin by sterilizing tweezers and a needle by soaking them in alcohol for ten minutes or holding them in a flame for thirty seconds. Before you start, clean the skin around the splinter with alcohol. You are now ready to "unroof" the shard.

Where to Start

Never start from the deep end. Always begin from the point where the shard went in. If you can't tell which is the deep end, try pressing a pen flashlight close to the sore spot. The light will pass through the skin and highlight the angle and depth of the fragment.

This May Pinch

Use the needle to break open the skin, so the splinter can be taken out more easily. Press your thumbnail against the base of the splinter at the deep end to nudge it toward the opening. Hold the tweezers parallel to the skin and grasp the splinter as far down as you can without causing further injury. Once the splinter is out, do not forget to wash the area one more time and apply antibiotic ointment and a sterile bandage.

If you can't get the splinter out after twenty minutes, stop jabbing at it and wait until it's covered by scab tissue. Then you can remove both the splinter and the scab.

 TOP TIP

Never start from the deep end. Always begin from the point where the shard went in.

YOU MIGHT *NOT* HAVE TO GET ALL UP IN THERE

Before you start poking around in your skin, try a less-invasive method: steam it out. Fill a glass or wide-mouthed bottle three-fourths full of hot water. Then place the stuck skin over the mouth and press it slightly. The steam will soften the skin, and if the splinter is wood, the steam will cause the wood to expand, which might allow it to pop out. If the splinter is in your finger, it may be even easier to get out. Just soak the finger in warm water and it might float out all on its own. If this method doesn't work, you're going to have to get a bit more surgical.

cavities, gingivitis, and other things
that screw up YOUR SMILE

You probably think you've got this whole brushing thing down to a science. How could you be messing up this thing you've been doing twice a day, everyday, for your whole life? (You are brushing at least twice a day, aren't you!?) Well, if you are getting bad breath, some pink in the sink when you brush, or disapproving nods from your dentist, then odds are you're screwing up this daily routine.

That's Only Six Minutes Per Day

The biggest mistake that people make when brushing is that they do not brush nearly long enough. **You should take a full 120 seconds in order to have healthy gums and minty fresh breath. This doesn't sound like a long time, but most people spend less than 30 seconds removing plaque. In a world run by D.D.S.s, you would be brushing your teeth three times a day: when you get up in the morning, after lunch, and just before you go to bed.** The middle brushing tends to get skipped because people are at work, but if you want your pearly whites to last a lifetime, keep a travel brush at work and pop into the restroom for a quick clean on your lunch break.

Doing Right by Your Pearly Whites

Brush, brush, brush, scrub, scrub, scrub, spit. Right? Wrong! There is a method to brushing that, when done correctly, will keep your chompers their chompiest. Angle the brush against the gum line at about 45°. Using small circular movements, first clean the outsides of your teeth, then the insides. Clean the insides of the upper and lower middle teeth by tilting the brush vertically. Finally brush along the biting services.

After you've finished with the surfaces of your teeth, clean your tongue. This will get rid of swamp breath. You can either use your toothbrush or buy a special tongue cleaner. Nowadays a lot of toothbrushes come with special tongue-scraping ridges on the back of their heads, so you can get two in one.

Failure to Floss

Wait! Don't wander off yet! You are not done. 👍 **It's time to floss. You may think this step is optional, but skipping it is just as likely to cause cavities and other grody ailments as skipping brushing altogether.**

To floss the right way, take 18 inches (45 centimeters) of floss and wind it around the middle finger of each hand. Hold the floss taut so you have about 1 inch (2.5 centimeters) between your fingers. Using a smooth seesaw movement, gently ease the floss between your teeth. Don't snap it to get it between your teeth, or you could damage your gums. Gently rub between the teeth a few times and get below the gum line. The back ones may be challenging to reach, but do not skip them. Wind the floss along so that you use a fresh piece each time.

OK, You Can Spit and Rinse Now

When you've finished, rinse your mouth with water to wash away the particles you just dislodged. If you like the

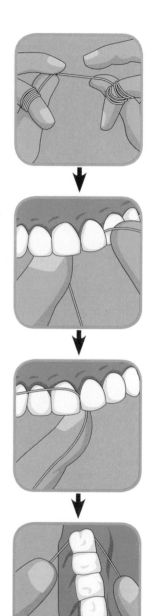

feel of mouthwash you can use it, but according to the FDA (Food and Drug Administration), there is no proof that mouthwash gives you healthier gums or cleaner teeth than rinsing with plain water. Just think, if you hadn't flossed, all that junk would still be between your teeth and gums, festering. Yuck! If flossing is a new addition to your routine, you're likely to have some gum bleeding. But once it turns into a habit, that will stop.

KEEPING YOUR BRUSHES KOSHER

Toothbrushes are germ scrubbers that go in your mouth. That said, you should take some precautionary measures to keep them as clean as they can be.

Screwup ⋯⋯⋯▶	Big Fix
• Using brushes with natural bristles sounds good, but they're actually gross because natural fibers trap bacteria.	• Buy brushes with synthetic-fiber bristles, because those will be nonporous and the bacteria will be easier to rinse away.
• Allowing your toothbrush to mingle with your family's brushes can cause germs to migrate to everyone.	• Store brushes upright and separately so they dry properly and everyone keeps their yucky mouth germs to themselves.
• Keeping your brush after you've been sick can make you sick again, because germs can survive on your brush and reinfect you.	• Replace your brush any time you get sick. You should also be replacing it every three months no matter how healthy you are.

don't FALL DOWN

First day with the new legs? Har har har. Walking on two legs as opposed to four has its evolutionary benefits. Thanks to our standing posture, we have free hands that can reach for books on high shelves or operate a smartphone. But there is a trade-off. We have a hard time keeping our balance.

Most Accidents Happen in the Home, but Not Because of the Home

The obvious advice is to check your house to be sure you do not have any loose throw rugs, slippery showers, or other hazards that could cause you to trip. This is obvious, but not necessarily as helpful as you'd think. A recent study by the Yale School of Medicine found that loose throw rugs, slippery showers, and other hazards were not responsible for most falls by the elderly living at home, those most prone to falls. People simply lose their balance.

Better Balance Means Fewer Falls

The good news is that **there are a number of exercises that you can do to keep yourself from tipping over. The purpose of the exercises is to relieve the tension that most people carry unevenly in our bodies**—thus throwing off their balance—and to strengthen the muscles for added support.

Work Out to Avoid Going Down

Here are some simple exercises you can do to up your chances of not falling down. All of them should be performed barefoot while wearing comfortable clothing.

ALTERNATING KNEE BENDS

1 Begin by standing straight.

2 Stand with your feet together and bend forward at your waist as far as you comfortably can. Let your arms and head hang down to release tension.

3 Now bend one knee slightly for about fifteen seconds while keeping the other leg straight. Then repeat the process with the other knee.

4 Do a total of three bends per leg. If you become light-headed, put your hands on the ground and look straight ahead.

WALKING THE TIGHTROPE

1 Stand straight again.

2 Now imagine you are going to walk on a tightrope of at least ten feet in length. You can put an actual length of string or another straight line on the floor or just do your best to imagine it. Stretch your arms out at shoulder height with your palms facing up.

3 With your eyes on the horizon, walk along the line. Walk to the end and then turn and walk

WHEN ALL ELSE
FAILS

Face it, you're still going to fall over from time to time. The cat gets underfoot, your flip-flop snags on a nail, you see Brangelina walking down the road—it happens. So here's another suggestion: practice falling. This is the idea of F. J. Leavitt of Ben-Gurion University in Israel. After studying the available medical literature, he recommends following the example of martial arts practitioners who practice falls to prevent injury. To learn the proper technique, join a karate class near you.

back. Focus on keeping each foot right on the line, and do not step until you are centered.

4 Repeat five times.

LEG SWINGS

1 Stand with your arms bent at the elbow and your hands resting on your hips.

2 Lift one of your legs in front of you as high as you comfortably can while holding it straight and keeping your toes pointed.

3 Now, without putting your foot on the ground, sweep your leg back and extend the leg behind you, keeping it up in the air. Flex your foot so the toes point down.

4 Do this ten times, then switch legs and repeat.

when **WORKING OUT**
doesn't work out

TOP SCREWUPS

- Pushing too hard too fast
- Doing exercises the wrong way
- Thinking pain equals gain

You look at yourself in the mirror one day and realize you've gone from having just a couple extra pounds to being really out of shape—how you failed to realize this as it was happening is a mystery. This will not do. In that instant, you decide that you are going to become as fit and healthy as you were in high school. No, fitter than that. You jog to the gym, start operating the bench press, and next thing you know you're lying down flat in your doctor's office. This does not feel much like health.

Take It Easy with a Buddy

Wanting to get too fit too fast is the biggest mistake people make when it comes to exercise. Instead of getting healthier, you end up getting hurt: pulled muscles, injured backs, overexertion, and accidents are the results.

Whenever you lift weights, at home or at the gym, you should have a spotter. If a certain lift hurts, try substituting another movement that works the same body part from a different angle. If your gym offers a free personal training session, take it so you can learn how to use all the weights and equipment properly.

How to Screw Up Your Workout

Even basic exercises can be dangerous if they're not done properly. Some of the worst offenders are:

TOE TOUCHES. The wrong way to do this is with the knees

in a locked position combined with rapid bouncing. It puts pressure on the lumbar vertebrae and can lead to back pain. Allow your knees to bend slightly and remain bent for three full breaths. Do not bounce.

SIT-UPS. These are also screwed up by keeping the legs straight and locked. This can lead to an increased curvature of the lower back. Bend your knees, keep your feet flat on the floor, and curl up to only a 30° angle from the floor—curling up the whole way may strain your back.

DEEP KNEE BENDS. Done incorrectly, they cause injury to knee cartilage. Be sure to bend the knees so that they are directly over your feet and your thighs are parallel to the floor. Do not extend your bent knee past your foot.

LEG LIFTS. The ones where you lie on your back and raise both legs at the same time are just bad. They can cause the pelvis to rotate and lead to a swayback, which means your spine curves in excessively. Don't do this exercise.

No Pain, No Gain? No Brains

A better saying might be "no pain, no pain." **There is a difference between feeling your muscles burn from working them out properly and feeling straight-up pain. When you start to hurt, rest, even if it's a muscle burn that doesn't indicate injury. Pain is your body's way of saying that you've gone too far.** You are either doing something that is too advanced or you shouldn't be doing at all. A good rule of thumb is to increase your activity a little bit each week until you reach your goal.

DRINK UP!

Anyone who ever told you that you should not drink liquids while exercising was wrong. If you do not replace the fluids that you lose by sweating, you are at risk of dehydration and heat stroke. Don't wait until you're thirsty to drink. By then you're already dehydrated, and exercise can blunt your body's thirst signals. A good rule of thumb is to drink two cups of water fifteen minutes before you start exercising and about a half a cup of water every ten to fifteen minutes while working out.

don't let crutches put you on
CRUTCHES

TOP SCREWUPS

- Using crutches when you need something more
- Using bad crutch technique

This can happen. Just ask any of the estimated 73,615 people each year who are injured by—as the National Electronic Injury Surveillance System categorizes it—"crutches, canes, or walkers." About the same number of people as are injured doing such risky-sounding activities as in-line skating or riding a horse.

Don't Get Tripped Up by Pride

One problem with crutches, according to Kris Schmidt of St. Mary's Hospital Medical Center in Wisconsin, is human stubbornness. People who should really be using a walker sometimes refuse to do so because they think it makes them appear weak or old. Instead, they ask for crutches. They get fatigued, and they fall down. **If you should be using a walker or a wheelchair, do so. If you do need to use crutches, spend some time learning to use them safely.**

How to Become Crutch Capable

1 While in a seated position, take both crutches in the hand of the side with the injured leg and push off the arm (or seat if there's no arm) of the chair with your free hand to stand.

2 Transfer one of the crutches to your free hand and get a good grip.

3 Place the tips of the crutches two inches (five centimeters) in front of your feet and about four to six inches (ten to fifteen centimeters) to the side.

4 Shift the crutches and the injured leg forward together to share the load, and then step forward with the non-injured leg.

   If your injured leg is unable to bear any weight, work with your arms and shoulders and swing the injured leg level before stepping forward with the other leg.

Do not expect to get around as quickly as you do without crutches. Take it slowly, and as you practice, your balance and coordination will improve.

YOU ALREADY HAVE ENOUGH PROBLEMS

There is, of course, a difference between your average in-line skater and your crutch-walker. The person on crutches already has some problems with his balance and health. This means that, contrary to common belief, a fall from a walker is often much more dangerous than a fall from a pair of skates. A young, athletic person who falls as she glides around a track will probably pick herself right back up and keep going. A ninety-year-old who slips with a walker can end up with serious and sometimes fatal injuries.

don't get scared by
HEALTH HYPE

Every year, hundreds of research studies are published in medical journals and are then picked up by the popular press. The studies that get the most attention are those that warn of a potential risk from something super common. The stories are often contradictory. One week there's a story about caffeine being a secret killer, but by the next week coffee fights cancer. Even worse are the stories about prescription medications. Is the drug that your doctor prescribed going to kill you or just your sex drive? How can you figure out what is true and what is just hype?

What Is Science Anyway?

"Science is the continual averaging of points of view until you get something of a consensus," *Health Magazine* editor Sheridan Warrick told the *Record* newspaper. "To journalists, on the other hand, consensus is the most boring and least newsworthy of all the things we could write about. Journalism loves conflict and contradiction."

Don't Believe Everything You Read

A recent study of the content of U.S. daily newspapers showed that thirty-five percent of all stories, and about forty-seven percent of front-page stories, deal with potential risks. This is not because we live in historically more dangerous times, but because risk is dramatic and more likely to engage readers and sell papers. Not only are the media often guilty of sounding the alarm before it is time, but also they often leave out relevant facts on the studies they report on and even, on occasion, report the actual findings incorrectly.

Weeding out the Truth

So before you stop taking your medication, start taking the latest trendy herbal supplement, or give up your favorite food, pause for a moment and try to evaluate the science in the story. Don't change your behavior based on a single uncorroborated study. One researcher's findings are interesting, but they do not prove anything until the results are repeated (or perhaps clarified or debunked) by another researcher. If the story reports on a conclusion without explaining how the study was designed and carried out, do not give it much weight. Without understanding exactly who and what was tested and how it was done, you cannot adequately judge whether the results apply to you and whether they are valid. Be more skeptical of news accounts about studies presented at conferences, rather than in professional journals, as conference papers are not necessarily subject to peer review.

Don't Just Read Articles About Articles

If the story cites research that is particularly relevant to you—for example, it is about a medication that you take—look up the original journal article. If you cannot find it online, you may be able to get a copy at your local library. The full article will tell you more than an article in the popular press. A scholarly journal article is a bit more difficult to read, but it will always give a

 TOP TIP

Without understanding exactly who and what was tested and how it was done, you cannot adequately judge whether the results apply to you and whether they are valid.

detailed explanation of the methodology of the study. Its conclusions will no doubt appear much more equivocal than the popular press version and will end with areas that need follow-up research.

Do What All the Commercials Say: Talk to Your Doctor

If you read a story that scares you, talk to your doctor about it. All medications have side effects, and taking them requires an analysis of the risks of taking the medication versus the dangers of not taking it. 🕐 **Your physician should be able to explain why he thinks the benefits outweigh the risks in your case.** Likewise, if you read a story or see a television commercial about a great new drug, or even a natural remedy, ask your doctor what she thinks of it in relation to your family history, other medications, or any other factors she has hidden there in your folder.

IS IT A SALES PITCH IN DISGUISE?

If someone is trying to sell you something, confirm his or her health claims with an outside source. An expert on germs whose research is funded by a bleach manufacturer may have a vested interest in reporting that bleach is the best cleaning solution. If your holistic health guru happens to sell a line of vitamin tablets, you should bear that in mind when reading his advice on how to stay healthy. If your favorite television doctor's program is full of sponsored product placements, you are smart to question whether the product is being recommended for health or business reasons. The financial connections may not necessarily nullify an expert's findings and advice, but you should take it into consideration.

YOUR
TRANSPORTATION

don't buy a **LEMON**

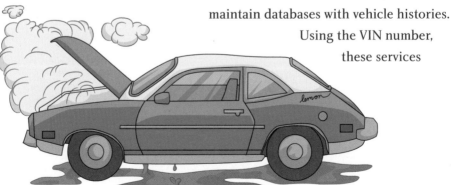

TOP SCREWUPS

- Shopping dumb
- Ignoring what you need for what you want
- Not having it checked out by a pro

Unless you enjoy paying thousands of dollars in repairs only to get stranded in the middle of nowhere by a car that just won't stay fixed, buying a car is not something you will want to do on a whim.

Do Your Homework

Make a list of what you need versus what you want. You may *want* a silver car with a great stereo and a sunroof, but what you *need* is a reliable car with great gas mileage. Be sure to keep these distinctions in mind so you do not become distracted by power windows and ubiquitous cup holders.

👎 **Before you start shopping, read *Consumer Reports* and look for pricing information in the *Kelley Blue Book*.** You should be able to find these online or at your local library.

Study History

The National Highway Traffic Safety Administration keeps records on recalls and crash-test results. There are also services such as Autocheck and Carfax, which maintain databases with vehicle histories. Using the VIN number, these services will tell you whether the car was ever damaged in a fire or flood, repurchased under a state lemon law, or totaled. A database search can also reveal odometer fraud.

How Old Is Just Right?

⚫ **Focus your search on cars that are two to four years old.** By then, the car has depreciated enough to save you money, but it still has a lot of life left in it. In addition to dealerships and private sellers, don't forget to check out public auctions. You can often find great deals on repossessed vehicles.

When to Shop

Do your car shopping in the evening of a clear day in the last week of the month, in late fall or winter. Sales are slowest in that season, and you can get the best deals. The last week of the month is when dealerships are under the most pressure to make their sales quotas, and by evening, often the sales people are tired and ready to go home, so they are apt to be more flexible about closing deals.

You want a clear day because rain can hide a vehicle's surface imperfections. Look for imperfections in the body that might indicate the car has been in an accident. Look inside the trunk and make sure the paint color there matches the body. If the doors, trunk, or hood do not open easily, there is a good chance the car was in an accident at some point.

THE MAGIC WORDS

If you've found a car that you love but you can't quite rise to the price the salesman is quoting, try asking, "What's your holdback on that car?" You're asking what their markup is, and it shows you're in the know. You can also ask what the invoice is. The invoice is the price at which the dealership bought the car. Of course, they need to make a living, too. So even if they are willing to tell you this number, they won't offer you that price, but you will be getting closer to knowing the absolute lower limit at which they can sell it.

What to Look for Under the Hood

Before you take a test drive, while the vehicle is still completely cold, look at the cooling system by unscrewing the radiator cap and siphoning off a little fluid with an antifreeze tester. The coolant should be translucent, not murky or cloudy. If it is, the radiator may be corroded.

How Does She Handle?

During your test drive, make sure no warning lights stay on. Check the accelerator and brake for responsiveness. Make sure the car holds its line on the road and does not veer to one side or the other. Listen for telltale squeaks and noises. A persistent click under heavy acceleration could mean the lifters or rods are worn, which would result in an expensive engine overhaul. Pay attention to the transmission and see if the car has trouble engaging when accelerating. Be sure to drive somewhere shaded or dark so you can take a look at the headlights and be sure they are bright enough. After you've driven the car, look underneath for leaks.

Have Your Guy Take a Look at It

Take the car in to your favorite garage and have them do a prepurchase inspection, which will likely cost between $100 and $200. Your mechanic can do a compression test to evaluate the output from each cylinder of the engine, potentially saving you from having to do some very expensive repairs in the near future. Also have the mechanic take a look at the brake disc pads and drums. These could be worn without producing sponginess or squeaking noises. The mechanic can also test the electrical system with a diagnostic machine.

drive a **STICK SHIFT**
without grinding and stalling

The biggest mistake that drivers make when it comes to manual transmission vehicles is trying once, looking like an idiot, and quitting in frustration. There is a learning curve, no doubt, but nothing worth doing ever came easily. Just acknowledge that the first few times you try it, you will not look cool. Keep at it. Once you've mastered the stick, you may not want to drive anything else.

Don't Start on the Highway

Start your lessons in a deserted parking lot, preferably in the company of a friend who can give you pointers without laughing at your first clumsy attempts (or at least one you can forgive for laughing). If you've never encountered a manual transmission vehicle before, take a moment to familiarize yourself with the pedals. You have a gas pedal on the right, the brake is in the middle, and that extra pedal on the far left is the clutch.

Before You Turn the Key

Begin with the car turned off and in first gear. You do not want the car to start rolling before you are ready. So before you step on the clutch, push the brake pedal with your right foot. Then, using your left foot push the clutch pedal all the way to the floor. When the clutch is depressed, the car behaves as if it were in neutral. In order to avoid some frustrated searches and grinding later, take a moment now to run through the gears with the clutch depressed so that you have a feel for where they are. Once you've done that, put the car in first gear and, with the clutch still depressed, start the engine.

Quit Stalling

Your big challenge now is to **start moving without stalling. To do this you need to find the point where the clutch engages the transmission instead of just revving the engine. Slowly lift up the clutch pedal until you feel the RPMs fall off.** The car might start to shudder. Press the clutch back in and try again until you have a feel for just how far you can release the clutch before the vehicle starts to stall.

This is the point at which you need to take your foot off the brake and slowly give it gas. This is a coordinated two-foot motion. As you let up on the clutch with your left foot, give it a little gas with your right. The car will probably sputter and stall the first few times while you're learning—you will laugh embarrassedly, get discouraged, feel frustrated, and maybe even pound the steering wheel with your fist, but you just have to keep at it. When the car stutters, press on the clutch, and then slowly let it out again. If you stall, push in the clutch and the brake, turn off the car, and start again.

Get It Rolling

First gear is only to get the car rolling, so once you are moving, you need to shift up to second gear. The guides will tell you to shift up to the next gear when the engine reaches about 3,000 RPM. The goal, however, is to listen and feel the car's signals so you do not need to look at the gauges. It gets easier from this point on because once you're out of first, the car's momentum will keep the engine from stalling.

Put on the Brakes

Now that you are driving, you will need to know how to stop. Don't worry, if you're about to run into something, you can always hit the brake and the car will stop. To stop properly, let off the gas and push in the clutch at the same time. With the clutch pushed all the way in, apply the brake with your right foot.

You can also slow the car by downshifting. Let off the gas, press on the clutch and shift down through the gears, fourth to third and so on. Let the gears slow the car naturally until you get into first. Then apply the brake.

An Uphill Challenge

One of the trickiest driving situations you will face in your new stick shift is a stoplight at the top of a hill. Remember that **your car will have a tendency to roll backward if you let up on the clutch and do not push the gas and start moving forward right away. The more familiar you become with the shifting of your car, the easier this will be. In the short term, you may want to use the parking brake, releasing it just as you feel the engine supporting the car's weight.** This is a tricky maneuver in itself, so you may just want to move to Kansas and avoid hills all together until you've mastered shifting.

THE MANUAL ADVANTAGE

Why go to all this trouble when you can just drive an automatic? A standard transmission car gets better gas mileage, and if you drive it right it will extend the life of your brakes. It can also cut a car's price by $800 to $1,200. Your car is also less likely to be stolen. Newspaper archives are full of accounts of would-be thieves who were thwarted because they didn't know how to drive a stick!

don't put your whole paycheck
in your GAS TANK

TOP SCREWUPS

- Driving
- Letting your car crap out
- Blaring the A/C
- Idling
- Driving like a maniac

The most effective way to avoid high gas prices, of course, is to not drive at all. Walking, biking, carpooling, and public transportation will save you money and can have side benefits, such as improved health or social interaction. If this isn't feasible for you, here are some of the ways you can still use your car without having to pump your paycheck into your tank.

Car Fitness

A car that is tuned up and in proper running condition will have better gas mileage. 👍 **Change your oil, oil filter, air filter, and spark plugs according to the schedule in your car's service manual.**

- Switching to synthetic oil can extend your vehicle's oil change interval by twenty-five to fifty percent, which can improve gas mileage by as much as ten percent.

- Use free-flowing air filters to reduce resistance to incoming air, and replace oxygen sensors on older, high-mileage cars.

- Keep your tires inflated. A properly inflated tire rolls more easily than a flat one. If the car runs more easily, it uses less energy. Make sure your car has radial tires because the sidewall of a radial is stiffer and will roll more easily than the softer sidewall of a bias ply tire.

- If your "check engine" light comes on, don't ignore it. It could mean that the vehicle's oxygen sensor has failed, which could reduce your car's fuel efficiency by much as forty percent.

Don't Drive a Gas Guzzler

If you care about fuel economy, don't drive an automatic. Cars with manual transmissions can get better gas mileage: two to five miles per gallon. (If you are not sure you can drive a stick shift, see pages 179–181 for tips.) And keep in mind that the heavier the car, the more energy it takes to move it down the road. If your SUV is always loaded up with sporting equipment and broken appliances you meant to take to the recycling center, you are spending a bit more than you would if your car were empty. Of course, if fuel economy is your focus, you should probably not be driving an SUV at all. The smaller the car, the more fuel efficient it tends to be.

Don't Be a Lead Foot

Aggressive driving burns up a lot of fuel. 👍 **You will get the best gas mileage if you can keep a consistent gas-peddle position.** This is why highway driving is more fuel efficient than stop-and-go city driving. Let off the gas pedal early and ease onto the brakes when you're coming to a stop. When you start moving, go easy on the gas and accelerate slowly.

Don't Overdo the Extras

Any device in the car that uses energy—the headlights, defroster, automatic seat warmers, air conditioner, and even the radio—reduces your gas mileage by some amount. Before you drive in silence to save gas, though, you should know that the radio draws so little energy that it is not worth worrying about (it could run for months on a pocket battery). However, leaving the rear defroster on the entire time you're driving, well after the window is frost free, can make a small difference at the pump.

Hot and Cold

Running the air conditioner, on the other hand, can be a big drain on your tank. Here's the catch, though: if you are traveling more than thirty or forty miles per hour, you reduce your fuel economy by driving with open windows because you increase the aerodynamic drag on the car. Bike racks, luggage racks, and those top-of-the-car storage bins also make your car less aerodynamic and cost you some pennies at the pump. **Park in a shady spot or use a sun shade in hot weather so you don't have to blast the air conditioning when you first get in.**

Running the heater, on the other hand, does not reduce a car's gas mileage by any considerable amount because the heat is generated by the engine as a byproduct of combustion. The only electricity you are using is what is needed to run the blower motor.

Idle Engines Are the Gas Pump's Playthings

There is a very common misconception that idling uses so little gas that you'd do better to leave your car running when you make a pit stop than to turn it off and start it again. The truth is, idling consumes up to one gallon of gas per hour. **If you're going to be sitting for more than a minute, idling will consume more gasoline than restarting the car.**

Think Outside the Car

There are also some tips to avoid money at the gas station that have nothing directly to do with your car. Start looking for a gas station when your tank is half full. This gives you a chance to comparison shop and stop at a station with the best prices.

Be sure you know your rates if you use gasoline credit cards. Their annual percentage rates are sometimes high. Some companies, however, offer incentives such as discounts to get you to use the cards. You might be able to save a penny or two per gallon with such a program, but it will only be a plus if you pay off the balance each month in full. If you don't, any savings will be more than wiped out by interest charges.

TOP TIP

Be sure you know your rates if you use gasoline credit cards . . . . You might be able to save a penny or two per gallon with such a program, but it will only be a plus if you pay the balance off each month in full.

DON'T TOP OFF THE TANK

Modern cars have an antipollution evaporative emission system that includes a canister containing charcoal. This absorbs gasoline fumes from the full tank. When the fuel runs low, the system sucks the fumes out of the canister and injects them into the fuel mix. If the tank is overfilled, liquid gasoline can pour into the canister and destroy the charcoal, which can lead to an expensive repair of the system.

find a **PARKING SPACE**
without losing your patience

You are having a stressful day, and you would like to just pop into the big-box store for a pre-roasted chicken and a gallon of ice cream. Your feet are tired, so you search for a place close to the door. You circle, and circle, and your low-gas light comes on. You watch a woman walk in with a cart and come back out, and you're still circling.

Lower Your Standards

The problem, paradoxically, is that you are trying to find the best spot. It turns out that  **people who actively look for the best space rather than just sliding into the first spot they see spend much more time getting to the store.** Not only do they burn up time behind the wheel with their searching, when they finally come to rest they end up on average no closer to the door than the people who did not go on the hunt for the best spot. There is a gender difference in this behavior, incidentally: women are more likely to drive around looking for a good spot than men are.

Don't Go for the Obvious

If your goal is to take fewer steps from your car to the entrance, avoid the row directly across from the door. If you were to take a look at a big parking lot from space—and you can try this now with Google Earth—you are likely to see that the rows across from the door have the most cars followed by the rows just to the side. The cars create something like a Christmas tree with a long row straight across from the door and each row to the side becoming shorter and shorter. The people who manage to get **spots in the row right across from the door are often farther away from the door than many of the open spots off to the side.**

👍 TOP TIP

If your goal is to take fewer steps from your car to the entrance, avoid the row directly across from the door.

CITY PARKING IS A DIFFERENT BEAST

"This is all well and good," you may say, "But I work in a big city. Where can I find a place to park?" Erik Feder, the author of *The Feder Guide to Where to Park Your Car in Manhattan* says that street parking can be had in even the busiest city. Learn all of the streets near your home or place of work where parking is never allowed. There is no point turning onto those streets. They will just waste your time. Make a list of the places where you might be able to park and go straight for them.

Roll down your windows so you can hear sounds that might indicate someone is leaving, for example the jingling of keys or the beep of an alarm being deactivated. Look for people with shopping bags who might be about to return to their cars. Believe that you will be lucky, and you may be able to stop your car and get out before the sun goes down.

PARALLEL PARKING
without rear-ending anybody

 TOP SCREWUPS

- Overestimating the size of the spot
- Starting at the wrong spot
- Not cutting the wheel when you should
- Going in at the wrong angle

You want to go shopping on Main Street. There is a spot right in front of your favorite boutique, but if you want it you will have to parallel park. You signal and watch the cars driving up behind you. Your heart starts to race. Parallel parking provides a wide array of possible screwups. Will you block traffic for miles? Will you sideswipe a car? Will you end up on the curb or wedged in at an angle you can't escape? Will you be a laughingstock to your passengers?

Turn-by-Turn Directions

1. First, be sure your car will fit in the spot. **The ideal parking space should be about five feet (one and a half meters) longer than your car and no less than two feet (sixty centimeters) longer.**

2. Now signal, and then **stop your car parallel to the one parked in front of the spot you wish to occupy and about two feet (sixty centimeters) away.**

3. Check your mirrors. If there are other cars coming, let them pass before you start to park.

4. Put the car in reverse.

5. **Before you start to move, turn the wheel as far as it will go toward the curb.**

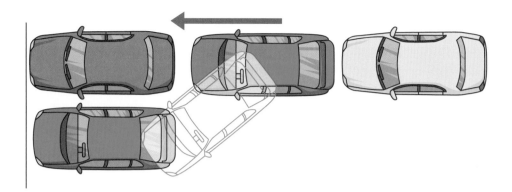

6 Once the rear edge of the passenger door is level with the bumper of the other car, straighten the wheel. 👍 **You should be at about 45° to the curb and about three feet (one meter) away.** The passenger door should be about six inches (fifteen centimeters) from the car in front. If the distances are off, pull out and try again.

7 👍 **When your front bumper is clear of the rear bumper of the front car, turn the wheel as far as possible away from the curb** and keep reversing slowly until your car is in the space. Don't go too far, or you'll hit the car behind you!

8 Straighten the wheel and move your car forward until you are centered in the space. You are aiming for a position six to eight inches (fifteen to twenty centimeters) from the curb. Be sure that you have left enough room for the cars in front and back of you to pull out.

UNDER PRESSURE

Like many things in driving, parallel parking can only be perfected with practice. If all of this is a bit much for you to master with a stream of traffic coming your way, you may want to rehearse until you get comfortable. Use an open space—such as a parking lot—and set up traffic cones or something similar to represent the parked cars.

MERGING
makes the world go 'round

You are driving along an expressway at normal highway speeds when suddenly you see brake lights. Everyone ahead of you is nearly stopped. A sign barely visible on the horizon tells you that there is a construction zone ahead. Three lanes will merge down to one. Meanwhile the cars inch along, changing from one lane to the other trying to get the advantage. You are probably annoyed with someone, either the slowpokes who gum everything up by merging before they have to or the selfish jerks who try to nose in at the last minute. You are not alone in your stress. A survey by the Texas Transportation Institute found that "merging difficulties" are the single greatest cause of highway stress.

Polite or Practical?

There are two main schools of thought when it comes to merging. One holds that it is polite and most efficient if drivers get into the lane that will remain open as soon as they see signs indicating that there will be a lane closure. The other argues that traffic will move more swiftly if drivers use all of the available lanes until they can't.

Who is right? According to Tom Vanderbilt, author of *Traffic: Why We Drive the Way We Do*, the late mergers win. Of course, this does come with a small caveat. Late merging works best if everyone merges late. This way all drivers take advantage of all the available lanes and use the full capacity of the road until they come together in an orderly "zipper merge," one car after the other.

The Later, the Better

In the 1990s, Pennsylvania engineers came up with a new strategy, the late merge. They designed signs that instructed drivers to USE BOTH LANES TO MERGE POINT. Finally when it came time for one lane to drop, there was a sign reading 🔄 **MERGE HERE, TAKE YOUR TURN.** The late merge concept showed a fifteen-percent improvement in traffic flow. There was less lane jumping, and fewer stops as people punished late mergers by refusing to let them into the open lane. Incidentally, highway construction zones are statistically more dangerous for you than for the workers. Of those killed in construction zone accidents, eighty-five percent were drivers or passengers.

Merge politely.

 TOP TIP

Late merging allows drivers take advantage of all of the available lanes and use the full capacity of the road until they come together in an orderly "zipper merge," one car after the other.

THE SCIENCE OF THE SNARL

What happens in a traditional merge is this. Traffic is moving along normally until drivers come to a sign warning of a lane drop. They are instructed to merge into the lane that will remain open. As the traffic slows and the line of cars backs up often beyond the sign announcing the lane closure, some drivers are unaware of it and continue in their lanes. The ones who have been waiting patiently sometimes view the passers as "cheaters" and try to prevent them from joining the slow lane. At the same time, some drivers in the slow open lane will try to merge into the freer lane that is going to close. As cars inch in and out of lanes, they are prone to rear-end collisions and near misses, which cause cars to hit their brakes.

DON'T GET HIT by a truck

TOP SCREWUPS

- Assuming you're visible
- Failing to yield
- Getting too close when it's too steep
- Getting caught in their draft

Driving as though a truck were just another car can mean sharing some time with a police officer filling out an accident report or worse. The biggest mistake car drivers make when they share the road with trucks is assuming that driving a truck is just like driving a bigger car. It's not.

Don't Assume—
It Makes a Crash Out of You and Me

Even though trucks are equipped with large mirrors, they can only do so much. Do not drive beside a big rig if you can avoid it. **If you want to know if the driver can see you, try to see his face in the mirror. If you can't, then he can't see you either.** Along with the sides, all trucks have a blind spot directly behind the trailer. Some drivers try to slip in behind a truck to save gas by riding in the truck's wake. Truckers hate that. Be considerate and don't ride where you can't be seen.

Don't Be Squashed Like a Bug Because You Refused to Yield

It seems as though this should go without saying, but accident stats show that lots of people don't know this. **If a trucker signals to change lanes and you are in the way, move out of the way!** Trucks cannot make fast corrections, so seasoned truckers are always looking for an escape route in case they need to get off the road quickly, for example if the truck's air pressure fails and the brakes suddenly lock up. Also keep in mind that a trucker in the left lane is always looking for a path to get back to the right. You can dodge more easily. Do so.

Don't Cause a Fire on the Mountain

⏺ **Use extra caution on hills. On a steep grade, the momentum on a heavy loaded truck can be great.** You may have noticed the "runaway truck ramps" when driving in a mountainous area. These exist because from time to time a truck going down a steep grade loses its breaks or otherwise loses control and needs the steep gravel ramp to stop it. You do not want to be in front of a truck at such a time or pulled over in this emergency-out lane.

Truck Storms

Don't get caught up in a truck-made weather pattern.

⏺ **Remember that trucks create wind gusts. Be sure to keep both hands on the wheel if a truck is passing you. If it is raining, be ready for a big splash.** Trucks can throw up a wall of water that temporarily reduces your visibility to zero. Give trucks extra space when it is wet.

WHAT'S GOOD FOR THE TRUCKER ISN'T GOOD FOR THE DRIVER

In bad weather especially, remember the golden rule: You Are Not in a Truck. Just as there are things you can do in your little car that truckers cannot—swerve in and out of traffic, parallel park—there are things a truck can do that you cannot. Because of their weight, trucks can drive on ice and snow long after your Toyota Camry has lost traction. Don't let the presence of trucks on a road fool you into thinking it is safe for you to drive.

don't **DRIVE BLIND** at night

Do you remember taking driver's ed? Your instructor gave you some information on how to avoid being temporarily blinded by the headlights of the oncoming cars. You laughed at the very idea. *Cars' headlights aren't that blinding,* you thought. Now if you're over thirty, you may be wishing you had paid a bit more attention.

Back It Up

As we age, our eyes' ability to see in limited light declines. It starts happening at around age thirty, but you don't notice it until a few years later when you're driving at night and you suddenly find it hard to see. **Don't drive like your eyesight is exactly as it was when you were twenty. You will need more following distance at night between cars.** In daylight, *three seconds* is considered a safe following distance, but at night you should increase it to five or more if you are tired.

Blinded by the Light

If an oncoming car's headlights are blinding, gaze down and to the right and keep your lane using the edge of the road or the line markings until the headlights have passed and you can look up again. Keep driving at the same speed. The drivers behind you may have also been temporarily blinded, and they might not see that you've stepped on your brakes. After you look back to the road, remember that it takes about six seconds for your eyes to readjust.

Mood Lighting

Dim your interior gauge lights slightly. The glow from a bright dashboard can fight with your eyes' ability to see outside at night. If you have a choice between straining to see the gauges and straining to see the road, choose the gauges. If you wear glasses, choose the kind with an antireflective coating. It cuts down on lens glare.

Don't Let Dirt Get in the Way

Don't drive at night with a dirty windshield. **The grime that is a small annoyance during the day can be deadly at night because it can cause a huge glare. Be sure you clean the inside as well as the outside of the windshield.** (Refer to pages 196–197 for tips on how to do this.)

TOP TIP

If an oncoming car's headlights are blinding, gaze down and to the right and keep your lane using the edge of the road or the line markings until the headlights have passed and you can look up again.

HELPING OTHERS HELP YOU

Many drivers make the mistake of not turning on headlights until it is quite dark. Even though they do not help you to see at dusk, they help other drivers to see you. To make sure your own headlights stay properly adjusted, take a moment after your headlights have been aligned to mark where the brightest part of each beam hits the back wall of the garage when the car is standing at a line taped to the floor. Then when you park in that spot, you can check and see if your lights are pointed in the same spot.

don't drive with a dirty
WINDSHIELD

TOP SCREWUPS

- Letting frost form
- Battling stubborn ice in the cold
- Trying to see around the bugs

As a general rule, it is helpful to be able to see the road when you are driving. This is hard to do when your windshield is covered in salt, snow, and/or bugs.

Frost Prevention

If you live in a northern climate, your biggest windshield issue will be ice and snow. **You can reduce the amount of time you spend scraping and sweeping by wiping your windows in advance of a snowstorm with a sponge dipped in salt water, then letting them dry.** The salt will discourage ice formation. The next time you go out to your car, the windows should not be coated in ice.

Deice with Ease

If the storm dropped a bit more ice than a little salt could fend off, you will need to do some scraping. Don't make life difficult on yourself by scraping the car while it is cold. **Start up the car, and let it warm up with the defroster running. Now go back in the house and whip up some homemade deicer. A number of combinations will work for this. Try a mixture of one cup of water, one cup of rubbing alcohol, and one cup of vinegar, or use fifty percent water and fifty percent ethyl alcohol, or fifty**

percent water and fifty percent vinegar. Another option is to come out with the salt. Pour the salt or one of these solutions over the windshield, wait a minute or two for it to work, and you may barely need to scrape at all.

Troubled by Bugs?

All you need to get them off is a couple of old mesh onion bags. The mesh gives you enough of an edge to scrape the gunk off, but it won't damage the glass. Apply a mixture of dishwashing liquid and warm water to the windshield to soften everything up, scrub with the bags, and then wipe dry with clean rags. When you are washing your windshield, don't forget to clean the wiper blades themselves, or they will just wipe dirt all over your clean windshield.

CAREFUL WITH THE SOLUTION

If you use a homemade or commercial deicer, be careful to apply it only to the ice on the windows. This stuff is all corrosive, and if you get it on your car's paint, it can eat away at your sweet cherry finish. Also make sure you have plenty of windshield washer fluid in the reservoir and carry an extra gallon with you. Road salt is great for keeping roads ice free, but it coats everything.

JUMP-START A CAR
without blowing it up

 **TOP SCREWUPS**

- Not knowing the warning signs
- Linking positive to negative poles

Car batteries contain an electrolyte solution that includes sulfuric acid. Under certain conditions—for example, extreme heat or cold—hydrogen liberated by electrolysis of the water in the battery can be detonated when given a jump start, and the battery can explode. This is what is technically called "a bad outcome."

One Urban Legend That's True

Yes, the horror stories about jumper-cable explosions are true. Most of the injuries caused by jump-start mishaps are eye injuries incurred when a battery blows up in someone's face. How often does it happen? Hard to say. When Cecil Adams, author of the "Straight Dope" newspaper column, researched this question, all he could say for sure was, "Some nontrivial number of people get injured by exploding car batteries each year."

Don't Be Scared

Just follow these instructions and you should be fine. The main thing you do not want to screw up is this: **When you look at the two car batteries you are going to be linking up and the casing is damaged on one of them, if either battery is visibly leaking, or if it looks as though there is any chance the battery's solution could be frozen, do not perform the jump.** Call a pro. However, it's normal for the batteries to have a little corrosion. It looks like

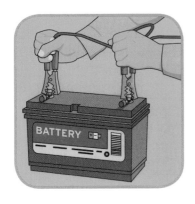

blue or green snow surrounding the battery terminals. Don't touch it with your bare hands. You won't blow anything up, but the chemicals will burn your skin.

What You Should Do

Make sure that the voltage on both batteries matches. Unless you are getting a jump start from an old collector's car, this will probably not be an issue. Turn off the car giving the jump, including headlights, radios, and any electrical equipment in the car. **Attach one end of the red jumper cable to the dead battery's positive terminal. Then attach the other end of the cable to the positive terminal on the starting car's battery. Now attach one end of the black cable to the negative terminal of the battery of the starting car. The other end of the black cable should go onto a metal bolt on the engine block of the car with the dead battery, not on the battery itself.**

Start Your Engines!

Start the car that will be giving the jump. After about five minutes, try starting the car with the dead battery. If it doesn't start right up, turn it off and wait another five minutes before you try again.

WHAT NOT TO DO

When you're jump-starting a battery, you may produce small sparks, so you do not want to do this task right next to a gas pump or anything that gives of fumes that could be ignited. Finally, do not lean over the engine and gaze at the battery during this process. If anything does go awry, you will want your face to be as far from it as possible.

don't get ripped off by
SLEAZY MECHANICS

Unless you are willing to crawl under the car and check things out yourself, you need a good mechanic; one you can trust to tell you what needs to be repaired without charging you for things that do not need to be done.

Just Like a Doctor's Office

Look for posted certifications that show that the shop's mechanics have completed training from accredited schools or programs. One set of letters to look for is ASE, which stands for National Institute for Automotive Service Excellence. Although there are good mechanics who do not have ASE certification and certification does not guarantee a mechanic will be good, at least you know that the mechanic has invested a certain amount of time and money into training, which is at least a sign of professionalism. There are ASE certificates for various automotive systems. Look for someone who has certification in the area for the specific repair you are seeking.

Utilize the Interwebs

A good resource for finding quality mechanics is the Web site of the Automotive Service Association (http://www.asashop.org/). The organization has a code of ethics that members are expected to follow and offers benefits such as technical training. It performs a pre-employment check of prospective employees and does screening of shops before letting them become ASA members. The organization checks for outstanding or unresolved complaints with the Better Business Bureau and the Governor's Office of Consumer Affairs. Its web page has a searchable database of ASA shops.

⊙ **Another good resource is the website for the NPR car repair radio show** *Car Talk* **(http://www.cartalk.com/content/mechanics-files).** The program has 4.4 million listeners on 600 stations nationwide. It maintains a database of mechanics recommended by its listeners. You can type in your zip code and the make of your car, and find local mechanics along with recommendations and comments from real customers.

Back Whence the Car Came—Maybe

Ideally, you are looking for a mechanic experienced in servicing your make and model of car. Some problems, such as computer systems that trigger warning lights, are best dealt with at a dealership service department. Overall, though, you will save a lot of money by going to an independent mechanic you trust.

It'll Take How Long!?

If a time estimate to complete a repair seems high to you, look in *Mechanical Labor Estimating Guide* by Mitchell or *Labor Guide* by Chilton. These directories list various repairs and the length of time they usually take to complete. Your mechanic will probably have a copy of one of these guides on the premises. If the amount of time the mechanic is estimating is substantially longer than the time in the guidebook, he is either trying to pad his billing, or he is not very efficient. In either case, it's time to find another garage.

WHEN ALL ELSE FAILS

If you do not have any friends who can recommend a good mechanic, one way to get an idea of the type of service you might get is to look at a garage's parking lot. If you spot a lot with a lot of government vehicles such as utility trucks, you might want to steer clear. Service contracts for government agencies always go to the lowest bidder. The shop may have bid lower than it should have, which means it might be trying to make up the difference with more costly repairs to other vehicles.

don't let your
BIKE GET STOLEN

TOP SCREWUPS

- Not locking it up (duh)
- Locking it to something that can itself be stolen
- Using a weak lock

There a many great reasons to leave your car in the garage and use a bicycle for your daily commute. It is better for your health; you're doing your part to cut down on emissions; and you're saving on gasoline and auto maintenance. It is even easier to find a parking place. The only problem is, it is much easier for a thief to walk away with your bike than your SUV.

Lock It Up No Matter Where You Are

The first piece of advice will seem obvious, but it is not. **Lock your bike.** Many bikes are stolen each year simply because people fail to lock them. This isn't quite as negligent as it at first seems. Most of the unlocked bikes are stolen out of people's yards or off their porches.

So don't assume that a criminal will not venture into your yard. Use extra caution in places with lots of bikes. Bike thieves like to do their shopping where they're most likely to find lots of poorly locked cycles from which to choose. College campuses are popular targets.

Don't Lock Your Bike to Something Easily Stolen

The second big mistake that bicycle owners make is locking their bikes to something that is not solid and secure. If you lock your bike to a wobbly pole, someone can come along and lift the pole out of the ground and slide your lock right off. **Your bike not only needs to be locked, it also needs to be locked to something that can't be taken away.** Don't lock your bicycle to parking meters or anything that is posted as illegal, or your bike may be "stolen" by the cops!

Tougher Than Steal

That chain bike lock you used when you were a kid is probably not enough to thwart a modern thief. **The best choice is a U-lock for the back tire and frame combined with a cable lock for the front tire.** Put the U of the lock through the back tire and frame around the pole you're locking it to. Run the cable lock through the front tire onto the U-Lock, and then lock the U-Lock.

ACCESSORIES TO THE CRIME

Don't forget the items that are attached to the bike. If you leave your water bottle and backpack on the bike, they might not be there when you come back. Be sure to take everything with you that you want to keep.

ride a **BUS OR SUBWAY**
without falling over

You enter a crowded subway car and all of the seats are taken. As the car starts moving, you lurch forward, take three quick steps and fall in the lap of a guy with three more tattoos on his face than are strictly necessary. This is not a good way to start your workday.

Subway or *Swan Lake*?

To keep yourself upright on public transportation, you need to learn to stand like a ballet dancer. Dancers train for years to achieve perfect balance. The skills they use can be easily applied to any situation where balance is needed.

- **Stand with your head held high and your abdomen and behind tucked in.** Not only will you look taller and slimmer, but you will also keep your axis straight, which will aid in keeping your balance.

- The key to not falling is the turn out. **With your feet about twelve inches (about thirty centimeters) apart, point your toes outward.** You do not have to turn out as much as a ballerina— a comfortable 45° angle will do. Dancers, and many athletes as well, use this stance because it provides stability and allows a person to quickly change direction and adjust balance.

- 🖐 **Let your knees bend slightly.** Do not lock them into place. You want to be flexible and absorb the motion. Imagine yourself as a surfer or a skateboarder.

Don't forget that even though you have mastered subway balance, the other passengers may not have. Pay attention because someone else might lose her balance and plow into you.

WHEN ALL ELSE
FAILS

If you don't have a handrail or pole available, look up. If you're of average height or taller, you should be able to brace yourself by putting your hand up and pushing against the ceiling of the train or bus.

don't give terrible DIRECTIONS

Have you ever been lost and stopped to ask directions at a gas station only to get an answer like this: "The expressway? Yeah, I think I know where that is. First you go up this road here, three or four lights. I think it's four. I don't remember the street name, but you turn right where the old Morris farm used to be. You can't miss it." In fact, you can miss it. With those directions you almost certainly will. Help your fellow travelers. Don't give directions this way.

Use Landmarks as Landmarks

When giving directions, it helps to bear in mind that the person who is asking is probably not familiar with the area. Landmarks are useful, but there is a right way and a wrong way to use them. The wrong way is to begin your directions like this: "Do you know where the high school is?" Your out-of-town guest most likely does not, and this will only scare them. **This is the right way to use a landmark: "Pull out of the parking lot here and turn right. Drive three blocks and you will come to Main Street. You'll recognize it because you'll see a big high school on the right."**

Keep It Simple, Stupid

Try to limit your information to that which will truly help the driver. Landmarks are useful because they stand out. If you list every thing a driver is likely to pass along the route, nothing will stick. What is more, the person asking for directions will become overwhelmed. 👍 **Limit your landmarks to things that help tell a driver where to turn, when to start looking for an intersection, or where to stop.**

Consider Multiple Entrances

If someone is asking for directions on the phone and they are at a gas station or a fast-food restaurant, remember that these often have entrances on more than one street. Be sure you know which way the caller is oriented before saying something like "pull out of the parking lot and turn right." You might be visualizing different streets. Instead say, "Pull out on Rochester Road and turn right."

Good Directions

They should sound something like this: "Turn right out of the parking lot. You'll be heading north on James Street. Drive three blocks. The cross streets are numbered, so you will pass Third and Fourth Streets. When you get to Fifth Street, you'll see a big church with a steeple on your right. Turn right on Fifth Street, and you will come to the doctor's office about three blocks down on the left across from the Drug Mart."

IT TAKES ALL KINDS

Different people process information differently. Some people like a route perspective, which focuses on turns and landmarks. Some are more comfortable with a spatial perspective, with directions like east and west as though they were looking at a map. You can help your traveler by mixing different modes to make one set of instructions that will make sense to different thinkers.

don't **BACK UP A TRAILER**
in the wrong direction

The problem with renting a trailer is that eventually you're going to have to back it up. You turn the wheel to the left, and the trailer jackknifes to the right. You overcorrect, and it wobbles to the left. Everything you do sends it veering off in exactly the wrong direction.

Mirrors Will Solve Your Mirror-Image Problem

You will have to outsmart your natural instincts and overcome your mirror-image steering confusion. To perform this maneuver, you will need to use your side-view mirrors. Going forward, align your vehicle and trailer so they're as straight as possible. Now, **put your hand at the bottom of the steering wheel at the six o'clock position. From this position, you can simply rotate the wheel the way you want the trailer to go. If you want it to go left, bring the hand gripping the steering wheel up to the left. If you want it to go right, swing your hand up to the right.** The trailer is not going to move perfectly straight, so you will need to go slowly and make constant small adjustments. That's it. You've successfully backed up your trailer!

THE PROBLEM IS ONE OF PERCEPTION

The trailer hitch is not operating in the same manner as a car in reverse. All of your training and your instincts are working against you. In your car when you're backing up, you turn the steering wheel and you back up in the direction you want to go. The trailer turns in the opposite direction of the car, a fact that is surprisingly hard to get used to, sort of like fixing the back of your hair in a double mirror.

YOUR JOB or YOUR COMPUTER

don't write a RÉSUMÉ
that gets overlooked

If you've been searching for a job for months without landing any interviews, the problem may not be your experience. It could be your résumé.

What Would *You* Look For?

The biggest mistake applicants make is to become so focused on the job they want that they forget to consider the perspective of the person doing the hiring. Take a look at that piece of paper. 👍 **Pretend you're a busy recruiter and you've never met the individual in question. The résumé is one of fifty on your desk. You want to get someone hired so you can check that off your to-do list.** What type of résumé will go in your interview pile? Most likely it is going to be a résumé that:

- Is not too wordy.

- Allows you to see the person's experience and accomplishments at first glance.

- 👍 **Has skills that apply directly to the job popping off the page.**

You and What You Do

Make it easy for the tired recruiter to imagine you in the job. Your résumé should have a title at the top. This does not have to be your current job title. Think about what you would answer when someone asked you what you do for a living. "I am a marketing manager." This is your title. Follow it with a brief profile that quickly sums up who you are, and most importantly, what you have to offer.

A Résumé Is Not a One-Size-Fits-All Proposition

A huge thing that job searchers get wrong is putting all of their attention into creating one résumé and then refusing to change it. **You need to customize it for each company to which you apply.** Read up on the company's mission and values; learn as much as you can about the position and what function you would serve in the company; and then tweak your résumé to show exactly how your particular skills and experience will fit in.

Always Follow Directions

If you have a beautiful functional résumé and Company X asks you to submit a chronological résumé following its online template, then you will have to use it even if you think yours highlights your talents better. Do not assume that they will make an exception and accept your e-mailed functional résumé because you are so wonderful. What you are really doing is automatically disqualifying yourself from the job. They want to know that you can follow basic instructions. It's time consuming and annoying to have to keep reworking your résumé, but they're the ones with the job. You need to show that you can take on the tasks they give you, not the other way around.

ARE THEY RIGHT FOR YOU?

If the previous employee was fired, you may be able to get an idea of what went wrong by looking at previous postings by the company for the same position. Try looking at past company newsletters, searching through old issues of professional journals or seeing if an archive search of old versions of the company's web page (use archive.org) will bring up an old version of the job listing. If any new qualifications have been added ("must be able to get along with others"), this could be a hint as to what went wrong. Look at this info as the company's résumé to you. Do you want to hire it as your company?

Don't Bore Them

Let's face it, saying you're "effective," "qualified," or "competent" is setting the bar pretty low. Instead of saying you're a "self-motivated, hard-working team player with an attention to detail," get specific. 🖐 **Let your accomplishments speak for themselves. Don't think you have any accomplishments? Think again. It's all in how you word it.** Instead of saying "Did effective cold calling for an advertising agency," say "I initiated 200 calls a day, which led directly to the acquisition of thirty new accounts, including three of the agency's largest clients."

Don't Enter with Entry-Level

If you really are just starting out, avoid using the expression "entry-level" in your objective statement. This screams, "I don't have any experience, but you can get me cheap!" This may in fact be true, but why make this the first thing you say about yourself? Anyway, you probably have more experience than you think. You don't have to only focus on paid work in the career field you're trying to enter. Did you lead a team as part of a volunteer project? Were you in ROTC? Think about everything you learned and the skills you used. There is a good chance you can find some experience that can be applied to the job.

Check for Typoos

Before you hit send and e-mail your résumé to your potential new employer, have a friend look it over. You might have looked at it six times and still not noticed that you listed your current job as "Copy Editer." A fresh set of eyes can catch embarrassing misspellings and minor things you overlooked.

don't BLOW YOUR CHANCES before you even get there

Your awesome résumé landed you an interview for your dream job but fears of coffee breath, convoluted HR questions, and your mind going blank plague you. You can't sleep the night before. You're groggy. As you get dressed, you find a rip in your interview outfit. You can't find your keys. Panic sets in. Don't let this happen to you!

Remember the Scout Motto

Take a lesson from the Boy Scouts and always be prepared. 👍 **Read up on the company on the web and through industry magazines. Have an idea of the company's mission and objectives so that you can express how your particular talents will be an asset.** Quiz yourself on some of the most commonly asked interview questions (you can find these online pretty easily). Have printouts of your résumé, make sure you know how to get to the office, try on your outfit the night before, and bring some mints to suck on before you go in. Deep breath!

Dress for the Job You Want

Don't wear your favorite old Bon Jovi T-shirt, but don't show up in a tuxedo either. 👍 **Your mode of dress should befit the job for which you are applying, plus a little extra.** If you're going into an office, you want to go for a tasteful suit (see pages 126–128) instead of business casual.

don't blow the INTERVIEW

👎 TOP SCREWUPS

- Giving a shuffling, awkward first impression
- Being too modest
- Not rehearsing answers to what they'll definitely ask
- Nodding and mumbling dumbly when your mind blanks

OK, you got there on time. You look great, your breath is fresh, your hair is managed. The person who is going to interview is walking toward you. Take a deep breath, smile, and . . .

Rock That First Impression

First off, don't have a seat first. 👍 **Remain standing until you're greeted by the interviewer in order to make the best first impression.** (Also see *First Impression* on pages 296–297.) You do not want her first image to be of you getting your things in order and adjusting your clothing. If you have a briefcase or portfolio with you, hold it in your left hand. This leaves your right hand free to shake without any awkward shuffling or pauses. So far, so smooth.

Don't take out your nerves or frustrations on the assistant. Remember, your interviewer works closely with this person. You don't want him to say, "That guy was kind of rude," when you're out of earshot. Thanking the assistant can go a long way.

Just Being Modest Can Just Cost You the Job

An interview is not the time to be humble. 👍 **You want to be confident and engaging. Sit straight in the middle of your chair with one arm on the armrest and the other on the table.** You'll look and feel more confident. Speak freely about your accomplishments and skills. Recent psychological research reveals that narcissists actually make a better impression in job interviews because they naturally promote themselves. What do narcissists do that non-narcissists do not? They tend to speak a lot, speak quickly, and smile at people.

Don't Blank on the Big Opening Question

Long before you are asked the first question, you should have rehearsed your pitch. Write out a sixty-second "commercial" about your reasons for pursuing the position and why you'd be a good fit. Make it specific to the job. Don't memorize it word for word, but read it enough so that you have internalized all the main points. This will be your answer when the interviewer opens with "Tell me about yourself." Do not go on and on. You want the interviewer to discover new and wonderful things about you as the interview progresses. Do not forget to thank your interviewer. Finish your meeting with a firm handshake and say something like, "I really appreciate you taking the time to talk to me about this position."

If Your Mind Does Snap Shut Like a Bear Trap

But if you do draw a blank, ask the interviewer to rephrase it. **It is much better to ask for clarification than to ramble through an incoherent half answer.** If you're tempted to give a yes-man answer, don't. Interviewers are smart enough to know when you're just telling them what they want to hear.

THE ART OF THE THANK-YOU NOTE

That night or the next day, write a thank-you note. It can either be written by hand and sent through the mail or typed and e-mailed. E-mail is faster, but your message will stand out more if you send it the old-fashioned way. By the way, your "thank-you" message will not be nearly as effective if your prospective employer's name is spelled wrong. Be sure to take a business card on the way out.

don't **ZONE OUT**
in business meetings

If you read business publications, you will find a lot of advice on avoiding dull meetings. Almost all of it is written from the perspective of the manager, but there are a lot more "managed" than managers out there. What if you have no power over how often you're called to meetings and how they're run? What if you just have to show up? How can you keep your focus?

You Can't Pay Attention to All the People All the Time

First, you should know that keeping your focus all of the time is an unrealistic goal. Jonathan Schooler of the University of California at Santa Barbara is one of the leading experts on mind wandering. (He is not an absentminded professor; he is a professor of absentmindedness.) In one experiment he found that subjects who were specifically asked to focus their attention still had their minds wander off at least five times during a forty-five-minute session. Schooler identified two different kinds of mind wandering: There is the kind of ambling when you are aware that you're thinking about something else and a kind when you are not even aware that you're not aware. Schooler gave this latter form the technical name of "zoning out."

Mind Games

Your mind wanders because part of your brain has made the calculation that your attention is not needed and your mental energy would be better spent in focusing on the big picture. In order to keep focus, therefore, you will need to convince yourself that what is happening in the room is useful and necessary. This may involve some trickery.

This Meeting Is Going to Rock, or at Least Tell Yourself That

Mood affects your ability to focus. If you know you're going to have a big (and potentially dull) meeting the following day, be sure to get enough sleep and try to go into the room in a good mood. 👍 **Put yourself in a "peak state" by sitting or standing up straight, throwing your shoulders back, and lifting your head.** This will get oxygen pumping through your body more easily.

Make It Apply to You

As the meeting progresses, look for something of value even if it is indirect. 👍 **If the conversation involves a completely unrelated department or work process and you are baffled as to why you're there, pretend you're a film critic and the meeting is a movie. Make mental notes about all of the things the facilitator is doing right and wrong.** This should at least keep your focus within the room.

WHEN ALL ELSE FAILS

It's bound to happen. You zoned out around hour two, and suddenly everyone is looking at you. Clearly you've been caught zoning out. There's no denying it. The best thing you can do depends on the room. If you're in a room of coworkers who you get along with and are generally reasonable, you can crack a joke. "I'm sorry, my brain apparently already went to lunch." If it's a stuffy meeting and clearly no one is going to be amused if you crack wise, you can try to look like you were at least zoning out professionally by saying something like, "I'm sorry, I was still thinking about the logistics of implementing that great idea Johnson presented earlier."

don't waste INK AND PAPER

TOP SCREWUPS

- Using more because you recycle
- Forgetting the second side
- Ignoring paper- and ink-friendly settings
- Printing more than you need from the internet

Whatever happened to the paperless office that all the futurists predicted we'd have by now? It hasn't materialized, and instead we have the ability to make gorgeous full-color presentations from our desks, thus increasing the amount of paper we use and throw away. You don't have to be part of the problem.

Recycling Isn't a Defense

Don't use your recycle bin as an excuse to print every little e-mail and memo. Researchers Jesse R. Catlin and Yitong Wang of the University of California–Irvine discovered that rather than serving as a reminder to reduce consumption, consumers seem to use recycle bins as a justification to use more resources. People feel less wasteful and guilty when they put the paper in a blue bin, and with a free conscience, they use more. **Remember that recycling isn't a one-to-one ratio. It takes a lot of energy to remake paper, and so each sheet of paper you recycle doesn't magically turn into a clean sheet. Conserving paper is one step better than recycling.**

There Are Two Sides to Every Paper

Don't discard paper that has a blank side. Instead, put one-sided paper in a box by your desk. Keep the printed sides all facing in one direction. When you clean out your old files, put the blanks in the box. You can throw in flat paper from your junk mail. It will not be appropriate for your important correspondence or presentations, but you can reach for this paper for your everyday, utilitarian print jobs.

Generics Can Cost You

With a quick search online, you can usually find all manner of generic and refurbished printer ink cartridges that are much cheaper than manufacturer brands. Although it seems thrifty to buy them, they can be unreliable. When *PC World* tested generic inks, they found that many could save consumers money and provided similar quality, but others clogged and leaked. Most internet retailers do not identify the brands of the refurbished or generic cartridges, so it is hard to know what you are going to get when you shop. **You're probably better off spending $25 on a fresh new cartridge from the manufacturer than throwing $10 away on a cartridge that doesn't print anything and makes a mess in your printer.** If you have a steady hand you might try an ink refill kit. They work and offer great savings—if you're not afraid of the messy process.

What You Print Counts for a Lot

Print in draft mode. **Most printers allow you to select from various levels of print quality. Draft mode is a little less pretty, but it uses less ink and also prints faster. Choose an ink-friendly font.** A font with a thinner print line, such as Century Gothic, can use thirty percent less ink than Arial. There is also

BE CAREFUL WHAT YOU REUSE

For security, do not put anything in your reuse box that you would not want just anyone to read. You do not want to print out directions for your coworker only to have her realize that it is printed on the back of a steamy sex scene from your novel-in-progress or a spreadsheet with the salaries of everyone in the office. To avoid paper jams, don't reuse pages that have folded edges or staples in the corners.

a special font called Ecofont that you can purchase. Each letter is full of little holes, like Swiss cheese. It comes with a software package that allows the user to print any font in a hole-filled eco-mode.

Don't print in color unless you really need color. Color is great for eye-catching presentations, business cards, flyers, and photo printing. Yet most of the time, when you print out a document for your information, color is just a waste of ink. Since 1996, the average price per printed page has risen by twelve and a half percent. Much of this is attributable to an increase in color printing.

You Don't Need to Print the Ads

Have you ever tried to print an article from the internet and been startled when it came out of the printer with ten pages of comments and brilliant color promotions and ads? A free web service printwhatyoulike.com lets you isolate the elements you need and print only those. It can also automatically print without images. Or you can select the text you want and copy and paste it into a word processor program. If you print a lot of online articles, these methods can save you a lot of ink and paper.

don't blow your chance to
GET A RAISE

The idea of asking for a raise makes most people nervous. You are opening yourself up to the possibility of rejection, plus there is money involved. A lot of people are so intimidated by the idea that they fail to ask all together and make less money than their bolder coworkers. Don't be one of those people whose low salary allows for someone else's inflated pay.

TOP SCREWUPS

- Asking at the wrong time
- Making it about your needs
- Referencing other people's pay

When *Not* to Ask for a Raise

Let's begin by talking about how not to bring up this touchy subject. Don't blurt out, "I want a raise," as your boss is walking into the elevator or putting a bite of food in her mouth. Make an appointment for a sit-down meeting. Think about when you have deadlines that might make your boss stressed. **A good rule of thumb is not to ask for anything from a busy person first thing on a Monday morning. You also want to avoid last thing on Friday when she is trying to clear her desk.**

Proper Raise Position

Make sure your boss is sitting down. Psychological studies have shown that you enhance your chances of persuading another person if she is sitting down or reclining, not standing. It doesn't matter whether you are sitting or standing.

It's All About Your Job

 When you make your pitch, remember to focus on what you do for the company, not what you need from the company. You get a raise based on the good job you're doing. Don't go in and talk about how your mortgage payment is always late and your kids need braces. That is not your boss's problem.

It's Not About Someone Else's Job

Don't talk about other people's performances and how much they make. You may have been inspired to ask for a raise when you glanced at some papers you weren't supposed to see and realized that Lazy Frank, who is always taking off early, is making twice what you are, but don't bring it up. **The issue is not that Lazy Frank is paid more than he is worth but that you are worth more than you are being paid.**

Make a Great Case

The way to do this is to write a performance review for yourself. Lay out how your position has grown since you started working. List your major accomplishments and the good they did for the company. Give concrete examples. Go over it in your head. You may even take a copy on paper to share with the boss when you make your pitch, especially if she has people above her she will have to answer to. Once you've made the case that you are too valuable to lose, ask for a raise. Then stop talking. People often get nervous at this point and keep chattering away until they have talked themselves right out of a raise. Be confident and let the silence work for you.

 TOP TIP

Once you've made the case that you are too valuable to lose, ask for a raise. Then stop talking. People often get nervous at this point and keep chattering away until they have talked themselves right out of a raise.

Let Them Make an Offer

Do some research and find out what the going rate is at other companies for your job description. Come up with a well-researched figure that you think is fair, and then ask for about two percent more. You need to give your boss a bit of wiggle room for the negotiation. Before you blurt out your figure, though, explain that you feel it is time for a raise and see what your boss offers. She might surprise you with a figure that was higher than you were ready to propose.

UMM, NO

Be prepared to take no for an answer, and don't take it personally. The company may be in the middle of a budget freeze, so it may be beyond your boss's power to grant your request at this time. If you do get a no, ask if there might be some other form of reward for your effort that might make you happy in the short term. Maybe you can get a few extra vacation days, a more flexible schedule, or if you have increased your workload substantially, maybe you can find a way to reduce it. There may not be much that she can do, but if your employer values your contributions, she will most likely try to come up with something to keep you happy. Do not threaten to quit or say you have another offer unless you actually do. Your boss might just call your bluff.

you don't have to **GO BLIND**
from staring at a screen all day

TOP SCREWUPS

- Having a bad setup
- Not taking breaks
- Failing to blink

There is an official name for that squeezed eyeball feeling you get after a day staring at Excel spreadsheets: Computer Vision Syndrome. The good news is that it is preventable.

Don't Suffer Because of a Bad Screen

First, **if you have not yet upgraded to a flat-screen LCD monitor, it is time.** Old-fashioned monitors refresh images more slowly, causing a flicker of images that contributes to eyestrain. Make sure you have your computer monitor positioned correctly. The top of the screen should be at eye level. If you cannot position your computer to avoid glare, consider investing in an antiglare screen cover. Now adjust the brightness of the display so that it matches, as much as possible, the surrounding brightness of your workstation.

Get That Far-Away Look

Take regular breaks from the computer. **Some experts suggest a 30-30-30 rule, for every thirty minutes of computer work, gaze thirty feet away for thirty seconds.** Others have proposed a 20-20-20 rule. The theory is the same. The main point is that you need to give your eyes regular breaks. Stop what you're doing for a short time and look at something in the distance.

Act Like a Human

Don't forget to 👁 **blink**. Studies show that people who work at computers blink less frequently than normal. This leads to dry eyes. Lubricating eyedrops can help.

DON'T SCREW UP YOUR EYES

If your eyes are already strained, here's how to replenish them at a glance:

Screwup ·······▶	Big Fix
• Your screen is way too bright.	• Adjust the screen so you don't have to squint at the darkness or open wide from the brightness.
• You have about a million hours of staring at the computer ahead of you.	• Take breaks every twenty to thirty minutes. Stare off into the distance, or better yet, get up and walk around for a minute. Getting off your butt will stave off other woes like hemorrhoids and muscle atrophy.
• Your eyes are completely bloodshot by the end of the day.	• Blink more. If that's too hard to do (it is a largely unconscious act), keep some eyedrops on hand.

don't lose your dissertation to a
COMPUTER GLITCH

There are few things more frustrating than completing the last paragraph of a twenty-page report only to have your computer inexplicably seize up and give you the blue or gray screen of death. Although most word processor programs periodically save and give you the option to restore, that doesn't always happen often enough (and it won't matter if you can't get your computer to turn back on).

Save It Yourself

If you're writing an important report, a novel, a dissertation, or a love letter, 🔘 **take the extra step of saving the document manually from time to time as you go.** Though this can save you ninety-nine percent of the time, it cannot ward off all data disasters. Bad things happen. You might be hit with the new hard drive–eating computer virus (see pages 228–229 to avoid this); a power outage could burn out your motherboard; your hard drive could go bad; or you could spill a cup of coffee over the keyboard and short out the system. There are many ways you could accidentally lose access to your data. There is really no excuse not to back things up.

Back That Thing Up!

In the old days, backing up data was a tedious process involving floppy discs and tape drives. Now there are external hard drives and online storage services that can back everything up automatically. 🕐 **Plugging an external hard drive into a computer's USB port is a quick and painless way to make sure you have another copy of your important data.** Combine this with a software program that performs this task on a regular basis, and you're good to go.

Put Your Head in the Cloud

Of course, having an external hard drive next to your computer won't do much good in the case of a fire or natural disaster that destroys everything in the room. 🕐 **To be sure you have your most important files after an emergency, you can back your files up to the cloud, i.e., the internet.** You can do this by subscribing to an online service that lets you load files to their server. There are many companies that offer free storage for up to a certain amount of data and then larger amounts for a fee. Not only does this keep your data somewhere other than your house, but you can also access it from different devices.

Double Down

No digital storage media has yet been invented that can last forever. External drives burn out, and web hosting sites suffer their own glitches or go out of business. Your best bet is to back up in a few places. It is a good idea to make more than one archive copy of your files and to check the discs to make sure they still work. In order to keep your old data, you will need to re-archive it from time to time.

DON'T GET COMPRESSED

These days hard drive space is not the issue it once was. Even though most backup programs give you the option to compress your data, you should not do it. To begin with, most photo and music files are already compressed, so you won't save much space. More important, if your files are compressed, you will need to use the same program to restore and back them up. If the program becomes outmoded or for some reason you no longer have access to it, it could make your data unusable.

don't catch a
COMPUTER VIRUS

You never open e-mail attachments from people you don't know, so you're safe from computer viruses, right? Wrong. It has been a long time since hackers have been using e-mail as their primary method of spreading viruses. Of course, using caution with e-mail attachments is still wise, but it is not enough to keep your computer safe.

Finding the Link to Viruses

These days you're much more vulnerable clicking on a link than opening an attachment. You may get an e-mail offering a deal from a site you regularly shop at or even saying that your account has been compromised. You click the link and it lands you at a spoof a site that either downloads a malicious payload or tries to steal your sensitive information. The most successful malicious code is designed to reside on your computer without your knowledge. The purpose is not to wreck your machine or get a bit of notoriety but to take a little bit of your computing power and link it with thousands of computers being similarly hacked. This sets up a super strong network that can be used to send out bulk e-mails, infect other computers, or steal information from remote computers.

How Do You Know if It's Legit?

The best way to tell if an e-mail is a fraud is to look at the address it's coming from. If an e-mail looks like it's supposed to be from eBay, but the email address is something like noreply@ebay.tz or mail1@eday.co, it's probably a scam. The safest thing to do is close the e-mail and go directly to the site (eBay, in this case) by typing in the URL. From there, you can log in to your account and see if there are in fact any fabulous deals or compromises in security.

Turn on the Hard Drive and Cough

There may be few telltale symptoms that the code is running. Modern viruses can block your antivirus program yet make it appear as if everything is fine. **If your computer seems to be running more slowly than usual or your hard drive is constantly spinning when you're not running any special programs, take it as a warning sign.** If your internet connection becomes noticeably slow, it could also be a sign that something is wrong.

Keep Up-to-Date

Of course you know that you need a good antivirus program and that you should update it regularly, but don't stop there. **It is important to update all of your programs with the latest security patches.** This can be time consuming, but it is much less of a bother than having to reformat and reinstall the entire operating system after a stubborn malware attack or having to deal with all of the repercussions if your identity gets stolen.

JUST LIKE IN THE MOVIES!

The most complex viruses are digital spies. They can capture files, take screenshots, copy online chats, and turn on computer microphones to record conversations. Security experts have discovered malicious software that target corporate and government computers in order to steal blueprints, plans, and other secret information.

do you forget your PASSWORD
every time for every site?

If you spend any time on the internet, you already know that you need passwords for everything: your favorite shopping site, your social networking site, your online banking and credit card accounts, even the newspaper you read online wants you to log in to post comments. So how do you remember all those passwords?

One Is Not Enough

The biggest mistake you can make is to choose one simple password and use it for everything. If you do this and a hacker figures out your Facebook password, then he can use it to access your bank account.

Make a System That Can Hang Tough

Fortunately, 👍 **you can store hundreds of different passwords in your head as long as you create a system.** Here is an example, but you should experiment and come up with something like this on your own. 👍 **Begin with a random but memorable base password and then add something to it based on the site you're accessing.** For example, lets say you decided to make a password out of the first letters of the names of the members of your favorite band when you were in junior high school. So you start with JJDDJ (for Jon, Jordan, Danny, Donnie, and Joe, the New Kids on the Block ♥). Then you tack on the first two letters of the service name. So your eBay password would be JJDDJEB. Or you could reverse it and use the service initials first as in FAJJDDJ for Facebook.

The Need for Numbers

Many sites require numbers as part of a password, so 👍 **come up with a number that you can remember, perhaps the digits of your birthday reversed.** If you were born on the 16th, you would use 61. Stick them between your root and the service initials so you come up with something like JJDDJ61CI for Citibank.

The Finishing Touches

When you are working on your password system, a good rule of thumb is to come up with something that will produce a code at least eight characters long with letters (both upper- and lowercase), symbols, and numbers. Some sites require this, and it's better to have all your passwords working on the same system than trying to remember which sites use what. Working from our NKotB example, pick one symbol to always use in between the base of the password and the number. Then decide if you want to use the base or the variable letters in uppercase. You will end up with something like JJDDJ#6ch (for your cheese-of-the-month subscription).

THE LAMEST PASSWORDS

Also, do not choose a lame password. After analyzing data from cases in which systems were hacked and passwords published, a security firm was able to make a list of the most common passwords. For your edification, here are the top ten. If you use one of these, you are inviting hackers to peek at your data:

1. password
2. 123456
3. 12345678
4. 1234
5. qwerty
6. 12345
7. dragon
8. (too dirty to tell you!)
9. baseball
10. football

don't drown in your **E-MAIL**

You know the agenda for the staff meeting is listed in an e-mail you got last week from Mary. Since then, though, she has cc'ed you on about thirty messages, and they are among another 1,245 messages in your inbox.

Get It Together!

Here is a strategy to get things under control. Think about the inbox on your physical desk. Your goal is to have everything out of it by the end of the day. Your goal with your e-mail inbox should also be to keep it empty. To do this, 👍 **you're going to need a system of organization to keep the messages from piling up. Start by creating a set of folders in your e-mail program. One suggestion is to create one folder labeled "follow up," one called "pending," and a third called "archive."**

- The follow-up folder is for messages dealing with tasks you must complete. They may require a long answer, or you may need to draft a document or research something in order to reply.

- The pending folder is where you put messages that you do not need to respond to immediately but that you need to keep "active" for the time being—for example, if someone promised to get back to you and you need a reminder to follow up.

- Finally the archive folder is where you put any messages that contain information you might want to retrieve at some point in the future.

Don't Overthink It

One archive folder may not seem precise enough, and you may feel the urge to create dozens of specific sub-folders in your archive. This is unnecessary. A recent study, conducted by IBM, found that people who searched through unsorted e-mail found what they were looking for faster than those who had an elaborate filing system. Unless your job is specifically project-based, allowing for a very obvious organizational system, the more the messier.

You Don't Have to Read Them the Second They Come In

One mistake when it comes to keeping your inbox under control is to constantly check messages, whether you have time to deal with them or not. **A better strategy is to only click the little envelope icon when you have at least a few minutes to read and respond**—unless, of course, it's screaming URGENT at you.

Subjects Matter

It is quicker to just hit reply, and you have no control over the subject headers that come to you, but **it makes everyone's life more efficient if you get in the habit of using succinct, specific subject lines.** A good example would be "Subject: Questions about page six of the proposal." A bad example would be "Subject: Can you look this over?" Even that, though, is preferable to "Subject: RE: re: re: Surfing cat video."

DON'T CREATE MIXED MESSAGES

It will help you sort quickly if you take measures to avoid subject-line drift. This is when your friend and coworker sends you her vacation snaps, and several messages later you find you are discussing changes to an important proposal all under the subject heading "fun in the sun." This not only makes sorting slow, it is also kind of depressing. Keep your work and personal e-mails separate.

E-MAIL GAFFES
can ruin your life

Your boss just sent an enraging e-mail to your entire department. You can't wait to pan him with your watercooler buddy, Reba, so you whip up a hilarious note in a reply, likening the boss to a malformed rooster with the brains of a toilet tank. It's poetry. You type in Reba's name and hit send. Oh, wait, no you didn't. The auto-fill filled in Reply All. Now who's got a septic system for brains?

Just Don't Write It

Basically, the best way to prevent humiliation with e-mail is to avoid saying things in e-mails that you don't actually want in writing. You really don't want a record of anything that is embarrassing, offensive, unprofessional, or just plain mean. You can missend it, IT's filters may flag it, or you might accidentally leave it up on your screen when you run off to a meeting. Also, remember that Reba has a Forward button, and you forgot her birthday last week.

That's Not Funny

Remember that e-mail interactions do not include most of the visual cues of face-to-face communication. Jokes can be misinterpreted. Before you write, think about how your message could sound to someone who doesn't know your emotional state or have all of the context that you have. Give it an angry read. If it can be misconstrued or you have to rely on emoticons, you probably need to rethink and rewrite your message.

DON'T SCREW UP

with YOUR MONEY

don't be taken in by
FALSE SAVINGS

Magazines, newspapers, and television programs are always full of ideas on how to save money. Most of them miss the mark. Invariably, the features tell you where to shop for the best prices. Rarely do they advise you *not to shop*. Not shopping, it turns out, is the only thing that is one hundred percent guaranteed to save you money. For those times that you do have to go shopping, here are a few places to be especially vigilant.

Outlet Malls

There is a reason outlet malls are usually located way out of town, and it has as much to do with consumer psychology as real estate prices. Being out-of-the-way makes it difficult for shoppers to compare prices. The more effort a person makes to get to the shop, the more he overestimates the amount of savings compared to local stores. After driving an hour or more to get there (and burning an hour's worth of gas), people want to believe the effort was worth it. What is more, they want to take advantage of the bargains while they are there so they don't have to make the drive often. They then "stock up" and buy more than they would otherwise. **If you do go outlet shopping, go with a list and stick to it. Walk away if they don't have what you want.**

Warehouse Stores

Warehouse stores offer huge savings to customers who pay a membership fee and buy in bulk. The shops take advantage of limited-time sales of bulk items, so what is available varies from visit to visit. While the per-item price of products is generally less than the same item in a grocery store, the bargain price and the sense that you might miss out if you don't buy today means that many customers end up confusing spending with savings. Not only do they buy things they do not need, but research shows that when consumers buy in bulk they use more of the product than they would have otherwise. **If you have one roll of paper towels, you are more likely to use it sparingly, but if you have a carton taking up space in your cupboard, you will naturally use the towels for every little spill. In this vicious cycle, more use leads to more buying.**

Collective Buying Sites

Sites like Groupon that offer deals for a limited time when enough people opt in lure shoppers with incredible bargains and a ticking clock. **You don't want to miss out on a once-in-a-lifetime chance to go horseback riding on a cruise ship for half of the normal price! Of course, you had not been planning to go horseback riding on the deck of the *Equestrian* for twice the price to begin with, so it is not exactly a savings.** What is more, it is estimated that about twenty percent of the vouchers people impulsively buy go unused.

ARE YOU EASY PREY FOR MARKETING?

Often the things that are presented as ways to save money actually end up costing us more. When you scour the coupon inserts and "friend" your favorite brands on Facebook to get special offers, you're constantly exposed to marketing messages and images of shiny new products. They make you are aware of things you never realized you needed before. That's what they were designed to do. Marketers want you to see an offer as an opportunity, not a buying decision.

don't owe your arm and your leg in
CREDIT CARD DEBT

There is no great secret as to how to stay out of debt. It's all about not spending more than you earn. We'll call this rule number one. As simple as this sounds in theory, modern life is organized to make it difficult.

It Seemed Like a Good Idea

It begins with something that sounds eminently responsible: establishing credit. Young people, especially those who go off to college, are encouraged to get starter credit cards in order to pave the way for later mortgages and car loans. This is smart and rational only if you pay off your cards in full each month. Unfortunately, most people do not. Thus they begin to drift away from rule number one.

Don't Fall for Imaginary Money

Being allowed to carry a balance can give you the illusion of more income. What do you do when you feel richer? You spend more. As you do, banks see you as an even more attractive customer and send an onslaught of credit card offers. The letters with these offers generally explain that you have been specially chosen for your excellent credit worthiness. This should not be enough to convince you that everything is fine with your finances, but interestingly it does. Psychological research has shown that if something is repeated often enough, you will start to believe it and doubt your own senses. **You may have a gnawing sense that you are falling deeper and deeper into a hole, but these constant letters from the financial experts (banks) reassure you that everything is fine and dandy. In fact, they say you are an especially fine example of a responsible spender. Do not listen to them.**

We Have Big Ole Pie-in-the-Sky Hopes

Credit card companies make profits on a simple fact of human nature: We are overly optimistic about our futures. We always believe we will have more time and more money in the future than we have today. So you charge a new sofa today forgetting that between now and the day the bill arrives you will continue to have expenses. The raise you're sure you will get this year is not guaranteed, and there is also no guarantee that your car will not break down.

Don't Trust Your Future Self

Knowing this, you should approach debt with the respect and caution it deserves. **Don't trust your future self to be more responsible or richer than you are today. If you can't afford to pay outright for that stereo today, there is no reason to think you will find it any easier to pay for it with interest a few months from now.**

THE GREAT WHIRLPOOL OF DEBT

The more cards you carry, the more you will be tempted to carry more and more of a balance on your cards. Eventually you will find yourself in a place where it is impossible to pay what you owe with what you earn. More debt becomes necessary just to get by. (It is at this point, too, that the love letters from the banks tend to stop coming.) This is why financial advisors always suggest making a budget. Having credit available makes it harder to be aware of how much money you actually have to spend.

don't ruin your **CREDIT SCORE**

If you never borrowed a thing in your life and saved up every penny you ever earned, you would not have a good credit score. The strategies that make you a good prospect for a lender are not necessarily the ones that make you the most financially secure. Staying out of debt in the first place may be a better goal than tweaking your score.

Who's Keeping Score?

A credit score is a measure of how good a prospect you will be for the companies that make a living buying and selling consumer debt. **When you are thinking about managing your finances, bear in mind that your credit score and your financial health may be correlated, but they are not entirely the same thing.** A common mistake that gets consumers into trouble is the assumption that as long as they are maintaining a decent credit score, this means that they are in good financial health and that they can go out and borrow more.

How to Score

You do not need to carry a balance on your credit cards to have a good credit score, but you do need to have open lines of credit and use them. If you know you have a problem keeping credit cards without overspending, this is one area where it is wise to consider whether your focus should be on your *credit score* or on your *spending habits*.

What's the Score For?

The score is important, however, if you want to get a mortgage or a loan with favorable interest rates. Fair or not, credit scores are used for all kinds of decisions that could have a huge impact on your life. Even potential employers sometimes use credit scores to get a sense of how good you are at managing money and how likely you might be to steal from them. They assume that someone who is up to his eyeballs in debt is more prone to such temptation.

A Perfect Score

FICO, which stands for Fair Isaac Company, does not actually calculate anyone's credit score. It developed the software the credit-reporting agencies use to assess your credit worthiness. Your FICO score is a number between 300 and 850. The higher the number, the better the credit risk you are deemed to be. There are three major credit-reporting agencies: Equifax, Experian, and TransUnion. Even though they are using the same software to make their calculations, they may not begin with the same information. One agency may give you a high score while another may have some incorrect information on its books and give you a low one. Only mortgage lenders generally check all three, so whether or not you get a credit card might depend on which company a lender contacts for its information.

DON'T PAY FOR YOUR REPORT

There are many companies now that ask you to subscribe to their monitoring services for a fee. This is not necessary. The Fair Credit Reporting Act requires each of the nationwide consumer reporting companies to provide you with a free copy of your credit report, at your request once every twelve months or if you are turned down for a loan or line of credit. The Federal Trade Commission's website has information on how to do this.

What's in a Score, and How You Can Ruin it

Your score is made up of the following elements: one-third is based on your payment history; another third on the amount you owe; and the remaining third is based on the length of your credit history, how many requests for new credit you have made, and the types of credit you use, as well as a number of other variables. Besides just having too much debt, the easiest way to screw up your credit is to make late payments. To be sure you avoid this, **consider consolidating your due dates so you never forget. Many companies let you change your billing cycle. Remembering you have to pay by the 15th and 20th is much easier than remembering to pay by the 2nd and the 8th and the 16th and the 28th.** Even seemingly trivial bills such as unpaid library fines and parking tickets can screw up your credit score if they go to collections.

What Will Make Your Score Happy Again?

Paying off installment loans—such as a car loan or a mortgage—does help your score but not as much as paying down your credit cards. Ideally, **to have a great credit score, you would have a couple of credit cards that you've kept open for years, use regularly, but never get near your credit limit. This is why it is a bad idea to close your credit card accounts. You do not have to use them, but as long as they're open, the ratio of presumably available credit to debt is high.** Lenders like this. You can improve your scores by limiting your use of active accounts to less than thirty percent of the credit limit, whether you pay off the balance in full each month or not. See if your credit card has a system to e-mail or text you when you get close to the spending limit you've set.

TOP TIP

Your score is made up of the following elements: one-third is based on your payment history; another third on the amount you owe; and the remaining third is based on the length of your credit history . . .

do not stay BURIED IN DEBT

In the off chance that you are already in debt, let's take a look at what you can do to avoid being in debt for the rest of your natural life.

TOP SCREWUPS

- Keeping your cards in your wallet
- Not knowing how much debt you're in
- Feeling defeated

Admit You Have a Problem

If you are paying one credit card with cash taken out on another or if you have an excellent salary and are still living from paycheck to paycheck, then something is amiss. If the thought of trying to get through a month without relying on your credit card sends a shiver down your spine, it is time to face the beast.

Quit Cold Turkey

Stop using your credit cards entirely. Not even for "emergencies" or "just to get through." You are probably quite skilled at justifying little emergency expenses, but you have to stop lying to yourself. If you are not entirely maxed out, congratulations, but pretend that you are. 👍 **Freeze your assets by putting your credit cards in the freezer. If you simply cannot use credit because it is not available, your habits will change by necessity.** You can make all of the same types of purchases with a debit card that draws straight from your available funds. If you haven't got funds available, you can't buy anything. Period.

Once you have figured out how much you need just to get by each month—don't forget to leave an emergency reserve in there in case the car breaks down . . .

What's the (Terrifying) Bottom Line?

Sit down with all of your statements and add up how much you owe. Most people try to avoid doing this and you may be a little bit horrified when you see the actual number. Lots of people run away and go buy lottery tickets at this point. This is a perfectly natural reaction, but not helpful. Fight it.

Get Real

Once you've gotten over the shock of how much you owe, take a realistic look at your salary. How much is coming in each month? This is what you have to pay for your living expenses and everything you owe. **First, figure out what you really need each month in order to eat, put gasoline in your car, cover medical expenses, and so on. When you assess your spending in a rational way, you may find that there are a lot of little things that you can do without, and these could add up to big savings.** Try to think of thrift as an exercise in creativity and resourcefulness, not as deprivation. For example, having to brown-bag it for lunch means you get to learn to cook!

Take It One Month at a Time

Once you have figured out how much you need just to get by each month—don't forget to leave an emergency reserve in there in case the car breaks down—see how much is left over to pay your creditors. There are two approaches to paying off your debts. Which one is best for you will depend on your personality. The first school of thought says to focus on the biggest debts with the highest interest rates first. Getting them out of the way frees up more of your capital to tackle the smaller debts. The other school of thought is that paying off the smallest debts first gives the debtor incremental victories and the emotional satisfaction of seeing one debt after the other eliminated.

Whatever you choose, 👍 **you will need to pay more than the minimum each month to make any real progress.** If you're able to do so without closing your accounts, it will help your credit score in the long run because the utilization of available credit is a big part of your score.

In Over Your Head

If you look at your debt and income and find that your minimum balance each month is more than you have available, it is time to call your card issuers and negotiate. Do not dread this call. 👍 **Most card issuers have programs available that reduce interest payments and help you pay off your debt.** Be honest about what you are able to pay each month. When you have taken advantage of their plans and reduced your interest and payments, you will most likely end your conversation feeling relieved. If you happen to reach someone who is unhelpful, end the call, take a few breaths, and try again later. You can also talk to nonprofit debt counseling services, such as the National Foundation for Credit Counseling (http://www.nfcc.org/).

DON'T LET IT GET YOU DOWN

Financial gurus often fail to address the very real emotional impact of indebtedness. It is common for people who are deeply in debt to feel depressed and helpless. Studies have shown that people who feel cash-strapped avoid all kinds of social activities, even those that do not cost any money at all. The only thing that being broke increases is television viewing. But remember the old cliché, there is more to life than money. Be sure that whatever budget you put in place leaves you enough wiggle room so that you can still lead a normal life, spend time with friends, and feel like yourself. Punishing yourself, wallowing in self-pity, or labeling yourself a failure will do nothing to solve your problem.

don't PAY FOR COLLEGE
for the rest of your life

 **TOP SCREWUPS**

- Not even applying for scholarships and aid
- Missing aid application deadlines
- Thinking you have to stay in-state
- Getting hurt by your savings

Don't pass up the chance to get the degree you want because you are afraid of the cost. If there is a will, you can find a way to get a diploma without spending the rest of your life working two jobs to pay for it.

Don't Get a Rash Thinking About Ivy League

One mistake that many people with lower incomes make is to not even consider high-tuition colleges. If you have the grades, don't shy away from an Ivy League school. Because of their loyal alumni, they often have large endowments to aid promising students. That means 👍 **if you qualify for need-based aid, you might end up paying less at a top-rated school than at a state school where aid is limited.**

It Never Hurts to Try

There is no real income cutoff for tuition aid, but you definitely will not qualify if you do not apply. Even if you are a perfect candidate for financial aid, you will not get it if you miss the deadlines. 👍 **Don't wait until an acceptance letter rolls in. Apply for aid at the same time you file the application to attend.**

You Don't Have to Stay Home

You may be able to pay in-state tuition while attending an out-of-state institution. 👍 **More than half of states provide reduced-tuition programs for students from** certain neighboring states when the program they want is not offered in their home state. For more information look up the New England Regional Student Program, the Midwestern Higher Education Compact, the Southern Regional Education Board, or the Western Interstate Commission for Higher Education.

Don't Save in the Wrong Places

Choose your college-savings plan carefully. There are a variety of tax-favored savings plans—such as 529 plans, Coverdell Education Savings Accounts (ESA), and Uniform Transfers to Minors Act (UTMA) accounts—but a study released in 2004 says they may actually do more harm than good, especially among middle-income families who are on the margin for aid. The problem is that savings increases a family's wealth, which can reduce a student's eligibility for financial aid. This reduction can cost more than one hundred percent of the amount accumulated in the tax-favored investment account. Savings in a UTMA account could cost as much as $1.24 for every $1 saved.

 You might do better saving through an IRA or another tax-favored retirement plan that is not assessed under financial-aid formulas. If you have a choice between paying down your mortgage faster and putting extra money into your IRA, consider the IRA. Equity in your home is often counted as an asset when determining financial aid, but retirement accounts are not.

SOMETHING FOR EVERYONE

Finally, don't try to figure this all out on your own. There are scholarships, savings plans, and tuition-savings programs that you may never have considered. There are scholarships especially for *Star Trek* fans, for students who have worked as golf caddies, for marble champs, and for people with an academic interest in sheep. A college tuition aid expert studies all of your financial options full-time. Take advantage of his expertise.

avoid IDENTITY THEFT

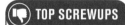
- Letting your secrets slip too easily
- Using hacked ATMs
- Not shredding everything
- Trusting people

Outside the realm of science fiction it is unlikely that a doppelgänger will show up in your house and take your identity—replacing you so that your spouse, kids, and employer don't know it's not the real you. Your personal information, such as credit history and bank account numbers, is another story. If you are not vigilant, this type of identification theft can easily happen.

Keep Them Secret, Keep Them Safe

If you are a victim of this crime, you will spend lots of time trying to convince various bureaucratic entities that you did not max out your credit card with online psychic readings and purchases from JetSki4Life.com. It can take a victim up to two years to get it all sorted out. Fortunately, there are some steps you can take to avoid this nightmare. **Be vigilant in protecting your important ID numbers, especially your social security number, credit card numbers, and driver's license. These are the keystones that an ID thief can use to build on. Be especially protective of your PIN numbers and never write them on your ATM cards or keep them in your wallet with the cards.**

What's Wrong with This Picture?

Before you use an ATM, look at it closely. Technologically savvy felons create skimming devices that fit over the card reader at an ATM to read the magnetic

stripe before it enters the real machine. This is combined with a camera that records time-stamped footage of victims punching in their pin so that the scammers can match up the information later on. Your best defense against the camera is to cover your hand when entering your PIN.

No More Junk Mail Is No Good

Be sure to shred bank and credit statements, as well as credit card offers that come through the mail. A thief can take these out of the garbage and sign up for the offers in your name. If you suddenly stop receiving mail, call the post office. Sometimes a crook will forge your signature and have your mail forwarded somewhere else in order to obtain information or hide evidence of identity appropriation.

Trust Almost No One

Do not give your personal information in response to an e-mail or a call that you did not initiate. Be aware that scammers will sometimes pretend to be from entities with which you do legitimate business. If you receive an e-mail that says there is a problem with your PayPal account, for example, and you are worried that this may be true, do not follow the link in the message. Instead, log into your account as you normally would. If there is a real problem with your account, you should have some kind of notification besides the e-mail.

GET A YEARLY CHECKUP

Check your credit report at least once a year. This will tip you off if any credit lines were opened in your name. If you discover anything out of the ordinary, put a fraud alert in your credit file by contacting the credit bureaus. When you have done that, any future credit application will have to be confirmed with you over the phone.

don't **RETIRE** only to find yourself working again

TOP SCREWUPS

- Finding yourself unexpectedly retired
- Starting your plan too late
- Forgetting medical expenses
- Living for a realllly long time

Most people dream of retiring to a sunny tropical beach where they will lounge holding piña coladas with paper umbrellas in them, not of greeting people at a box store in order to pay a stack of late bills. Here are some tips that can help you plan ahead and achieve the retirement of your dreams and not your nightmares.

The Best Laid Plans

When it comes to deciding when to retire, your answer should be based on your bank account, not your birthday. Your end goal with retirement planning should be to create the level of financial security that will allow you to have a secure and comfortable life.

That said, don't assume you will have the luxury of deciding when to retire. Two in five people retire sooner than they expected because of illness, layoffs, or other factors. You do not want to find yourself with a forced retirement and a pile of credit-card debt instead of a 401k. Your best option will vary depending on your goals and financial situation. **Your best bet is to get professional planning help and start earlier rather than later.**

Help Is Out There

If you are already retired and struggling to make sense of it all, you do not have to figure it all out alone. If the various Social Security options get confusing, there are a number of telephone hotlines that provide free or low-cost legal advice to people over 60. Some will even review legal documents you send to them. You can find a list at: http://www.seniorlaw.com/hotlines.htm.

Stick It Out

If you do have a choice, **try to stay on the job a few extra years. Don't retire just because you're offered an early retirement package that sounds appealing.** Stick to your plan. Not only does working longer allow you to put money away instead of drawing it out, but the amount of Social Security benefits you receive also increases about eight percent each year.

Plan for a Loooonnnngg Retirement

The average life expectancy of a woman in the United States is 84 and for a man it is 81, but you could be one of the lucky ones who lives to 95. **Plan as if you were going to live to be 95 to be sure you don't outlast your nest egg.** Keep your annual drawdown rate to four percent of assets. At that rate, if you start withdraws at age 65 you will have a cash flow until age 95.

Your Arm Trouble Could Cost You Your Leg

If you live in the United States, be sure to save enough for medical costs. Most people expect that Medicare will simply cover everything. Often it does not. The average couple retiring in the United States in 2012 at age sixty-five is expected to spend $285,000 in health-care costs over the course of their retirement.

TOP TIP

When it comes to deciding when to retire, your answer should be based on your bank account, not your birthday.

RETIRE TO WHAT?

Remember that a career is about more than just money. If you love your job and you're not sure you're ready to stop working, then don't. Even if you are ready to stop punching in each day, think about the nonfinancial benefits working gives you. Then make a plan to address some of what you'll be giving up. You may discover that there is only so much leisure you can handle.

don't screw up YOUR WILL

TOP SCREWUPS

- Not having a will
- Hiding your will
- Not matching your other assets to your will
- Being vague

The whole idea of a will is to make life easier for your loved ones. The last thing (and I really do mean the *last* thing) you want to leave your heirs is a mess to clean up.

You Never Know When You Will Go

The biggest mistake people make when it comes to a will is not having one at all. You are young and not planning to die anytime soon, but who is really? Don't wait for the right time. If you die "intestate"—that means without a will—all your assets will be distributed under state law. This may or may not be where you would like it to go.

It's Not a Treasure Map

So you've made a will. Congratulations! Don't make the mistake of hiding it. Sometimes people hide their wills away because they don't want relatives to take a peak and learn what they will or won't be getting until it is time. If you hide it so well that no one knows about it, it is the same as not having one.

On a related note, it is good to give your executor a heads up that he or she has been named. This person will be responsible for handling the transfer of all your assets, which is a big responsibility. Be sure you have chosen someone who is willing and able to do it.

IRA Trumps Will

Just because you have made out a will, don't assume you've taken care of everything. 🕐 **There are some assets a will does not cover. For example, your IRA.** The person you name as the beneficiary in your IRA documents will receive the funds regardless of what it says in your will. The same is true of many insurance policies. Property that is held jointly will go to the surviving co-owner, even if you name someone else as a beneficiary in your will. Doing this will just result in confusion and legal battles.

Everyone Will Want Your Autographed Justin Bieber Poster

Just because you don't have a fortune doesn't mean there won't be disputes over your estate. If your will states that your personal items are to be "divided equally" among your children, it won't keep them from fighting over a particular heirloom. A much better strategy is to 🕐 **ask them what objects they value while you're still alive and then either give them the items before you die, or list each item specifically in the will with explanations as to why you've given what to whom.**

WHAT *WILL* YOU DO?

Here are the most common ways to screw over your loved ones from beyond the grave. Don't let this happen to them! (Unless, of course, you want to leave them with one final pain.)

Screwup ·······▶	Big Fix
• Dying unexpectedly with no will in place	• Make your will right now.
• Hiding your will so greedy relatives won't bump you off to get their hands on your collection of Beanie Babies	• Leave your will's whereabouts with someone you like, and leaving the bloodsuckers nothing.
• Not making sure your will jives with your other documents—legal unpleasantries ensue	• Make sure all your policies, assets, and accounts match what you lay out in your will.

Everything that is listed in your will must pass through probate, which can be expensive and time consuming. Instead of transferring all your property through your will, you might want to set up various trusts, which can reduce your tax burden and bypass the probate process.

It's Not Any Fun

As unpleasant as it is to contemplate, while you are working on your will, you should also 👍 **draft a health-care proxy that will name someone to make medical decisions for you in the event that you are unable to do so yourself.** Include end-of-life directives that lay out what types of medical life support you wish to receive in case of a terminal illness. This can relieve some of the burden on your family that comes with making these hard choices.

NOT THE PLACE FOR YOUR EPITAPH

The will is not the place to list your burial and funeral instructions. Most wills aren't read for some time after the person has died. You will probably be in the ground before this happens. Use a separate document to detail your funeral wishes. (See pages 326–327 for more info.)

YOUR VACATION

LUGGAGE without lugging

 **TOP SCREWUPS**

- Overpacking
- Packing messily

The word "luggage" dates back to the late sixteenth century, and as you may have surmised, it comes from the verb to "lug," and it originally meant "a bag that is inconveniently heavy to carry." There is no reason it has to have that connotation today—at least not if you do things right.

How Much Is Too Much?

A handy rule of thumb is that if you have to sit on your bag to get it closed, you're probably taking too much stuff. There are good reasons to pack light. Not only are airlines charging you for checked bags and making sure your carry-on is not over the weight limit by an ounce, but overly heavy bags are also a leading cause of injury among travelers. More than 13,000 people are injured by luggage in the United States each year. Carry-on bags alone harm about 4,000.

Pack Practically

You do not need to take along every piece of clothing you like. 👎 **Bring enough clean underwear for every day of your journey, unless it is very long and you will have a chance to do laundry. For outerwear, just choose a few items that can go from day to night. Pick neutral colors so that you can mix and match a few key pieces to make unique outfits.** Clothing made of synthetic fabrics are less prone to wrinkling and tend to be lighter than natural fabrics, making them a good travel option. If you think you might need to do some hand washing on your journey, these will also probably dry more quickly.

Roll without Wrinkles

The biggest mistake amateur packers make is folding clothing to keep it wrinkle-free. You want to do just the opposite. 🕐 **Once you've selected the clothing you want to take with you, roll it all up. Roll everything from socks to suits. Rolled clothing does not move around as much in the suitcase, which is what causes clothes to wrinkle.** What is more, you can fit more clothing into a smaller carry-on bag. Rolling does not actually give the clothes a smaller mass, but it is a more efficient use of your luggage space. Remember, of course, that even though you can fit more into the bag, it will not make it any lighter. So do not use this as an excuse to ignore the first rule about taking less stuff. (For all kinds of tips on efficient packing, including how to bundle roll your travel wardrobe, visit www.onebag.com.)

TSA LIGHTENS YOUR LOAD

If you're traveling by air, Transportation Security Administration (TSA) regulations allow only a small amount of liquid to be brought onto a flight in your carry-on. Remember the 3-1-1 rule: You're allowed to carry liquid and gels only in 3.4-ounce bottles or smaller, and all of these bottles must be packed in a 1-quart, clear, plastic, zip-top bag; 1 bag per passenger. You will want to keep this on top of the other stuff in your carry-on because you'll have to take it out and put it in the screening bin. This may seem like a hassle, but it's actually forcing you to pack lightly, literally.

don't get stuck in the
MIDDLE SEAT

TOP SCREWUPS

- Not choosing a seat assignment
- Not checking on your seat at the airport
- Getting on a plane that is almost all middle seats

You're flying cross-country in the middle seat. Your bag is stowed under the seat in front of you, which means you can't stretch your feet out—unless you call putting your tootsies a couple of inches forward stretching. Your neighbors have taken both armrests, and now the guy in the seat in front of you decides to lean his seat all the way back. This is not the best way to fly.

Assigned Seats Aren't All Bad

You have a good chance of avoiding the dreaded middle seat if 👍 **you choose your seat assignment when you book your flight.** Never wait until you arrive at the airport if you can help it. When booking online, many airlines allow you to see a diagram of the aircraft and which seats are still available. If you can, choose a seat in a row that is three across where only one seat is already reserved. The middle seat between two people traveling alone is least likely to fill up, so if the flight isn't full, you may get some extra breathing room.

No Backsies

Even if you do choose a seat when you book online, the airline might just "reclaim" your seat for favored customers. 👍 **Be sure to check in at the airport an hour or more before departure.** If you do find you're in a seat you don't like, go to the airline's desk as soon as someone shows up there and see if you can get a seat change. This is when all of the reserved seats of passengers who do not show are released.

Know Your Craft

You can also improve your chances of getting a good seat by flying on the right type of aircraft. You should know, for example, that you are nearly three times more likely to get stuck in a middle seat on a 747 as you are on a 767. **An Airbus 300 is also a good choice for the middle-seat phobic.** There are a number of websites (seatguru.com is one) that provide seating charts and tips to find the seats with the most legroom and so on.

👍 **TOP TIP**

When booking online, many airlines allow you to see a diagram of the aircraft and which seats are still available.

THE SILENT WAR

The middle seat is stressful because you have to spend so much time pretending you're not sandwiched between two strangers, all while fighting a war on two fronts: the armrest war. While trying to still pretend the armrest invader is a non-person, you try to slide your arm into the space and dislodge her. Both parties are well aware of the contest, but neither is likely to acknowledge it verbally. If you are a woman, you have an extra incentive to avoid the middle seat—as if you needed one. The odds are five-to-one that you will not come out the winner of the armrest war if the passenger next to you is male. You can, of course, throw off the balance of power by politely saying to one of your neighbors, "Excuse me, may I use this armrest?"

arrive REFRESHED instead of harried and JET-LAGGED

You've flown to Paris for that dream vacation, but you spend the entire first day asleep in your bed. You wake up that night and head out for a huge meal that is everything you could hope for. Then your stomach rumbles, and you feel ill because you ate a five-course meal when your body says you should be asleep. You're muddle-headed, and your body temperature is off-kilter.

All Out of Whack

Each person's body operates with its own circadian clock—that is, an internal sense of time and what the body should be doing at certain times of day. Scientists believe that there are different mechanisms at work when your internal clock is advanced and when it is delayed. This is why it is always harder to advance, as you do when traveling west to east, than to delay, as you do when traveling in the other direction. Beyond that, different organs in the body adapt to time shifts at different speeds. This means that your body processes are no longer coordinated.

Trick Yourself Ahead of Time

Set your watch to the time at your destination as soon as you begin your flight and start "living" that time right away. Sleep, or stay awake, and eat as though you were already there. If it is daytime in your destination, stay

 | NEW YORK | LONDON | MOSCOW

awake. If it is night, try to sleep. Airline meals are usually serviced based on the time zone you're leaving. Bring your own snacks or wait until a time that is appropriate in your destination time zone to eat the meal they give you (this will work for something like a sandwich but not a hot dish).

Beat Your Body Clock

One recent study suggests that you can 👍 **reduce the shock to your system by "phase-shifting" your meal times over the course of a week before your departure.** If you can, arrive a day early to give yourself time to adjust.

Flush Out the Jet Lag

Jet lag is exacerbated by dehydration, which many people experience during a flight. 👎 **Drink plenty of liquids and try to avoid alcohol and coffee.** Then eat a high-protein breakfast on the first day in your new destination. The protein will help you through the first day. Eat carbohydrates before bed when you arrive. It will help you go to sleep and be loaded up for the next day.

THE PLACEBO EFFECT

Although some people swear by melatonin tablets, recent studies have found no evidence that it is effective in preventing jet lag. You may get a small placebo effect, but this should just show you how important your perception can be. If you don't think you'll be jet-lagged, you probably will actually feel less jet-lagged.

don't spend your whole vacation
in the **BATHROOM**

Most people have heard not to drink the water in more exotic travel locations, but a lot of people get some sort of stomach ailment while traveling just about anywhere. There's no worse way to see a tropical destination than from the inside of a bathroom stall. Good thing you don't have to!

Soda Is Good for You This One Time

Bottled drinks, such as cola, are somewhat acidic and do not provide a hospitable environment for microbes, but **be sure to order your drink without ice. Ice is, of course, frozen local water.** If you're at a restaurant, you can politely ask for bottled drinks to be opened in front of you. Otherwise, if your water bottle comes out sans cap, it may just be tap water after all. **You'll also want to have bottled water in the hotel room for brushing your teeth.**

What's Happening in the Kitchen?

Most travelers' intestinal maladies derive not from contaminated water but from poor food-handling practices. Harmful microbes that are introduced to food breed quickly, producing a larger infective dose than you are likely to find in water. **Don't eat salads or other fresh fruits and vegetables that have been washed in local**

water or raw fruits that you have not peeled yourself.
If you can, eat in places where you can directly watch the
food being prepared.

You've Gotta Eat Something

You may be tempted to avoid eating all together. This is a
mistake. Eating the right food can help shorten a bout of
intestinal distress. A bland diet of bananas, rice, apples,
and toast puts soluble fiber in your system and slows the
passage of food through the intestinal tract. Be sure to
get enough fluid. When you have diarrhea, you run the
risk of dehydration. If your diarrhea lasts for more than
seventy-two hours, if it is accompanied by abdominal pain,
or if it is accompanied by a high fever or dizziness, seek
medical attention.

OUT IN THE WILDERNESS

If you're roughing it, you may not want to
have to lug heavy water bottles into the
woods, along with all your other gear. Good
thing it does not take a great deal of effort
to make most water safe for drinking. All
you have to do is bring it to a good rolling
boil. Many guides suggest to keep the
water boiling for twenty minutes, but this is
not necessary and just wastes fuel.

don't lose your shirt in
LAS VEGAS

 **TOP SCREWUPS**

- Going in thinking you won't lose your shirt
- Allowing yourself to go off budget
- Gambling on the Strip

You already know that you are almost guaranteed to come out of a casino poorer rather than richer. Yet you book a Las Vegas vacation anyway, determined that you will be the exception to the rule. You will not. Put that idea out of your head. This does not mean you can't pop into a casino to experience the thrill from time to time.

Pretend It's the Price of Admission

Playing the slots is not a retirement plan or a way to get out of a financial bind. It is a form of entertainment. 👍 **Think of a gambling outing as a trip to a ball game or an amusement park. These outings can cost a lot of money, but you plan ahead, choose an event you can afford, and afterwards enjoy the memory of a fun experience.** Think of the money you want to gamble as what you are willing to pay for your evening's entertainment. You may be OK spending $100 on a fun night out, but $1,000? No way!

Give Yourself No Choice

Make a budget. If you spend all of it, that is fine. If you have a tendency to think, *Oh just another $20 can't hurt,* then 👍 **only take cash with you and leave your cards at home or in the hotel room.** This way you can't spend more than you intend to, no matter how much all of the free cocktails make you want to.

What Are the Odds?

To get an idea of how much money you will need for an evening of slots, remember that it costs about $9 an hour to play a nickel machine with a three-coin maximum. A quarter machine will cost about $45 an hour, and a dollar machine $180 an hour.

Let's say you've decided you can afford to spend no more than $300 a day on gambling during your Las Vegas weekend. You will not have much fun if you walk in and place one $300 bet and lose right off the bat. Instead, make bets of no more than one percent of your budget. If you are ahead, you can raise your bets a bit. Never chase after money you've lost. Take a deep breath and walk away. You should also walk away if you find you are ahead. If you won $100 and then lose $20, quit while you're ahead. Use your winnings on a relaxing dinner, and then move to another table for a new game if you still want to play.

Little-Known Fact

Visit the theme casinos on the Strip for the shows and the ambiance, but 🖐 **do your gaming at the smaller casinos a bit off the main tourist path.** The big casinos have a steady stream of tourists and don't need to offer the best odds.

DON'T GET CHEATED BY DIRTY CHEATERS

Whether you are playing in a casino or informally with your buddies, here are a few tips to avoid being cheated. You can tell if cards have been marked by rifling the deck and watching the design on the back. If it has been marked, it will move like one of those animated flip books. Test for loaded dice by dropping each die into a tall glass of water. Do this several times with different numbers on the top. If they turn when sinking so the same two or three numbers always show up, the dice are loaded. If it would be a bit too conspicuous to do the water trick, hold the die loosely between your thumb and forefinger by the diagonally opposite corners. A loaded die will pivot when the weighted side is on top.

don't accidentally order Lassie from a menu
in a FOREIGN LANGUAGE

If you're traveling in a foreign nation, as shocking as it may seem, you are likely to find yourself in situations where there is no one around who speaks your language. You may even find yourself at mealtime wandering into a quaint little eatery and being presented with a menu full of incomprehensible symbols. You are hoping to eat something a bit more like a hamburger and a bit less like flambé of worms. How can you ensure this happens?

Play-Act Your Food

Your server will generally catch on fairly quickly to the idea that you are hungry. She will have figured this out from context, as you are both in a restaurant. She will also, through similar deductive reasoning, work out that you are not from around there. If you are lucky, the menu will have a few pictures, and you can point at something that you recognize. If not, you may have to resort to mime and sounds. This tends to be easier for meat eaters. It is a lot easier to mime a fish or cluck like a chicken than it is to pretend to be broccoli.

Bring a Pocket Translator

You can circumvent some of the mime  **by bringing a guidebook or multi-language dictionary with you.** Then, you should be able to communicate a few key ingredients by pointing to them in the book.

🔊 You can also download translation apps for your phone, some of which will even speak for you.

Know the Basics

Of course luggage gets lost, phones get forgotten, and other unforeseeable circumstances can lead to you being hungry and without your translation method. So 🔊 **it always pays to learn at least a few phrases in the local language.** If there are certain foods you want to avoid—for example if you have an allergy or you simply have no desire to ever try a poodle steak—those are some of the first words you should learn.

Lost in Translation

Remember, though, food language can be tricky. In English, a hot dog contains no dog, head cheese is not cheese, and sweetbreads are not sweet bread. It is the same in other languages, as well. Just because you know the words does not mean that you are certain to understand how they are being used. Michael Lonsford, a writer for the *Houston Chronicle,* discovered this when he used his memory of high-school Spanish to order "huevos" off an Argentine menu expecting to get scrambled eggs.

"Señor, in this country, huevos is another name for the bull's . . . um . . ." a helpful English speaker finally told him.

Even if you know that a word means "ham" or "beef," you can't be sure if it will show up cooked or raw unless you can identify the other terms around it on the menu.

WHEN ALL ELSE FAILS

The best approach is to be open to the adventure of it all. You're traveling, after all, to experience another culture. You may not come to love broccoli with ice-cream sprinkles (as Julie Subotky, author of *Consider It Done,* was once served), but you will have a great story to tell when you get home.

how to look decent in your
vacation **PHOTOS**

TOP SCREWUPS

- Sucking it in
- Taking it too seriously
- Being uptight
- Striking the wrong pose

You're walking along a scenic vista, enjoying a stress-free vacation when your husband runs up, camera in hand. Instead of smiling broadly with the joy you're feeling about the mountains and sunset, you're now sucking in your stomach and thinking, *Is my skin too pale? If I tilt my head this way, will I have a double chin in the picture?*

Let It All Hang Out

One of the worst things you can do is suck in your gut and hold your breath. You'll look uptight and uncomfortable. Study after study has shown that people rate others as more attractive when they do one simple thing: smile. The trick is that you need to have a genuine smile. People can sense the difference, even in photographs. **If the camera seems to capture a true moment of joy, people will love the way you look. So relax when the camera comes out, and give in to the fun you're already having.**

Forget Your Hang-Ups

If you're stressed about your looks, your fear of looking bad will become a self-fulfilling prophecy. **So relax your face and your mind. Think about something funny.** A great photo is full of motion and action. Instead of standing in a stiff pose next to a statue, do something silly. You don't want the statue to appear to be more lively than you.

A GOOD TIME

don't eat it at the SKATING RINK

TOP SCREWUPS

- Lacing up the wrong way
- Being afraid to fall
- Having bad posture

Your friend invites you to an afternoon at the skating rink, and your heart sinks. Last time you tried skating, all the other people at the party sped along the ice backward and forward, racing and doing turns while you held onto the side railing, afraid to let go. "It's my weak ankles," you muttered, vowing never to strap anything with a blade to your feet again.

Laced with Fear

Even *you* can learn to enjoy skating if you know just a few of the basics. Let's start with your "weak ankles." If you feel as though your ankles are wobbly on the ice, chances are it has nothing to do with your legs and a lot to do with how you fit and lace up your skates. Your instinct when confronted with all of those long laces will be to tie everything evenly from bottom to top, but this is not right. Instead:

- **Tie the laces as tightly as is comfortably possible at the ankle and then looser above the ankle.** You want the ankle to be well supported, but you do not want the top of the boot to be so rigid that you cannot bend.

- Do not forget to keep the tongue in the correct position: in the middle of the opening between the sides of the boot. Keep it flat and in place as you lace.

- When you've finished lacing, try to bend so your knees are over your toes. If you can't, the top is too tight. Sit down, unlace, and try again.

OK, so You Will Eat It at First

When you venture onto the ice, remember this:

🖐 **You are going to fall. It is inevitable that a beginning skater will fall at least once. So just relax and don't be embarrassed.** It is part of the learning process. Being relaxed is one of the keys to skating. It will also hurt more if you fall when all your muscles are tense. Don't let the fear of falling keep you from moving. Believe it or not, falls taken at speed are usually less painful than the tumbles you have when you're standing still. Try to land on your side when you go down, and get up quickly so other skaters do not trip over you.

Taking a Stance and Moving Forward

As you edge your way onto the slippery surface of the ice, 🖐 **keep your knees slightly bent and your shoulders a little bit forward, in line with your knees.** Congratulations! You are standing up on the ice. Now you will want to move forward. Shift your weight over onto your left foot and push your right foot outward in a diagonal stroke. (If you're a leftie, it might be more natural to start with the opposite foot.) Repeat with the other leg. Move your body with your strides. The more confident you become, the longer you can stride and the faster you will move.

DON'T FORGET THE BRAKES

Before you get moving too fast, remember that you will have to stop. Make a few practice stops before you get up to Olympic speeds. To stop, place one foot behind you with the front point digging into the ice. Then you can drag the back skate along the ice to slow yourself down.

get your **BOOMERANG**
to come back

What do you call a boomerang that doesn't come back? A stick. Boomerangs look so simple and straightforward when you see people use them on television. In cartoons all you have to do is bend any stick and throw it, and it will come back and whack you in the head. In real life, operating a boomerang is a bit trickier.

More Like a *Bummer*ang

The most common boomerang screwup happens long before the object is released from the thrower's hand. If you want a boomerang to return, you have to buy a well-designed boomerang to begin with. This is harder than it seems. Many of the boomerangs you find at toy stores will never come back, no matter how great your technique may be, because they do not have the right design. Steer away from the flexible plastic "boomerangs." They do not hold their shape, so the best you can hope for is that they will curve slightly before falling out of the sky. 🖒 **You want a boomerang with arms shaped like airplane wings, curved on one side, flat on the other.**

It's All in the Hand

A boomerang is a flat object, not round like a baseball, so you may be tempted to throw it as if it were a Frisbee. This is the wrong way, and it could set up a dangerous flight pattern. Instead:

1 🖐 **Hold the boomerang by one tip with your thumb on the rounded side. The boomerang should curve so the top wing points forward.**

2 🖐 **Aim at a spot slightly above the horizon and throw with a smooth, hard motion.**

3 🖐 **Snap your hand at a slight angle, about 65 to 70 degrees to the horizon.**

Don't expect the boomerang to land right at your feet on the first try. If it circles back to your general vicinity, you're on the right track. It takes a lot of practice to make it come right back to its original position.

When It Does Come Back Around

Until you've gotten fairly skilled, it is a good idea to let the boomerang fall rather than trying to catch it on its return. If you do want to nab it from the air, use some patience and don't grab until the right moment. Notice the trajectory of the object in flight. As it completes its turn, it will start spinning horizontally and much more slowly. This is the time to trap it. As it drops to about chest level, step forward, place one hand above the boomerang and one hand below it, with palms parallel to the boomerang. Then clap your hands together as if you were catching the boomerang between a couple of pot holders. Keep your body to the side of the flight path. If you miss, you do not want to be slapped in the face by a big wooden stick.

FROM THE I-SHOULDN'T-HAVE-TO-TELL-YOU-THIS FILE

Practice in an open area like a park or a football field. Until you're a master—and even once you are—your boomerang might not fly exactly where you expect it to. You don't want to toss it around windows, cars, or your grandmother's china cabinet.

don't get beaten at ROCK, PAPER, SCISSORS

There is a great opportunity for glory in front of you. You and your friend both want it, but only one of you can have it. You throw what you think is the most powerful of the three objects: the rock. Your friend lays his hand flat creating "paper." Paper covers rock, you lose. Was it just your dumb luck, or did you somehow screw up?

No Such Thing as Random

Even though Rock, Paper, Scissors assumes that our throws will be purely random and that everyone has basically the same chance, recent studies have shown that human beings are terrible at being random.  **Learn the common patterns, and you can beat your competition and maybe even head to the World Rock, Paper, Scissors Championships.** (Yes, there really is such a thing.)

Rock is for Rookies

That is rule number one. Inexperienced players tend to open with rock. So if you throw paper, you win. Now,  **if you're playing with a pro who knows the "rock is for rookies" rule, try throwing scissors.** Your opponent will either open with paper or scissors, so you'll either cut his paper or tie his scissors.

People Hate Being Predictable

They will almost never throw the same thing three times in a row. You can use this to your advantage. 👍 **If your opponent throws paper twice his next move is almost guaranteed to be something else.** That leaves only two options: scissors or rock. Throw a rock. You will either smash his scissors or tie his rock.

Sore—and Predictable—Losers

👍 **If your opponent has lost the last round, he will often come back by throwing the move that would have beaten the last round.** For example, if you smashed his scissors with your rock, he will throw paper on the next move. In this tendency, people are not much smarter than monkeys. Believe it or not, a team of researchers at Yale taught rhesus monkeys to play Rock, Paper, Scissors, and they found that they also tended to react to a loss by playing the move that would have won the following round. (In case you're wondering why scientists were teaching monkeys to play this childhood game, they wanted to examine how the monkeys responded to the disappointment of losing. Surprise! They didn't like it.)

WHEN ALL ELSE **FAILS**

If you have trouble outthinking your opponent at the breakneck speed of Rock, Paper, Scissors game play, you can increase your odds by priming your opponent to throw what you would like. When you bring up the idea of playing the game, keep making a gesture for the move you would like your opponent to play. The other player will often subconsciously accept your nonverbal suggestion.

don't get trounced at SCRABBLE

You have a master's degree in English literature, and you were a sixth-grade spelling champion. Surely your stellar vocabulary gives you the advantage in Scrabble. Not necessarily. Scrabble is not so much about the words a reasonably educated person would use in conversation or writing; it is about game words—words like 👍 **zax** (a hand tool used by a slater for cutting), **zo** (a Tibetan yak), **seniti** (a monetary unit of Tonga), and **ka** (to the ancient Egyptians, a spiritual part of a human being or a god that survived after death and could reside in a statue of the dead person).

The *Players Dictionary* Is Scrabble Scripture

There are more than 100,000 words in the *Official Scrabble Players Dictionary,* and even more words are allowed in international tournaments. If you're offended by the concept of "arf" (the sound a dog makes) or "hm" (as in "I'm thinking") as legal words, then Scrabble is not your game, because if it is in the *Official Scrabble Players Dictionary* you can play it.

Make Your Qi Short and Sweet

👍 **The key to Scrabble triumph is in the two-letter words. Not only do the twos help you fit into tight corners, but they also help you line up parallel plays, where you form two or more words along two axes.** The National Scrabble Association says learning the twos will increase your scoring by an average of thirty to forty points a game. Next, you will want to learn the twenty-one legal "Q" words that do not need a "U." Believe it or not, the typewriter word "qwerty" counts, as does "qi" (the circulating life energy in Chinese philosophy).

Rack 'em Up!

Once you've mastered a few of the valuable uncommon words, it is time to play. ⦿ **Be strategic with the letters in your rack. The least-valuable letters in terms of scoring and playability are Q, V, W, B, F, O, and P. Try to get rid of them as quickly as you can, but hold onto S, E, R, D, and Y.** These are useful as "hooks." You can use them to turn someone's "twerp" into "twerps" and build a whole new word with the S. The ideal ratio to maintain is four consonants to three vowels. The only duplicate letters worth keeping are E and O (O is better in pairs than on its own). Look for any letters that form prefixes (like "pre") or suffixes (like "ed") and set those to one side.

Advanced Play

Top players keep track of all of the letters that have been played using tracking sheets. This gives them an idea of what letters are left in the bag and on their opponent's rack. You might also want to write down all of the tiles on your rack on each turn so you can see what words you missed and improve.

SCRABBLE AS SPORT

The champs make an almost full-time job of memorizing the tricky and useful words. (Players at this level take their game rather seriously. In 2011, at the World Scrabble Championships in Warsaw, Poland, two competitors nearly came to blows when one accused his opponent of stealing a "g" tile and asked the judges to strip-search him. They did not.) Top players are often mathematicians or computer programmers. They look at the board and the tiles and consider the probability that the symbols will come together in a way that will allow them to create high-scoring combinations, preferably over the coveted "triple word" spots.

don't get stuck on 43 down—master
the **CROSSWORD**

TOP SCREWUPS

- Using pen
- Going in order
- Misinterpreting purposefully confusing clues

Is your table covered in newspapers with half-finished crossword puzzles? Perhaps this means your crossword technique needs a little work.

Don't Be a Hero

Use a pencil. Everyone makes mistakes, and those boxes are too small to accommodate ballpoint pen cross outs. The harder puzzles—especially the ones that torment you on Sundays—sometimes have multiple answers that fit, but only one that works with the other answers. You might feel certain now, but you need some wiggle room.

Start Simple and Go from There

Instead of going through all of the clues in order, for example all of the acrosses and then all of the downs, **work outward from your first completed word.** It will be easier to find right answers quickly if you have at least one letter to help you. Fill-in-the-blank clues are generally among the easiest to solve, so scan the list and start with those. Next concentrate on the short answers. Once you have taken up the crossword habit, you will start to notice familiar words that tend to creep in. Puzzle makers need words that begin and end with vowels, so you're likely to come

across epee, aloe, Arlo, anoa, esne, and similar words in your crossword travels. The more puzzles you do, the more "freebies" like this you will discover.

Clues Inside the Clues

 The wording of the clues will give you some idea as to the form of the answer. For example, if the clue contains a foreign word, the answer is likely to be in a foreign language. If the clue contains an abbreviation, the answer probably does, too. If the clue ends in "ing," or is in the past tense, the answer will also. Thus, if your clue is in the plural you can take an educated guess that the last letter of the answer will be "s"—but remember to use your pencil in case it's a tricky one like data or sheep.

Keep an Open Mind

When it comes to interpreting a clue, the most obvious read isn't necessarily the right one. Some words—such as golf and love—can be read as a noun, a verb, or an adjective. Some are cryptic clues. For example, "She meets him halfway across the living room" seems like nonsense at first, but if you look halfway across "living room" you'll see "groom." Don't get locked into one meaning, and—this is where the pencil comes in—if you're stuck, go back and reconsider the answers you've already filled in. One of them might be wrong.

 When all else fails, consult your crossword puzzle dictionary. (By the way, if you are looking for a 14-letter word that means "crossword puzzle fan" the answer is "cruciverbalist.")

TOP TIP

Fill-in-the-blank clues are generally among the easiest to solve, so scan the list and start with those. Next concentrate on the short answers.

THE META-CLUE

As you fill in the puzzle, try to get an idea of its overall theme. Not all crossword puzzles have them, but most do. Figuring out the theme will help you with the long words. The long answers are likely to be a multiple-word phrase involving some sort of word play. They are the most likely to represent the puzzle's theme.

don't carve an ugly
JACK-O'-LANTERN
(unless that's what you're going for)

It's Halloween, and your neighbor's porch is covered in jack-o'-lanterns that glow with bats and witches and goblins. Over at your house, your carving skills are the only scary thing going on. Why is it that your pumpkin is always uneven and caved in on one side?

Don't Start with the Seeds

The big mistake that most pumpkin novices make is to start by cutting off the top and hollowing out the inside before they even start to put on a face. Instead, 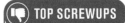 **try keeping the top attached and wait until you're done carving the design to hollow out the inside.** You will have more control cutting on a solid pumpkin, and if the stem is attached, you will have something to grab onto.

Leave the Big Knives for the Horror Movies

Use a small, sharp knife. Not only are big chef's knives hard to maneuver, they require more force, which makes them more dangerous. With a small knife and a vegetable peeler, you can produce a variety of effects by stripping off the outer orange flesh from one side of the pumpkin to create a soft canvas that is easy to carve and that gives off a glow when it is lit.

Not an Easy Canvas to Work On

If you're anything less than an artist, you should 🔘 **start with a stencil or drawing. Pictures from children's coloring books work well.** When you choose the image you plan to use, remember that straight lines are easier to cut into a pumpkin than curved ones.

Don't Start Hacking Away

Before you dive into your design, 🔘 **tape your picture on, then use the tip of a sharp pencil to make a dotted line around the lines of the image.** This will be transferred onto the pumpkin. Then all you need to do is cut along your dotted line.

Pumpkin Patches

If you make a mistake and cut off a piece that you didn't mean to, don't worry. It is repairable. Grab some toothpicks and use them to tack the pieces back onto the pumpkin. You can also use staples that you push in with your hand. This could make your jack even scarier, depending on the image!

The Postmortem

Here is a step that most people skip: Once you've finished carving your design and cleaning out the pulp and seeds, wash and rinse your creation inside and out. Then dry it thoroughly. A clean, dry pumpkin will last longer. A thin coat of petroleum jelly on the cut surfaces will also extend your jack-o'-lantern's life.

PLAN FOR THE CHAOS

Unless you want to clean up orange pulp for days, it is best to carve pumpkins outside or lay down newspapers where you will be working. Keep some towels nearby to dry your hands of pumpkin guts at regular intervals. This is not only more pleasant, but it also keeps the knife from slipping out of sticky hands.

don't screw up the PUNCH LINE

TOP SCREWUPS

- Forgetting the punch line
- Taking way too long
- Trying too hard

You're telling a great joke you heard. You get to the punch line with a great flourish, "So he said, 'It's a knickknack, Patty Whack, give the frog a loan.'" No one laughs. In fact they are looking at you as if you just arrived from Mars. "Um, did I mention the bank teller's name was Patty Whack? Maybe I forgot that part."

Wait, Wait, Let Me Start Over

This may sound obvious, but in order to tell a joke you have to remember it. The biggest joke disasters happen when you launch into your humorous tale only to discover that you have not quite committed the pertinent details— for example, the punch line—to memory. So 👍 **as soon as you hear a joke that you might want to tell later, write it down.** You don't have to write down every word as your funny friend told it. Think of it like a recipe. There is a list of ingredients, the story points, that you have to include in order to have the recipe come out right.

Don't Let It Get Stale

👍 **Don't wait a year until you trot out your joke, or you'll never remember it. Tell it frequently when you first hear it so that you can command it to memory.** Do yourself a favor and try to remember whom you have already told it to. Jokes are funny due to an element of surprise that causes delight. Your sister will be far less delighted by your joke on the eighth telling. If you are the sister, by the way, it is bad joke-listening etiquette to cut the storyteller off and blurt out the punch line. Spare your raconteur's feelings, and let him get to the end.

It's a Joke, Not an Opera

Telling a joke is not like reenacting the *Barber of Seville*. 👎 **You need to be brief, upbeat, and to the point. Don't embellish.** Get to the punch line in as few steps as possible, but be sure you don't leave any important bits out. Make eye contact with your listeners. Unless you are a natural comic or have a degree in theater, don't try to mime the action or perform accents and voices. Those are just other things to screw up.

You'll Laugh, I Swear! Why Aren't You Laughing?

Even a decent joke will have trouble getting a laugh if you have oversold it. Don't start by saying, "I heard the funniest joke. You will really laugh." You are setting the bar awfully high, and you're making it even harder for yourself to clear the hurdle because you've taken away the element of surprise. The corollary to this is that you should not apologize in advance for your joke by saying something like, "I heard this joke, but I don't know if it's funny or not. What do you think?" Rather than announce you have a joke, just start telling the story.

If you are repeating a joke you heard from a television host's monologue, say so. Don't pretend you wrote it or it happened to you. Otherwise you may be called out when one of your friends says, "That wasn't you, that was George Carlin. I saw it on YouTube."

what the fork is all this
SILVERWARE for?

If you're more accustomed to pizza than you are to caviar and escargot, you may find yourself a bit daunted by a formal table setting with rows of unfamiliar silver. Don't worry. Knowing which fork to use when is easier than it appears.

It's Surprisingly Simple

There is a simple rule that will keep you from committing a cutlery gaffe. **Start from the outside and work your way in. That's it.** The fork or spoon that is farthest away from your plate will be the first used. As you work your way in, there may be the odd exception—for example, a soup spoon may be needed before you get to the next fork on the far left—but it should be fairly obvious that even the rich do not use forks for soup.

Formal Fork Form

There are two ways to hold a dinner fork. Americans generally use the utensil with the dominant hand and the tines pointed up. The European method keeps the fork in the left hand with the tines pointed down. Many well-traveled North Americans use the European method to demonstrate their culture and breeding. This is not required.

Whose Lipstick Is on My Glass?

When the center of a table seemingly has a ring of glasses that go the whole way around, it can be hard to tell whose wine you're drinking. **Your glasses are the ones on the right side of your plate. You may initially encounter a stunning array of up to five glasses. Your water glass is laid at the one o'clock position right above the dinner knife.** You may also have a small aperitif glass, a red wineglass, a white wineglass, and a champagne flute. Don't worry. Your server will fill the glasses that match your drink orders and remove any that are not needed.

The Subtle (and Pretty Silly) Rules

The bread is one place where you may mess up your etiquette. **It is considered a faux pas to bite into a whole roll or slice of bread. Rather you should put the roll on your bread place and then tear off bite-size pieces to butter and eat.** Another place that you might reveal a lack of culture is in your napkin use. Once everyone at your table is seated, unfold the napkin and lay it across your lap. If you're in a really swanky place, the waiter may do this for you. **When you leave the table, gather up the napkin and set it to the left of your plate. Do not leave it on the seat of your chair.**

THE FRENCH DISCONNECTION

In France, diners often set their bread directly on the table in the spot where this plate would be. Waiters on the continent use crumb collectors to sweep crumbs off the table after the bread course. Another thing the French do differently is serve the salad after, rather than before, the main dish. The French word "entrée," which North Americans use to describe the main dish, means "entrance." In French-speaking countries (and ritzy French restaurants), it refers to the opening course, what we might call an hors d'oeuvre.

don't mess up your MARTINI

To make the perfect martini you must ignore everything you have learned from watching James Bond movies. That means you don't need a fancy shaker, but having a nice set of classic martini glasses is still fun.

The Real Deal

The proper martini, experts say, is stirred, not shaken. Shaking a martini adds water and makes the drink weak. Martini connoisseurs will also tell you that a real martini is made with gin, not vodka. So begin with a bottle of gin, a bottle of dry vermouth, a pint glass, and lots of ice.

Smooth as Ice

The most important thing to make a martini memorable is that it must be sufficiently chilled. Begin by filling the pint glass with ice. Next pour in two and a half ounces of gin followed by one half ounce of the vermouth. Now stir. Stirring dilutes the ice just enough to chill the mix but not enough to water it down.

Another option is to pour the vermouth straight into the martini glass, swirl it, then dump it right out into the sink. This will leave a delicate whisper of the flavor behind without risking muddling the flavor of the gin.

Have Some Chilled Glasses on Hand

When you've gone to all the trouble of making a martini the right way, the last thing you want to do is ruin it by pouring it into a warm glass. If your glass is room temperature, the liquid's temperature will rise, and you'll lose the whole chilly effect. **Plan ahead by putting the glasses in the freezer, or you can chill them by filling them with ice just before you start to mix your drinks.** A vintage-size (four to six ounces) glass is the perfect size for a perfect martini. Larger glasses just let the cocktail warm up before you finish.

TOP TIP

Martini connoisseurs will also tell you that a real martini is made with gin, not vodka. So begin with a bottle of gin, a bottle of dry vermouth, a pint glass, and lots of ice.

DRESS YOUR MARTINI TO IMPRESS

To really impress your guests, garnish your martini with a twist of lemon. Start by cutting the ends off your lemon. To separate the fruit from the rind, slip a spoon between the rind and the fruit and run it around the lemon on both ends. Lay the hollowed out rind on its side and make one long cut so you can flatten the rind out. Now roll it up tightly. Push a toothpick through the rind to hold the roll in place. Now you can slice through the rind to create twists. An average lemon will yield about eight twists. Before you artistically place the twist, rub the peel gently over the rim of the glass so your guest will taste the oils when sipping the cocktail.

open **CHAMPAGNE** without
putting out anyone's eye

You are celebrating a big occasion: New Years, a wedding, a sporting victory. At your big event, the last thing you want is to open the bottle the wrong way and send the cork flying like an unguided missile into the face of the honored guest.

The Right Angle of Attack

You do not want the bottle to be vertical when you're opening it, or you might shoot yourself in the face. If it is too close to horizontal, however, the gas will float up and form a bubble in the bottle's shoulder. When you open the cork, the bubble will expand all at once and shoot the liquid out of the neck. It's impressive looking, but messy, and you waste some expensive champagne. **So the angle you're looking for is 45°. This tilt will ensure that the gas stays in the neck where it belongs.** Of course, you do not want to aim the neck directly at any person or anything fragile. It is considered a social faux pas to destroy your Aunt Minnie's collection of Precious Moments figurines.

Giving Off an Air of Cool

Now that you have ensured that you will not do bodily harm with your effort, it is time to focus on looking cool. Stand with confidence and do not wince in anticipation of the pop. Hold your head high and smile. If this is difficult, you may want to practice at home by opening cheap sparkling beverages and those rolled biscuit tubes that pop.

It's All in the Twist

To avoid losing your grip and accidentally dropping the bottle on your feet, 👎 **you want to twist the bottle, rather than the cork, in order to loosen it.** If you twist the cork instead, you need to reposition your fingers several times. In order to do this, you need to loosen your grip. If it pops while you have a loose hold, the bottle might slip through your fingers. So twist the bottle slowly until the cork eases out. If it stays put, rock the cork with a forward-backward motion to loosen the stickiness between the cork and the bottle. If you do everything right, the cork will come off with a little hiss and not the dramatic blast that you see in the movies. This might not seem as satisfying, but the champagne will taste much better because it will keep its bubbles.

WHAT TURNS A CORK INTO A MISSILE?

The projectile quality of champagne is caused by a buildup of gas in the neck underneath the cork. When a carbonated beverage (champagne or any other) gets warm, the gasses expand. There are documented accounts, in fact, of soda bottles spontaneously exploding on extremely hot days. This is one of the reasons for the ice bucket. Keeping your champagne cool reduces the pressure on the cork and keeps the bubbly bubbly. A bottle of warm champagne might send its cork flying the moment you've removed the foil wrap and the wire muzzle. (It's called "le muselet" in French, and that is the term you should use if you want to convince your guests you're knowledgeable about champagne.)

don't suffer from post-party disorders, aka **HANGOVERS**

Everyone knows how to avoid a hangover. Don't drink too much alcohol. Everyone also seems to be unable to follow that simple guideline all of the time, hence the thousands of folk remedies to drive away those morning-after headaches and upset stomachs. Most of them don't do much of anything. But a few do . . .

It's Not the What, It's the How Much How Quickly

Now let's assume that you have decided to go out on the town (via taxi or with your designated driver, of course) and booze it up for the night. How can you plan ahead to avoid unpleasantness the next day? Let's start with what won't work. Chances are you've heard that mixing different types of alcoholic beverages makes you sicker than sticking with one. There is a small amount of science behind this. Different drinks contain different chemicals in addition to the ethanol that gets you drunk. Mixing them could have unforeseen effects. Research has shown, however, **that the most important factor in whether or not you get a hangover has to do with the total amount of alcohol you consume and how fast, not what mixes you pick.**

So What *Is* True?

When you have nothing but alcohol in your system, it is absorbed rapidly by the small intestine, so **never drink**

on an empty stomach if you don't want to end up yacking up later on. Eating after you're already drunk doesn't help nearly as much as, but man is it fun.

Water, Water Everywhere If You Had Too Much to Drink

Dehydration is one of the main causes of hangover symptoms. Most of the herbal concoctions and tablets that claim to fight hangovers seem to work only because you take them with water. 🌓 **The best thing to do is to start drinking water before you even pick up that cocktail. Then alternate each alcoholic drink with a glass of water.**

The Morning After

As far as a cure the next day goes, 🌓 **drink a lot of water or an electrolyte solution (such as Gatorade) to reverse the dehydration. Even though you may not feel like it, eat a well-balanced breakfast.** Alcohol raises your insulin levels, which can make you feel weak and tired. Eating will raise your glucose levels. Coffee will just increase your dehydration and make you more wide-awake hungover. Avoid it. You might also try taking a vitamin and mineral supplement. As the alcohol was busy dehydrating you with extra trips to the lavatory, it was also washing away vitamins. For your headache, take ibuprofen but not acetaminophen. You may still have alcohol in your system, and acetaminophen combined with alcohol can cause liver damage.

YOU PROBABLY WON'T LISTEN TO THIS, BUT IT WOULD HELP

If you're a smoker this tip might be hard, but try to avoid the combination of tobacco and alcohol. It seems that smoking makes you want to drink more, and drinking makes you want to smoke more. This is because alcohol makes your veins expand and nicotine makes them contract, so one always makes you crave the other because your body is attempting to even out.

don't be a WINE OAF

👎 TOP SCREWUPS

- Thinking everyone else knows what they're doing
- Mismatching food and wine
- Not knowing what the description is describing

To the uninitiated, wine can seem like a dreadful trap designed to snap and reveal you for the uncultured clod you are. There are all those French names, the descriptions about a "muscular brooding wine with chocolate undertones," and the little presentation ritual where the waiter lets you examine the bottle. What are you supposed to do with the cork anyway?

After All, It's Just a Drink

 Relax—almost everyone is faking it a little bit, too. Unless you are a professional sommelier, no one is going to expect you to know all of the ins and outs of wine. The fun thing about wine—once you let yourself relax and enjoy the experience—is that you can always add to your wine knowledge later. There are always greater levels of connoisseurship to which you can aspire.

Making a Match

When it comes to food pairing, you've probably heard the rule: "reds for red meat, whites for chicken and seafood." That's a start, but there is a lot more to it. You don't have to find just the right match, but a few additional guidelines will make you appear more savvy. **The general rule of thumb is not to overpower your food with the wine or lose the subtlety of a delicate wine with an overly aggressive dish.**

With heavy, meaty dishes with strong, spicy flavors, choose a bold red wine, like a Cabernet Sauvignon or a Malbec. If it is exceptionally rich and savory though, like cheese or foie gras, try a sweet wine, like a Madeira, instead.

A good medium-bodied wine, such as a Pinot Noir or Merlot, pairs well with a lighter red meat dish or a stew. For lighter dishes like chicken, fish, or vegetables, order a Pinot Grigio, a dry Riesling, or a Sauvignon Blanc.

Is This Wine Mad at Me?

What does it mean to say a wine is "brooding"? Is it annoyed and planning to act up? What about an "elegant" wine? When it comes to wine descriptors, things can get a bit murky. If a wine is said to be "brawny" or "muscular," it is a red wine with a lot of tannins and perhaps a high alcohol content. "Brooding" wines are usually red with dark fruit flavors. Their "elegant" cousins are light on the palate. You may also hear wines described as "racy," "linear," "focused," "feminine," or "austere." When wine writers are pressed to explain what they mean, they tend to come out with another list of adjectives and talk of "crisp edges" and "dark notes."

👍 **The easiest way to start to get a feel for these words is to do some sampling and experience it yourself.**

OK, You Picked a Wine

Once you've made your way through the minefield of choosing a wine, the waiter will go away and then

DON'T FEEL LIKE YOU'RE ALONE

Reading the descriptions of wines on a menu or in a wine shop, you will probably be confronted with all manner of adjectives that do not seem like they refer to foodstuffs. To decipher it all, ask the sales clerk. They will know about food pairing and can refer you to the type of wine that is in your price range. If you're at a nice restaurant, you don't really need to have much knowledge at all. Just ask your wine steward or waiter what wine he would recommend with the dish you've ordered. Don't be ashamed to ask the price. Being shy can cost you upward of $50 a glass.

The cork presentation is vestigial, like your appendix. You can, however, glance at the cork to see if it is wet (or colored if it is a red) partway up. This will let you know that the bottle was properly stored on its side . . .

bring the bottle to the table and show it to you. This is to confirm that it is the wine you asked for. Nod. Next comes the part where he presents you with the cork. What are you supposed to do with it? Nothing. The ritual of presenting the cork began in the nineteenth century. There was a lot of wine fraud back then with sneaky merchants trying to pass off cheap wines by putting them in the expensive bottles. Wine producers responded by printing their names on the corks. You do not have to worry about any of this today. The cork presentation is vestigial, like your appendix. You can, however, glance at the cork to see if it is wet (or colored if it is a red) partway up. This will let you know that the bottle was properly stored on its side, with the cork being constantly wet for a tight seal.

Is the Wine Bad or Is It Just Bad?

Once the cork moment has passed, the waiter will pour a little wine in your glass for you to sample and make sure the wine is in good condition. It may taste bad to you, but that doesn't mean it's spoiled. If you made a choice you don't like, you're stuck. If you're drinking vinegar, you can send it back. How do you know the difference? Well, 🖐 **the odds that your wine will be off—or "corked" as they say—is quite remote. If it is, it will be clear right away because it will smell like vinegar or mold.** In any case, always hold the wine glass by the stem. This avoids warming the wine and keeps ugly fingerprints off the glass. Make small concentric circles with your glass to gently swoosh the wine around. This releases the bouquet, which you can give a little sniff if you would like. After this, the waiter will finish pouring a serving of wine into your glass.

YOUR RELATIONSHIPS

don't blow your
FIRST IMPRESSION

👎 TOP SCREWUPS

- Looking like a hot mess
- Smiling like a salesman
- Making poor eye contact
- Sitting down
- Being a bad mover and shaker
- Forgetting someone's name

How long does it take for a stranger to form judgments about you? A team of Princeton psychologists suggests it takes no more than a tenth of a second. Other researchers have found that people categorize objects as soon as their senses perceive them, and there is no reason to believe that it is any different when we see people.

Sloppy Doesn't Bode Well

The blink of an eye provides little time to notice much besides how someone is groomed. If you show up in torn, dirty sweatpants with your hair uncombed, you'll have a rough time making a good first impression.

Show Off Your Pearly Whites, But Not All of Them

Smiling conveys openness and warmth, but it has to be the right kind of smile. If you immediately jump to a full-on grin, you will come across like a salesperson, not a potential friend. Instead, 👍 **you want to give a "slow-flooding" smile—a smile that builds slowly.** If you are not sure whether you can flash a natural-looking smile on command, try this: Stand in front of a mirror and repeat the word "great" in a number of funny voices. This should make you smile. The next time you meet someone, think "great" and a natural smile will come to your face.

Make a Note of Eye Color

🤍 **While you're noticing a person's eye color, you must gaze into her eyes, which will make you seem trustworthy.** Poor eye contact will make you seem dishonest, but don't carry the noticing thing too far. If you stare too long, you'll make the other person uncomfortable.

Don't Be a Slouch

🤍 **Use open body language. Keep your arms uncrossed and your hands unclenched. Point your heart toward the heart of the other person. Stand up when you meet someone new.** You may have heard that men should stand for greetings, while women should remain sitting. Forget that. Regardless of gender, anyone who is able should stand up and make eye contact. If you're in a booth at a restaurant and can't get up, extend your hand and say, "Excuse me for not standing. Pleased to meet you."

A Proper Handshake

🤍 **A good shake lasts about three seconds and is firm but not too tight.** In North America you should shake two or three times. In some parts of Europe a single firm shake is customary. To cultivate warm feelings in your handshake partner, gently touch his wrist with your forefinger. Aim for the spot where you would take a pulse. Gently touching this sensitive spot tends to foster a feeling of closeness even though the recipient is generally not aware of the reason.

 TOP TIP

. . . researchers have found that people categorize objects as soon as their senses perceive them, and there is no reason to believe that it is any different when we see people.

FRIENDLY SEE, FRIENDLY DO

People are more apt to like a person whom they perceive as similar to themselves, so mirroring someone's gestures and body language will put them at ease. If your new friend talks with her hands, do the same. If she speaks softly, speak softly. If she laughs a lot, you laugh a lot. After a few moments of matching, change your movements. If the other person follows suit, she feels in sync with you.

never say "I'M TERRIBLE WITH NAMES" again!

TOP SCREWUPS

• Forgetting someone's name

You are speaking to a charming man all night at a party. Your friend comes over and you need to make the introduction, but uh-oh, what's this guy's name!? You're looking awkwardly back and forth between faltering grins. It's getting uncomfortable. Party foul in 3–2– . . .

It's Not Your Fault

Well, it's not exactly your fault that you forgot his name. You probably don't remember his name because he told it to you too soon. People usually walk up and introduce themselves by name. This is proper etiquette, but terrible for name retention, because we best remember things in context. Before you know anything about a person, you have nothing to pin the name on. If you had heard your new friend's name about five minutes into the conversation, there is an almost 100 percent chance that the name would register.

HELLO my name is **?**

Repeat Repeat His His Name Name

You need to get in the habit of considering every name a valuable bit of information. You may not plan to speak to this guy again, but you never know what life will bring. The more you train your mind to consider names important, the easier you will find them to remember. **Repeat the name as soon as you meet someone: "It's nice to meet you, Mike." Then use the** name frequently in conversation. **"What a coincidence, Mike. I was at the same concert."** Remember back in school when teachers had you repeat times tables by rote to memorize them? Same idea. Repetition helps you remember.

Something to Remember Him By

Even though you don't know much about the person yet, you will need something to connect the name to in order to file it away. 🔵 **Focus on a feature, what the person is wearing, how he stands, a facial feature— something that is prominent. Don't worry about whether or not it is flattering—you do not need to share it. You just need to remember.** If Wanda is the one with the wrinkles, think, *Wanda-wrinkles*, or *Wanda-winkly* if alliteration helps you. The sillier and more creative you are, the more likely you are to remember.

If the person's name has another meaning, you're in luck. You can picture Bob bobbing in the water, or Joy laughing, or Jack propping up a car on a jack.

Help a Person Out

👍 **If you're the one who is being introduced and you get the feeling that someone can't remember your name, do him a favor and say your name before he has to ask.** Extend your hand and say, "Hi, I'm John Jacob Jingleheimer Schmidt," or whatever your name is. The person introducing you will remember your kindness. Then you can help the person you're being introduced to remember your name by dropping it again later in the conversation. "I said to myself, Barry, you really have to learn to remember names." This way you can save them the embarrassment you've just learned to avoid.

WHEN ALL ELSE FAILS

You are at one of the many social engagements that graces your calendar and are chatting happily with an old friend when an acquaintance spots you from across the room and waves. As he starts to move in your direction you search your memory banks for his name. Gabe? Gabriel? George? Something with a G. As the G-man approaches, you break into a sweat. You are about to have a clumsy moment of awkward introduction. Don't panic. If there is no one else around that can you can ask before he comes into earshot, and if your friend was not considerate enough to wear a name tag, you don't have to resort to subterfuge. The best thing you can do is simply ask.

don't fear the TELEPHONE

There are some people who have a warm and effortless phone manner. Then there are those people who seem to lose the ability to speak as soon as a receiver comes into their hand. "Um, yeah . . . Well, I'd, um, better let you go." If you suffer this technophobia, here's how you can become a smooth operator.

Don't Fall Flat

It is easy to come across as a bit low on energy on the telephone, even when you speak in your normal voice. The other caller can't see your face, which means he loses a lot of the emotional cues that would come across with your expressions and gestures. To make up for it, **you should add about thirty percent more expression to your voice than you would use face-to-face.** It may seem a bit unnatural at first, but it will sound normal to the other caller.

Make Them Feel a Little Special

You can make the caller feel important with a simple trick. **Use a normal energy level when you first pick up the phone, then shift into your high-energy telephone voice only after the other person has given her name.** "Ellen! Glad to hear from you!" The person on the other end of the phone will have warmer feelings toward you when she senses you are pleased to speak to her. Use your conversation partner's name a bit more often than you would in face-to-face conversation. People love to hear their own names, and you will seem more engaged and energetic.

Don't Be Surprised By Voice Mail

Avoid stumbling through an awkward voice mail message or the inverse awkward "Oh, I thought I was going to get the machine" moment by preparing in advance for both possibilities. Have a voice mail message ready, but also plan your opening conversation with a real live human being.

Never Sure How to End a Phone Conversation?

Early on, try to get an idea of what the other person was doing when you called. For example ask, "Have I caught you at a bad time?" The other person might say, "Oh no, I was just reading a book." Then you can end the conversation with, "OK, I will let you get back to your book." Do you have a friend or associate whom you dread calling because you will never get off the phone? Try to time the call just before he goes out to lunch or leaves the office. This will give him a reason to cut the conversation short.

Don't Give Them Half Your Attention

Remember, just because the telephone is ringing doesn't mean you have to pick it up. That's why voice mail was invented. 🕐 **If you are in the middle of a project that requires all your attention, let the phone ring and call the person back when you are able to focus.** If you pick up you will just sound distracted and unprepared. It is also perfectly legitimate to politely tell a caller that he has reached you at a bad time.

WHEN ALL ELSE FAILS

If you still dread that phone conversation, you can plan to call when you are sure you'll get voice mail and mention that there is no need to call back. There is even a sneaky way to be sure you get voice mail when calling someone's cell phone. A service called slydial (www.slydial.com) will send your call straight to voice mail without ringing. No fair using this to avoid difficult conversations though. If you plan to break up with your girlfriend, you will have to do it face-to-face.

avoid the sidewalk **DO-SI-DO**

TOP SCREWUPS

- Passing by too closely
- Not looking in the right spot
- Waving to someone who isn't who you thought he was
- Looking *and* not looking

There are few things in life that are so simple that they cannot be messed up. Case in point, walking down the sidewalk. What could be easier? Yet you have, no doubt, had this rather undignified experience. As you walk along, you spot another person heading in your direction. You dodge to the left, but he does, too. You change course to the right, and at the very same moment, he veers right, too. You step left again, and he steps left. You continue this dance until you and your sidewalk nemesis plant your feet and someone gestures for the other to go first.

More Rules Than the Playground

Passing on the sidewalk, it turns out, is a complex social game with its own unwritten rules and regulations. Although it is unlikely anyone has ever told you in so many words, in the United States and Canada (spatial relationships vary by culture) **you are expected to acknowledge a person you pass with eye contact at about the eight-foot mark (roughly two and a half meters). If the person coming your direction is an acquaintance, you should look down and pretend not to have spotted her until you get to that magic distance.** Otherwise you will have to contend with another gaffe: having to keep on recognizing the person with gestures, waves, and silly expressions for the entire, horrifying length of your walk.

Send a Message

If your passing counterpart is a stranger, 👍 **the eight-foot mark is where you negotiate passage. You do this by making eye contact and then looking down to the path where you intend to walk.** For this to work, the other person must pick up on the signal and move out of the way. If you glance at the wrong moment, you miss your partner's glance, or both signal the same direction and refuse to yield, you will collide.

Or Don't

It may seem counterintuitive, but the best way to get out of a corri-do-si-do is to avoid eye contact. Without any nonverbal communication, there is nothing to interpret and nothing to mess up.

HEY, WATCH IT, MISTER!

Men are more apt to crash into another person on the sidewalk than the ladies are. The reason is twofold: Studies have shown that men pass at a closer distance than two women or a man and a woman. Maybe because they are said to have better spatial reasoning than ladies, they think they can get away with a close encounter. Or maybe they're playing a little game of macho chicken since they are also more likely to be guilty of failure to yield.

don't get **UNFRIENDED**

 **TOP SCREWUPS**

- Being gross
- Trying to sell something
- Complaining nonstop
- Using Facebook as a soapbox

Rejection never feels good, no matter where it comes from. Study after study has shown that being dumped as a friend on a social network has real psychological impact, and not just because you're forced to utter the ostensibly silly phrase, "She unfriended me," to your friends.

Not Everyone Likes Toilet Humor

Think twice before posting that hilarious bathroom joke you just heard. Your sense of humor may not translate well to everyone. The social media research company NM Incite did a study of friending and unfriending behavior. The top reason that people ended a social network relationship was they were sick of seeing offensive posts. Fifty-five percent of those surveyed said they had dropped a friend for that reason.  **Save the gross jokes and four-letter words for real-life situations with friends whom you know will not be offended.**

Don't Peddle Your Wares

Thirty-nine percent of NM Incite's respondents had deleted a friend for trying to sell them something.  **It is OK to mention your new line of handbags, but do not make all your personal status updates thinly veiled commercial messages, or you will lose friends and followers.** Instead set up a page for your wares and update people through that. They'll be more receptive to something that's upfront and hate you less.

No One Likes a Negative Nancy

Some people turn to social networks as a place to vent frustrations and elicit sympathy. If you only post your complaints, however, you are likely to add social rejection to your long list of problems. Twenty percent of the respondents in the NM Incite poll said they had unfriended someone because their posts were too depressing. 👍 **If it is sympathy you seek, you're much better off calling or e-mailing one specific friend.** A blanket call for emotional support is not likely to produce satisfying results in any case.

👎 Lighten Up on the Politics

A survey by the Pew Internet & American Life Project found that eighteen percent of those surveyed said they had blocked, unfriended, or hidden a friend on a social network over a political post. Passionate political posters tend to be more liberal or conservative than the average joe, which makes it far more likely that they will be out of step with a large portion of their friends. Only one in four users in the survey said they "usually" or "always" agree with their friends' political posts. Most people will not respond to tell you they disagree with your politics, but when they do the result can be a friendship rift.

ARE THEY *REALLY* YOUR FRIENDS?

Before you get too upset about that online rejection, you should bear in mind that many of your contacts are probably not "friends" in any real sense of the word. According to a recent study by Robin Dunbar, an Oxford University professor of Evolutionary Anthropology, the human brain can keep up with only about 150 meaningful relationships. If you have more than 150 Facebook friends then you most likely do not even remember who some of them are. If you find that your college roommate's friend, whom you met twice twenty years ago, has decided she does not need to keep up with your day-to-day activities try not to take it personally.

don't spend **DATE NIGHT** alone

You are smitten with a charming, attractive woman. Every time you are around her you get butterflies in your stomach, but you still manage to make some witty banter. You really want to ask her out. How are you most likely to screw this up?

You're Not Asking for It

It sounds overly simple, but one of the main reasons that people do not get dates is that they talk themselves out of asking in the first place. Nothing ventured, nothing gained. Ladies, this goes for you, too. There is a school of thought that a woman should never ask a man out on a date because she will come across as overly assertive. This is believed to be a turnoff. In fact, when a Colorado State University researcher tested this hypothesis, she found that both men and women of college age favored women whom they rated as either "assertive" or "moderately assertive." In fact, they rated women who were not assertive unfavorably.

Don't Hold Yourself Back

Don't use big excuses to talk yourself out of asking. 🖓 **You may not have to have a lot of money for a first date, but you have just enough imagination to choose something fun and interesting.** A bike ride can be a great way to spend time with a person, and it even gets the heart pumping a bit, which might just increase her attraction to you.

It's Not What You Say, It's What You Do

Don't waste time rehearsing your opening line. Magazines like to run stories on terrible pickup lines because they are entertaining, not because they make or break your chances for a relationship. **The first impression you create has much more to do with your demeanor and your tone than what you say.** It is more important to use good timing than to say something memorable. Good timing, by the way, is before your potential new girlfriend gets away.

Don't Let Your Body Say Something Creepy

Whatever you say, make eye contact, smile, and speak slower than your normal pace. This gives the other person time to switch her focus to you and gives you more time to think and possibly avoid putting your foot in your mouth. Your goal is to get a conversation going. Use body language that conveys you are a nice person and not an ax murderer. Present an upturned palm midconversation or shrug your shoulders. This says, "I'm harmless."

No Guarantees

Be prepared for rejection. Sad but true, she may not feel the same spark. Not all risks end in reward (or they wouldn't be risks). Feel good about yourself for taking a shot, and hopefully you'll have better luck next time.

 TOP TIP

. . . one of the main reasons that people do not get dates is that they talk themselves out of asking in the first place. Nothing ventured, nothing gained. Ladies, this goes for you, too.

DON'T BE A PLAYER

Asking someone out doesn't mean you have to pretend to be outgoing if you are not. Nor should you play hard to get. (The object of your desire might interpret this as plain old disinterest.) If your goal is to meet someone you're compatible with over the long haul, you need to pair up with someone who likes your real personality. While one person will be intrigued by your shyness, another will be thrilled you made the first move. If you're a naturally assertive person and he is the type of guy who thinks this is pushy, you're probably not going to be happy together in the long run anyway.

don't blow your FIRST DATE

TOP SCREWUPS

- Doing something boring
- Buying an iced coffee
- Missing clues
- Giving creepy gifts

Let's begin with the assumption that you want for your date to like you and keep interacting with you after the first date. This means you have to be charming and bright, or at least not embarrassing and dull.

Going to See *Saw XXVII* Is a Bad Idea

Sitting in a dark room staring at a screen does not give you much opportunity to get to know each other. If you really want to be attractive to your potential partner, **go somewhere active and get his or her blood pumping. Go dancing. Ride a roller coaster. Go biking. Try climbing a rock wall. All of these things get the heart racing, which is just what you want.** Your date will subconsciously connect that excitement with you. Psychologists call it "misattribution of arousal." You can call it "awesome."

If You Don't Want to Seem Super Serious

Meeting for coffee is a great nonthreatening start. It is economical, low pressure, and if you choose a coffee shop near another attraction, you can go on from the coffee shop to another activity if you're really enjoying each other's company. What is more, coffee is a stimulant. It gets the heart pumping (see the point above) while, at the same time, allowing for an in-depth, getting-to-know-you conversation. If that isn't enough to convince you, a 2008 study by a pair of Yale psychologists found that holding a warm object can make us feel "warmer" toward other people. In the experiment, those asked to hold a warm cup of coffee were significantly more likely than subjects holding iced coffee to rate other subjects in the experiment as "caring" and "generous." We are such easily influenced creatures.

Read Your Date Like a Book

There are some subtle body language cues you can look for to figure out if you're blowing the date. To start, know the difference between a polite smile and the real thing.  **If your date is happy to be with you, the corners of her eyes will be squinting. Depending on her age, you may see crow's feet. If the smile has not reached the eyes, it is probably plastered on for your benefit.** You can also check interest with a quick glance at the feet. If your date's toes are pointed in your direction, that's good. If they're pointed another direction, it means she is planning her escape route.

Don't Oblige Her with Flowers

You do not need to spend a lot of money to impress your date. Be careful with gifts. Early in your courtship you may want to buy flowers and gifts to win your beloved's favor. This is not a bad thing to do, but the reasons are a

BELIEVE IT OR NOT, HE'S MORE NERVOUS THAN YOU ARE

If you are a straight woman, you can take comfort in the fact that studies show your date is probably more nervous than you are. Conventional wisdom aside, men are not nervous about whether they will have sex and how they will perform. Rather, they are afraid they won't know what to do or say. This makes sense because men are more likely to have done the inviting and chosen the event, so they feel more of the responsibility for how well the evening goes.

bit more complicated than you may think. Giving a gift will probably have more of an effect on you than on the person who you are treating. Studies show that giving a gift will make you feel more committed to the recipient and that it will improve your self-esteem. The effects on the recipient are much more mixed. It might make her happy or it might lead to negative feelings of pressure to commit.

THE DELICATE ART (OR MANIPULATION) OF CONVERSATION

If your goal is something more than a quick fling, you can plant the seeds for long-term love with your conversation. You do not need to talk about marriage and babies—in fact, this is almost guaranteed to cause panic in a first date. Thoughts of love relate to an abstract future, so ask about abstractions and the future. What are her dreams and goals? What is her philosophy of life? Ask "why" instead of "what."

On the other hand, if you want to elicit lustful thoughts, you should keep your conversation focused on specific present things—lust is about the here and now. You can prime your date to think in terms of one or the other and adjust what psychologists call the "construal level" of the experience. Talk about recent past activities, what excites her now and how things in the environment taste, feel, smell, and look.

don't screw up
MAKING OUT

When you kiss your beloved you want him to say, "Wow!" not, "Eewww!" Your date might be too polite to tell you that your technique could use some work. Here are a few things to ponder as you lean in for a smooch.

You're Not Kissing You

Romantic partners are always prone to one particular error. They project their own tastes and desires onto the object of their desire. Your partner is different from you and likes different things, which is, after all, part of the attraction. Kissing can be complicated because men and women report that they like different things. (Your partner is, of course, an individual, not simply a member of his or her gender, so personal preferences may vary.) This means, assuming you will be kissing each other, that there will have to be some empathy, imagination, and compromise at work.

Men Are from Mars, Women Are from All Over the Place

A woman's area of kissing pleasure is, generally speaking, more diffuse than a man's. 👍 **Many women love to be kissed on the neck and ears, not just the lips. Men often find this hard to believe because the same kisses do nothing for them.** A woman who loves to be kissed on the neck will undoubtedly assume everyone loves it just as much as she does. She will behave accordingly. While she is kissing his neck with gusto, his lips are getting cold, and he is getting bored.

According to William Cane—who surveyed more than 100,000 people on the subject for his book *The Art of Kissing*—if you ask women what the biggest kissing error is, they will tell you that it is an overly enthusiastic tongue. Women do not like it when a guy uses his tongue like a dart or flicks it in and out of her mouth like a snake. Men, on the other hand, are more likely to say that the biggest mistake women make is not opening their mouths wide enough. These two facts taken together paint a clear picture. He wants a passionate French kiss, and she wants him to rein in his tongue activity.

Meet in the Middle

So what is the solution to this conundrum? Variety. 🙂 **A combination of soft lip and tongue kisses and kisses on the neck (for her) will produce the most satisfying results.** Foster closeness with your partner by kissing often, without seeing sex as the ultimate goal. Couples who engage in more nonsexual kissing report greater relationship intimacy and less stress.

WHY HE'S ALL TONGUE

You may be interested to know that scientists speculate that when a man is trying to get his tongue in a woman's mouth, it is in an unconscious attempt to transfer testosterone to her and increase her sex drive. It's nature.

WORST-CASE SCENARIO

don't get eaten by a **BEAR**

You may have heard that the best thing to do when you are confronted with a bear is to lie down and play dead. This can be a good plan, but not always. Your bear strategy has to be tuned to the type of bear and the circumstances.

Know Your Bears

There are basically two types of bear attacks: defensive and predatory. If you encounter a grizzly bear, any attack is likely to be of the defensive variety. That is, the animal attacks because it

feels threatened. A "play dead" approach can therefore work, since bears don't feel threatened by dead people. Black bears are another story, though. Usually they run away from humans, but when they do attack it is usually predatory rather than defensive. In this case, playing dead doesn't work. It just makes you easier prey.

How to Scare a Black Bear

Your reaction to encountering a black bear should be, therefore, the opposite of your reaction to a grizzly. Instead of playing dead, you should **shout, bang on pans, and generally make as much noise as you can to scare it away.** Hopefully you planned ahead and packed some pepper spray. (You did, right?) If the bear continues to advance and make threatening gestures, you should spray it.

Fight the Flight Instinct

One thing you should never do is run from a bear. Bears can run faster than you can. **If your encounter is with a grizzly, back away so that she doesn't feel threatened. You might speak to the bear in a soothing voice to let it know you are human.**

Try Complimenting Her Hair

If you stumble on a bear with her cubs, she will try to defend them. She will stand up on her hind legs. Do not panic. Do not behave aggressively because this may further upset her. Back away while speaking in a soothing voice.

SHOW YOUR FEAR

If you are good tree climber, you can try to get up in a tree. Black bears are good climbers, and a grizzly could probably get to you before you got up in the branches, but your goal is to show the bear that you are trying to get away—not to attack. Hopefully once she sees you climbing, she will leave you alone.

don't make a
HEART ATTACK worse

 **TOP SCREWUPS**

- Panicking
- Not getting help fast enough

If you think you might be having a heart attack, don't panic. This is hard to do, but fear will only make your heart race more and use up more oxygen, which is already in limited circulation.

Stop Everything

Don't try to find a place to sit. Just 👍 **lie down on the ground with your legs elevated to keep as much blood pooled around your heart as possible and think calming thoughts.** If you have a watch with a second hand, focus on the second hand. For each second think or quietly say, "Heartbeat." Repeat. Breathe. This will increase oxygen delivery to the heart.

Don't Worry About Being Right

If there are people around, 👍 **tell someone that you are having a heart attack and ask him to call an ambulance even if you're not sure if you're actually having a heart attack. Who cares if you're wrong?** No matter what's actually happening, something is obviously going haywire, and you need immediate assistance. If it turns out not to be anything serious, this is absolutely a time to be safe rather than sorry.

Take an Aspirin ASAP

As soon as possible, 🕐 **take one 325-mg aspirin tablet, or four 81-mg baby aspirins.** Heart attacks are caused by clogged blood vessels that supply oxygen to the heart muscle. Aspirin doesn't remove the blockage, but it does keep blood from clotting and adding to the blockage. If you have adult, rather than children's aspirin, do not swallow it whole. Chew it up.

Get Some Air

Assuming you do not have an oxygen mask handy, 🕐 **have someone open the windows to increase the room's oxygen level. Coughing can keep you from fainting and keep you conscious until someone can administer CPR.** Breathe, and then cough every three seconds. Take a breath in through your nose, think "heartbeat, heartbeat, heartbeat," and then cough as an exhale. Do your best to remain relaxed until help arrives.

THE ONE TIME VEGAS CAN SAVE YOUR LIFE

By the way, do you know where the safest place in the world is to suffer a heart attack? A Las Vegas casino. This is according to the New England Journal of Medicine. Survival rates are greatest when a heart-attack victim is defibrillated and receives chest compressions fast. If you are treated within one minute, your chances of survival are around ninety percent, but they drop ten percent every minute after that.

Because Las Vegas is a popular tourist destination for senior citizens, local paramedics began urging casino owners to train casino workers in CPR and to install automated external defibrillators like fire extinguishers. Casino floors are also outfitted with security cameras to stop cheaters. Thus, when a casino guest grasps his chest and falls, someone sees it. At MGM's Mirage casino, a trained staff member will arrive with a defibrillator in about 2.8 minutes. Even if you were already in a hospital, you might not get someone to your bed that fast. In a city like New York or Los Angeles, your chances of surviving cardiac arrest are less than three percent. On the Las Vegas strip it is now fifty-three percent. Even in a hospital your odds are not as good.

what not to do if someone
feels FANT

A number of things can make a person feel light-headed and even pass out. They include having an irregular heartbeat, having low blood pressure, hyperventilating, having a bad drug reaction, and even suffering a spasm in a blood vessel in the brain.

Old Wives' Tale

Someone may have told you that the right thing to do when a person feels faint is to have him sit down and lean forward with his head between his legs. That person told you wrong. Yes, sitting down with your head level with your knees can relieve dizziness, but if a person feels that way, there is a chance that he will pass out. A person who faints in this position is likely to tumble out of the chair right onto his head.

Get Low

So a better idea when feeling faint is simply to 👍 **lie down on a bed, couch, or even the floor until the dizziness passes.** This should only take a minute or two. If the faint feeling goes on longer than that, it is important to seek immediate medical attention.

All Those Movie Scenes Are Wrong

Another bad idea when someone has actually passed out is to revive a person by splashing water on his face.

This is an old folk method that has the potential to be dangerous. Even though a splash of cold water on the face will stimulate nerve endings on the skin and send an alert signal to the brain, it is not effective enough to be worth the risk that the victim will breathe in the water. A person who is unconscious cannot control his throat muscles, and he could choke on anything that goes into his throat.

👍 **You can gently apply cool water to the person's face, but do not throw it at him.**

Just Nip? Not a Good Idea

You've probably also seen a number of flicks in which some passed-out person is revived with booze. Usually a grubby antihero pours a little mystery alcohol into the injured party's mouth from a flask that no one is surprised they have. The alcohol method is bad all around. In addition to the swallowing danger already mentioned, alcohol lowers blood pressure, which can only make a fainting spell worse.

WHAT ELSE NOT TO DO

There are a few things you should not do for someone who has fainted. One thing that never hurts to do is call a doctor.

Screup ··········▶	Big Fix
• Propping up her head but not her feet.	• Keep the unconscious person lying down with her feet elevated a few inches above the floor.
• Elevating her feet after a head injury.	• Don't elevate her feet if the faint was caused by a head injury. In this case, do not move her, and immediately get help.
• Keeping her head faceup.	• Keep the airway open and turn her head to the side so she does not choke if she vomits.

don't **FREEZE** to death

 TOP SCREWUPS

- Thinking it can't happen here
- Ignoring long-term risks
- Rubbing snow on you (seriously, who came up with that?)
- Keeping on trucking
- Panicking

One of the biggest mistakes you can make is to assume that the cold does not affect you because you do not live in a "cold city." As counterintuitive as it may seem, according to William Keatinge, an expert on the effects of climate on health, people who live in countries with mild winters, like Britain and Greece, have a high winter mortality rate compared to countries known for their severe winters. In fact, the United Kingdom has between 40,000 and 50,000 premature deaths every year in the winter months—even Yakutsk, Siberia, the coldest city on earth, sees fewer excess deaths in winter.

A Slow Freezer Burn

Do not assume that you were not harmed by the cold just because the effects were not immediate. Many winter deaths are not caused by hypothermia. Extreme cold strains the body, weakens the immune system, and causes a series of changes in the blood. These changes increase the chances of blood clots forming, which can lead to heart attacks and strokes a day or two after exposure. Deaths from heart disease can occur a few days after exposure. This lag time is what can lead people to fail to see the connection between weather and an illness.

Warmth in the Pits

Whether you live in Buffalo, New York, or Atlanta, Georgia, **when the temperature dips you need to** take it seriously and dress in layers. If you're caught in the cold, stamp your feet to stay warm. Movement burns calories, which creates warmth. Of course, there are limits to how much warmth you can create. Tucking your hands under your arms can ward off frostbite. There are major arteries in your armpits that carry warm blood from your heart. A similar junction can be found in your groin, but tucking your hands there is not always practical for social reasons.

An Abominable Myth

One thing you should never do if you think you are getting frostbite is to rub the area with snow. Where this myth began is a mystery, but the last thing you want to do with frozen skin is chill it more. Instead, ✋ **you want to bring the area back to normal temperature by immersing it in warm—never hot—water.** Frostbitten skin cannot feel pain. If the water is too hot, you might burn yourself without knowing it.

It is also a myth that you lose most of your body's heat through your head. It is, of course, important to keep your head and ears covered on a cold day, but only eight to ten percent of your heat emanates from your head. If you're buried up to your neck in snow, a good hat will not do much to keep you warm.

Calories Over Temperature

Hot drinks like coffee and cocoa are pleasing on cold days, but the effect is more psychological than physical. **If you want a drink to keep you warm, drink anything—cold or hot—with a lot of sugar in it. Sugar gives you a burst of warming calories.**

Don't panic. Most people who die in cold water are not actually suffering from hypothermia— their body temperatures are close to normal. They are killed not by the cold but by terror. They think they have minutes to live, and they panic, and die from heart attacks.

Don't Drive Yourself to Death

If you are caught in a blizzard while driving, it may be tempting to try to tough it out and keep going until you get to your destination. But if you can't see, hurtling a steel box across the ice, even at a slow speed, is a terrible idea. **If you're blinded by a whiteout, pull over and put on your hazard lights so other cars can see you. If you have a cell phone, call emergency services. Unless you can see a building very close to you, do not get out and walk for help.** You can easily get turned around and lost in a whiteout. Police and rescue vehicles are far more likely to find you and come to your aid if you're in your car.

Keep yourself warm by running the car with the heater for about ten minutes each hour. Do not run it longer, lest you run out of gas or fill the car with carbon monoxide gas. If the snow is heavy go out and check occasionally to be sure that the exhaust pipe is free of snow. If it is blocked carbon monoxide can seep into the car. If it is blocked entirely the car will not start.

Panic Is the Enemy

What if you fall through ice into cold water? Don't panic. Most people who die in cold water are not actually suffering from hypothermia—their body temperatures are close to normal. They are killed not by the cold but by terror. They think they have minutes to live, and they panic, and die from heart attacks. Gordon Giesbrecht, aka Dr. Popsicle, an expert on hypothermia from the

University of Manitoba in Winnipeg, says you have about ten minutes of meaningful movement to get out of your situation and then another hour before you will lose consciousness.

The key is to survive the first minute. ⏱ **When you plunge into the cold, the shock will cause you to gasp for air and start hyperventilating. If you do not fight the panic and control your breathing, you may inhale freezing water. Once you have your breathing under control, you have ten minutes to swim to safety.** After ten minutes, your muscle and nerve fibers become too cold to function properly. If you are not able to get out of the water and you are running out of time, try to freeze your arms to the ice so you do not sink when you lose consciousness. This is one area where being overweight is an advantage. If you have extra body fat you will live a bit longer in the cold.

THOSE BRITS THINK THEY'RE SO COOL

People in Siberia take their winters seriously and are raised from childhood knowing how to protect themselves from the cold. When Keatinge and his peers studied the community of Yakutsk, they found that people wore an average 4.26 layers of clothes with an outer layer made of fur or other thick material. Yakutskers wear fur hats that cover their ears and often the sides of their faces. In fact, researchers found that throughout Europe, when the temperatures dip, most people wear hats, gloves, scarves, and thermal attire. The British, meanwhile, mostly just wear coats and sometimes just a jacket.

oh, crap! there's a
BURGLAR in the house!

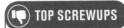
Of course you hope it will never happen to you, but your best defense against a home invader begins with advance preparation. Mistakes in this area can have deadly consequences.

Never Confront a Burglar

He may be armed, and it is much better to lose a television set than to lose your life. **If you come home and find evidence of a break-in, don't go inside. Walk away from the house and call the police.** If you can't walk away from the house, because you're already in it, you'll need an escape plan. Don't wait until it happens to make it. The same planning will be useful in the event of a fire. Think about the layout of your house with special attention of doors and windows that can be quickly opened from the inside. These are your escape routes.

Face-to-Face Moment

If you do find yourself face-to-face with a burglar, stay calm. Most burglars will not attack. Instead, they will simply try to get out of the house as soon as they can. Speak in a normal voice and avoid eye contact if possible. Do not do anything that could escalate the situation. For example, do not attack or try to hold the invader until the police arrive. Fight only if you are attacked. If you come out with a gun or a baseball bat, the criminal is more likely to become frightened and respond with violence.

what not to say to a
GRIEVING FRIEND

When someone close to you suffers a loss, you are likely to feel as though anything you say and do is wrong. The emotions are so raw and so huge, and your ability to take away the pain seems so small in comparison. It is important to realize that making your friend feel better at such a time is an unrealistic goal. It is not your job to fix anything. The most important thing you can do is be present and listen.

> **TOP SCREWUPS**
>
> • Comparing her grief to yours
> • Spouting clichés
> • Disappearing
> • Talking just to fill silence

It's Not About You

Keep the focus on your friend. You may have experienced grief in the past. Remember that each person's grief is unique. When the grief is new, do not say "I know how you feel," or "That's just how I felt when my mother died." Do not offer advice. **Think back to how you felt in the past and tap into what helped you. Do whatever it was that helped you for your friend without the words, "You know what helped me?"**

Allow Silence

Give your friend time to cry and to sit with her emotions. Don't interrupt or rush to respond. Putting a hand on your friend's arm can be highly supportive, but do not rush to hug a person who starts to cry because this can be interpreted as an effort to stop the tears.

DON'T AVOID YOUR FRIEND

Don't allow your discomfort at possibly saying the wrong thing keep you from approaching a friend or acquaintance who has suffered a loss. **Even a clumsy effort will be appreciated more than leaving a friend alone with her grief.**

don't screw up your FUNERAL

As a general rule, it is a good idea to avoid making major purchases that cost thousands of dollars while emotionally distraught and in a rush. Unfortunately, this is often how funeral plans are made. Imagining your death or the death of a loved one is not one of life's great pleasures, to be sure, but by planning ahead you can be sure you will be a rational consumer (or will have helped out your family in making your arrangements) when the time comes.

As Unavoidable as Death

Most people don't have any idea how much funerals cost until they're faced with the situation. This is a mistake. **Do some research. Know which costs are optional and which you can't avoid. Funeral homes have a "nondeclinable charge."** It includes costs such as planning, securing copies of the death certificates, sheltering the remains, and the logistics of coordinating with the cemetery or crematorium. These are the most basic fees, and generally unavoidable. On average, this cost is about $2,000.

The Bagpipes are Optional

Beyond this, the costs of a traditional funeral may include embalming; dressing the body; the use of a hearse; and costs for burial, entombment, or cremation. You will pay separately for the casket of your choosing, space in a cemetery, rental of a visitation room, and fees for religious professionals for the service. Extras, such as flowers, obituary notices, and acknowledgment cards, can bring the price up quickly. Which of these services you select is a matter of personal preference and budget. **You have a right to choose only the goods and services you want, and the funeral director must provide you with a written price list for every item.**

You Don't Need the Chemical Treatment

No state requires embalming of the body. The least expensive option is usually a "direct burial" or "direct cremation," in which the body is buried or cremated shortly after death with no formal service by the funeral home. A memorial service can be held later. If you do not plan to have a viewing, you do not need to pay for dressing the body or cosmetics. It is also legal to bury a body in something other than a traditional casket. Some religious traditions require a body to be interred in a shroud or plain pine box.

Factory-Direct Savings Aren't Just for Furniture

If you do wish to have a viewing, **you can save money on caskets by purchasing them directly from the manufacturer.** There are many sites on the Internet that will allow you to comparison shop for caskets and have them shipped overnight for a fee.

DON'T TAKE YOUR SECRETS TO THE GRAVE

Be sure your family knows about the arrangements you've made so you don't pay twice for your funeral. Also remember that when a person dies the bank usually seals their safety deposit box until legal proceedings take place. This might be a long time. Therefore, do not keep original wills, cemetery deeds, or burial instructions in there. Your family may not have access to them until you've already been buried somewhere else.

INDEX

Select Bibliography

Anderson, Kurt. *How to Back Up a Trailer and 101 Other Things Every Real Guy Should Know.* Avon, MA: Adams Media, 2008.

Asbell, Bernard and Karen Wynn. *What They Know About You.* New York: Random House, 1991.

Axen, Jennifer et al. *Anything You Can Do I Can Do Better.* San Francisco: Chronicle Books, 2006.

Behind Closed Doors. Stamford, CT: Boardroom, Inc, 2004.

Bottom Line Year Book 2012. Stamford, CT: Bottom Line Books, 2011.

Bried, Erin. *How to Build a Fire and Other Handy Things Your Grandfather Knew.* New York: Ballantine Books, 2010.

Bykofsky, Sheree and Paul Fargis. *The Big Book of Life's Instructions.* New York: Galahad Books, 1995.

Cohen, Brett. *Stuff Every Man Should Know How to Do.* New York: Quirk Books, 2009.

Compton, Nic et al. *The Indispensable Book of Practical Life Skills.* Long Island, NY: Ivy Press, 2009.

Ettus, Samantha, ed. *The Experts' Guide to 100 Things Everyone Should Know How to Do.* New York: Clarkson Potter, 2004.

Harrison, George H. *Squirrel Wars: Backyard Wildlife Battles & How to Win Them.* Minoqua, WI: Willow Creek Press, 2000.

Hunt, John F. *Stuff Guys Need to Know.* New York: Citadel Press, 2001.

Katayama, Lisa. *Urawaza: Secret Everday Tips and Tricks from Japan.* San Francisco: Chronicle Books, 2008.

Lagatree, Kristen M. *Keeping It Together.* New York: Random House, 2006.

Post, Peggy. *Excuse Me, But I Was Next.* New York: Harper Collins, 2006.

Powell, Michael. *100 Things You Should Know How to Do.* New York: Sterling Publishing Co, 2008.

Rinzler, Carol Ann. *Feed a Cold, Starve a Fever: A Dictionary of Medical Folklore.* New York: Facts on File, 1991.

Rosen, Courtney and the eHow Editors. *How to Do Just About Everything.* New York: Simon & Schuster, 2000.

Sherwood, Ben. *The Survivors Club.* New York: Grand Central Publishing, 2009.

Subotky, Julie. *Consider It Done: Accomplish 228 of Life's Trickiest Tasks.* New York: Random House, 2001.

Waggoner, Susan. *Classic Household Hints.* New York: Harry N. Abrams, Inc, 2007.

Walbaum, John T. *The Know-it-All's Guide to Life.* Franklin Lakes, NJ: The Career Press, 2003.

Wolke, Robert L. *What Einstein Told His Cook.* New York: W.W. Norton, 2002.

13 Things They Won't Tell You

From the wildly popular *Reader's Digest* column of the same name, this book is a collection of more than 1,000 trade secrets for living smarter, richer, and happier. We asked hundreds of working professionals in dozens of fields: What are the things you wish people knew? What should they know? What do you think people would be shocked to know? You won't believe how many secrets they told us that will save you money and time, get you better service, and help you avoid being scammed.

ISBN 978-1-60652-499-2 • hardcover with jacket

Available at www.13thingsbook.com and wherever books are sold.

How to Do Just About Anything

Now you really can do it all! Inside this book are loads of professional secrets and shortcuts for almost every task that you face in modern life. Whether it's a home repair, a better gardening technique, a cooking shortcut, or even how to win a game of chess, this book has outstanding advice, put simply, as only Reader's Digest can do it. Plus, you'll find surprising skills and little-known techniques that provide as much delight as they do help.

ISBN 978-1-60652-414-5 • paperback

Available at www.rd.com/doanything and wherever books are sold.